THE OTHER HALF

Roads to Women's Equality

CYNTHIA FUCHS EPSTEIN is an Assistant Professor at Queens College. In addition to doing research on the status of women in America, she has written many book and articles, including *Woman's Place: Options and Limits of Professional Careers.*

WILLIAM J. GOODE is Professor of Sociology at Columbia University. He has written many books and articles on changes in family life and marital relations.

THE OTHER HALF

Roads to Women's Equality

Edited by
CYNTHIA FUCHS EPSTEIN
WILLIAM J. GOODE

Prentice-Hall, Inc.   A SPECTRUM BOOK   *Englewood Cliffs, N.J.*

Current printing (last number):

10 9 8 7 6 5 4 3 2 1

C–13-642983-1

P–13-642975-0

Library of Congress Catalog Card Number: 71–153436

Printed in the United States of America

PRENTICE-HALL INTERNATIONAL, INC. (*London*)
PRENTICE-HALL OF AUSTRALIA, PTY. LTD. (*Sydney*)
PRENTICE-HALL OF CANADA, LTD. (*Toronto*)
PRENTICE-HALL OF INDIA PRIVATE LIMITED (*New Delhi*)
PRENTICE-HALL OF JAPAN, INC. (*Tokyo*)

CONTENTS

INTRODUCTION 1

1 THE POSITION OF WOMEN TODAY 7

The Status of Women in Modern Patterns of Culture
by Jessie Bernard 11

Civil and Social Rights of Women by William J.
Goode 21

2 PERSPECTIVES: BIOLOGY, PSYCHOLOGY,
THE ARTS AND WOMEN'S DESTINY 33

What Do You Mean "The Sexes"? by Jessie Bernard 39

Sex Differences: Biological, Cultural, Societal
Implications by Florence A. Ruderman 48

The Possible Biological Origins of Sexual
Discrimination by Lionel Tiger 55

Down with Myth America by Sandra Shevey 62

Sexual Politics by Kate Millett 65

3 HOW ARE WOMEN EMPLOYED? 73

The Wife Problem by William H. Whyte, Jr. 79

The Socio-Cultural Setting by F. Ivan Nye and
Lois Wladis Hoffman 87

The Declining Status of Women: Popular Myths and the Failure of Functionalist Thought by Dean D. Knudsen   98

Women in Science: Why So Few? by Alice S. Rossi   110

Women and the Professions by Cynthia Fuchs Epstein   122

4 THE CHANGING POSITION OF WOMEN IN CHANGING SOCIETIES   131

Leads on Old Questions from a New Revolution: Notes on Cuban Women, 1969 by Virginia Olesen   134

Elements and Types in Soviet Marriage by Kent Geiger   143

5 FEMINIST MOVEMENTS IN THE UNITED STATES: BEFORE AND AFTER   155

The Origins of American Feminism by William O'Neill   159

Women's Lib: The War on "Sexism" by Helen Dudar   165

6 AN EVEN NEWER LOOK FOR THE 1970s: PROGRAMS AND PROPOSALS   177

Equality between the Sexes: An Immodest Proposal by Alice S. Rossi   180

The National Organization for Women (NOW) Statement of Purpose   193

Redstockings Manifesto   199

Dangers in the Pro-woman Line and Consciousness-Raising by The Feminists   203

THE OTHER HALF

Roads to Women's Equality

INTRODUCTION[1]

The quiet ones are in revolt. Women have turned to the unfinished business of their own equality and the world now witnesses a new revolution.

The claims of women are being made in a worldwide atmosphere of revolt. In our time, colonies have insisted on their independence; national groups like Wales, Scotland, and Biafra have demanded independence; castes have fought for equality; authoritarian political regimes have been challenged; ethnic groups once subordinated have asserted their right to respect and power.

The issues of the "women's problem" are the basic issues of power and privilege, domination and subordination, dependence and autonomy. We hope that this book, by bringing together analyses of current issues, sociological studies of women's position in society, and historical perspectives on the present movement, can shed light on some far-reaching and fundamental forces in our time—forces that have deep historical roots and that have been exerted in all societies.

As the pressure toward attainment of freedom is great, so is the resistance against granting freedom. All of us are participants in today's struggles. There is no way to escape these conflicts and polemics because the problem is part of our lives and we are obliged to understand it, and to search for its solution as wisely as possible. It is our lives that are at stake.

Although the "women's rebellion" is becoming visible in many parts of the world, it is growing most rapidly and gaining the most power in the United States. This is both puzzling and obvious because, from many viewpoints, American women have more privileges than women anywhere. They certainly have more physical comforts and none are required to walk behind their husbands or to wear the veil. They do the purchasing for the family and are free to venture outside the home without seeking permission. They can vote, hold office, buy or sell property, even organize and lead a corporation. Their welfare is protected by laws that forbid discrimination against them. It is not surprising, then, that many men, feeling the pressure of work and seeing the

[1] The editors wish to thank Carol Ann Finkelstein for her able assistance.

proportionately greater leisure of women, wonder, "What do they want now?"

There is no doubt that women's lot has generally improved from the times when they could not vote, have their own bank accounts, or go to graduate school. But it is also clear, as so many analysts of revolution have shown, that a long-term improvement in social conditions that falls short of the ideal instills further hope of achieving that ideal —especially when it had seemed futile before. Even those who believe that American women enjoy an enviable situation are aware that unequal pay for equal work is injustice and that women do not have equal access to employment. While women may have accepted this injustice before, the improvement in their condition has led them to believe that they deserve more.

Some analysts further suggest that long-term improvement followed by a decrease in rewards creates a greater revolutionary potential—and it can be argued that during the 1950s and 1960s women actually lost ground, if one evaluates their participation in politics, the professions, graduate education, and even government. Thus, with such a decline after a long upward trend, we should not be surprised that American women are organizing to obtain equality.

Both the conditions to which women object and the new rebellion against them can be found throughout the world. Although some have proclaimed the Eastern European nations to be a model of the future, since women are expected to work and since the theme of equality is heralded in government pronouncements, that situation is not as favorable as described. These women are better represented both in the professions and in government than American women, but they too feel the pressure of inequality and protest the lack of attention given by their societies to such needs as providing adequate child care and homemaking assistance. Women in the Communist countries may easily enter professions, but they must also face the problem of doubling their burden, since they are expected to take care of the home as well. In Russia, where 75 percent of Soviet doctors are women, they may obtain free training and later acceptance as physicians, but individually they face the dilemma of finding adequate help for their children, in addition to performing well in their jobs. They can not depend on domestic help, and they enjoy few of the mechanical aids found in American homes.

It is not surprising that this problem remains unsolved—"equality" and "freedom" are persuasive rallying cries, but translating them into satisfactory plans is difficult. The analyses and data presented in this volume emphasize the issues—from many points of view—and show where some of the hard choices must be made. For example, it is clear that, historically and cross-culturally, the more interesting and sought-after jobs and activities are labeled "masculine." Women actually do heavy work in most societies, but their tasks are usually less fun. In any society—and especially in our own, with its complex set of bureaucratic and technical routines—there will be many boring, repetitive, and uninteresting tasks. If these are simply given to men, have we solved the problem? Or should we instead (as some analysts suggest later in the book) transform the society so that there is equal sharing—or instead aim at eliminating many of the less interesting tasks?

The fundamental change is that these *conditions* have become *issues,* that women who were vaguely dissatisfied suddenly understand that they share common problems with other women and that something should be done. In the past, policymakers have not concerned themselves with programs that would ease the strain of housekeeping for the tens of millions of women who both work and maintain homes. The stress was there, but it was not viewed as a social problem. Although large social problems do not often get "solved," it seems likely that *this* problem will not become part of a passing fad, a modish topic of conversation; it has become salient as a condition that must be remedied.

From reading newspapers and social science literature people today are increasingly aware that much of our behavior and many of our attitudes are shaped by prior social forces. Although most of this awareness presently applies to *individuals,* more and more people now understand that it applies also to *groups* of people, to classes, to ethnic groups—and, of course, to both sexes. Not only women are torn (as noted by several authors in this volume) by their wish to seize new opportunities and *also* to conform to traditional feminine roles. Men, too, are subject to the cultural definitions that determine how they are supposed to behave and feel. Like most, our society expects men to be strong and protective, to be firm husbands and fathers, and to place a primary focus on work and career. Men who, by personality and interest, are more devoted to home than to work are chided as much as women whose interest in homemaking is minimal or whose devotion to childcare is casual or weak.

Individuals have suffered anxiety and unhappiness because cultural definitions of the behaviors and feelings of men and women do not always "fit" their personalities and temperaments. In most traditional societies, the high-spirited young woman with talent and initiative was pressured into submission. The patriarch who could not dominate was a disaster to his family. The options that many modern women and men demand would permit people to find their own molds and their own ways of fitting together in a domestic unity.

Ideology always runs faster than practice, and faster even than private attitudes. In the United States, political leaders must give lip service to equality for women, and many husbands know that domestic harmony will be disturbed if they do not agree. As one tough-appearing TV interviewee commented, when a roving reporter asked *his* opinion of the women's liberation movement: "I just dunno. My old woman'll break my head when I get home if I say the wrong thing." The wise man will keep his traditionalist masculine views hidden when among professional women.

But ideology is nonetheless powerful. Mary Wollestonecraft, John Stuart Mill, Marx, and Engels all offered persuasive ideological statements. Increasingly throughout the nineteenth century social analysts realized that women needed economic independence if they were to obtain freedom. Without independent levers, without the ability to own property or to control it, they could not assert other rights—political, educational, or familial. Moreover, since economic independence carries a moral authority, a value of its own, women could never demand or gain respect or deference *as persons*.

Ideology does contribute its own effect: To the extent that people believe in equality, they are moved by arguments that laws be changed to permit women to own property independently, to obtain custody of their children, to spend their own income, and to vote. These actions, in turn, affect still other practices and economic forces.

Although the problems of equality are (as several articles in this volume show) fraught with conflict, because sometimes what one individual gains another loses—as the young gain power, the old lose respect—we can not assume that men refuse to grant freedom only because they want to continue their oppression. Nor is it wise to view the women's movement for equality as a simple reaction against the discrimination and injustice imposed by powerholders. Women themselves cooperate to reinforce traditional images and ideologies. They, too, purchase "masculine" toys for their sons and "feminine" toys for their daughters.

Moreover, relatively few women feel oppressed in the United States today. Perhaps equally important is that those who do are often unable to affix blame to any one man or even to any particular group of men. Many women are perfectly satisfied with, and perhaps prefer, the character of their lives because they believe that home is their rightful place. They see men following strained schedules, living shorter lives, working at uninteresting and routine work, and see little gain in adopting the pattern of life that men experience. For them, options to enter "the rat race" are of no advantage.

Whether men would gain from the changes in equality that tomorrow will bring is not entirely clear. Historical evidence suggests that oppression is costly to the whole nation, and that liberation frees both the oppressed and the oppressor. It is possible that this conclusion will apply to the situation of men and women.

Just how radically the society must be changed to give freedom to women is not yet clear. (Chapter 6 presents some of the proposals for the solution of this problem.) However, those who feel that all this agitation is unnecessary should consider the fact that, although some women will never want to engage in work that seems to degrade men (as men will not want to be degraded by doing "women's work"), they should not be pressured or persuaded to avoid the areas of "men's work" in which the most honor and respect could be earned. It is also necessary to remember that, although women in Western societies are relatively free, in many parts of the world, they are virtually enslaved. The struggle is a collective one, for women everywhere.

The studies and analyses in this book illuminate the interplay between the larger social structures of any nation and the daily interactions of men and women within those structures. Some of the arguments assert that it is impossible for women to become truly equal; but the main emphasis of these works is that changes are already being made.

Chapter 1 focuses on the present position of women, and points out both the resistances in the social structures and some of the patterns that have been altered a good deal. Like those of men, women's attitudes and habits are so ingrained that even when freedom is offered, some women continue to feel that their choices are considerably limited. Ideologies concerning woman's place and models of appropriate behaviors are supported by the daily confrontation with barriers. On the other hand, with each grant of new options, more women are attracted, and they do not willingly return to old ways.

Central to these problems is the age-old question, made especially sharp with new scientific knowledge and the new industrialism that no longer demands physical strength, of the *biological* basis of the allocation of tasks to the sexes. If biology does determine this allocation, then little can be done to solve the problem. Some authors in Chapter 2 discuss this perspective from several viewpoints: If women were less supportive and submissive, would this have a destructive psychological impact on men? Are the main organizations of the society based on a

kind of "male bonding," as Lioner Tiger suggests, so that female participation would be disruptive? On the other hand, Feminist writers argue
that physiology does not determine social structure, but rather that
beliefs about physiology are determined and maintained by society,
even when those beliefs are untrue.

Even if some of the biological differences between men and women
do shape their destinies, most social scientists have concluded that
much of a person's daily life is determined by social experiences. In
the future, the debate will continue. Which are more important: the
myths, literary views, commentators' opinions, sermons, and sober
reports of social scientists or economic and political actions? Those who
accept the first position must concede the daily importance of the
harsh financial and legal realities; but those who argue the second must
agree that both laws and economic decisions are based on how women
(and men) are socially defined—what traits are ascribed to them. The
later essays in Chapter 2 focus on perspectives on women as viewed in
literature, the movies, and the social sciences.

Although their lives differ in many ways, most women marry and
become mothers, whether or not they seek careers. Most women also
work outside the home at some point in their lives, and they form an
increasingly larger part of the labor force in all countries. Chapter 3
probes these aspects of women's lives.

The last three chapters focus on the radical programs for women's
development in Cuba and the Soviet Union; on the feminist agitation
of nineteenth-century America; and on the new proposals offered by
various emerging groups in the contemporary United States. Together,
these chapters furnish a long-term perspective on the slow, but acceler-
ating, changes in the position of women, and, therefore, of men. They
also reemphasize the depth of the problem and the ways it influences
all of our lives.

I

THE POSITION OF WOMEN TODAY

To analyze accurately the position of women today may be impossible, for an adequate treatment of women would require a full-scale analysis of men as well. The contemporary discussion of the position of women does, however, limit the focus of such an inquiry by centering on the difference in their positions.

Many women have learned, to their anger, that, while men view themselves as persons, as ordinary people, they feel women are different, incomprehensible. ("Why can't a woman be like a man?") The point should be underscored: *Men* are not different; women are.

Since women are different, they must be treated differently. One might suppose, if these differences were so obvious, that all societies would treat women in much the same manner. But the characteristics that set women apart from men vary from one society to the next, from one point in time to another. The upper-middle-class Victorian woman was thought to be frail and subject to frequent "vapors." No upper-middle-class woman has vapors anymore. They have evaporated. In Western society, women are thought to be too weak to carry heavy loads, but in peasant societies, it is taken for granted that they carry wood and water and engage in heavy farming. In Iran, men are considered emotionally delicate and poetic while women are considered tough and practical, and while women are considered more poetic than men in the United States, it is agreed that serious poets are more likely to be men.

Several authors in this book argue that whether the position of women is higher or lower, and whatever their peculiar traits, societies are similar in defining the most interesting and challenging positions, the top jobs in the society, as *not* appropriate for women. A noted revolutionary leader of a new social movement was asked recently, "What is the position of women in your organization?" "Prone," an-

swered the chief spokesman for the new equality, without any sense
of inconsistency.

It is generally assumed that women simply have no ability for the
challenging and highly rewarding work that men value. Often, the
definition states that it is unfeminine, indelicate, or unladylike to
engage in the activities men favor. If that were so, there would be no
need for prohibitions against women's participation in them at all.

From time to time, a philosopher or social analyst (Plato is a striking example) has suggested that women be given equal opportunities
and, upon proving their merit, receive the rewards men get. If women
were inferior, as has been almost universally believed, there would be
no threat in the experiment. If, as many men suspect, at least *some*
would merit high posts, then justice would be attained; however, most
of these suggestions have been ignored, and when not ignored, have
been derided.

It is not surprising that women would react against such rejection
and unite to change the definitions, as have most other subordinated
groups.

The social bases of the agitated present-day position of women that
led to the emergence of the women's social movement is analyzed and
described in this chapter. It focuses not only on the changes in women's
status, but also on the complex contradictions, tensions, and internal
discord that form its base.

Jessie Bernard notes that the *legal* restrictions on women are now
relatively few in the United States. Yet *informal* attitudes and values,
traditions and conventions, understandings and assumptions in the
society still substantially circumscribe women's world.

The limitations are of many kinds and are typically imposed by men
through force of habit rather than intent. In the everyday associations
of businessmen and professionals, men often get together without ever
considering that women of comparable interests and training might
like to be included. In the early days of student revolts, it was assumed that men would be the leaders and planners, while women
would serve food and run the mimeograph machines. In hiring and
promotion policies, women have typically been bypassed, since it was
assumed that their commitment must be low and, therefore, it has been
expected that they would probably drop out or underperform, although
their talents may be high. In childhood play, all this is prefigured, since,
as Bernard notes, it is part of the social institutions: boys organize;
girls join or not, *if* they are invited.

Men alone cannot be blamed. Central to the woman's position are
her own contradictions and inner tensions. Slaves always yearn for

freedom. Although the woman knows freedom is good, she is socialized to accept willingly her subordinate position in society. She further creates her own barriers to opportunity. As Bernard notes, women are not often committed to exploiting the opportunities open to them. The dedication of the woman has always been revocable. At juncture points in their careers, men do not ask themselves, "Ought I to quit now and devote myself to family life?" Because men have no such choice, they can more whole-heartedly throw their energies into their work. For them, society permits no alternative.

Still more fundamental to this situation is the fact that American women are not only given the option to lay their talents aside if they are not related to playing the woman's role; they are rewarded if they do so. Society gives approval to women for their domesticity, tender and protective relations with men, and rearing of children. Approval is *not* given to women, as it is to men, for achievements outside the home; if approval is given, it is usually tempered by the insinuation that the woman ought to have been doing something else. Thus, the reward system operates to support the woman's internalized commitments. Women are tempted by the new opportunities of the modern world, but they do not feel compelled to seize them.

Whether as Bernard suggests, the post-World War II period *was* different in tone and quality from the preceding generation of progress toward equality can not be decided as yet. True enough, the birth rate violated demographers' expectations and remained high, even after the first year or two. During the war itself, women were urged to participate in the great world; after the war, women were urged to stay at home and be "creative homemakers." In her book *The Feminine Mystique,* Betty Frieden argues that women did respond to these messages and renounced the world outside the home. But then they concluded that the advice was wrong; home life was not fulfilling enough.

While such comments and data may apply to the upper-middle class, educated women, a small minority of the total, it is not clear that any major change occurred among the vast majority of women, who have always been oriented toward the home.

In a selection drawn from a larger monograph on worldwide changes in family and society over the past half-century, Goode integrates several bodies of information that throw light on egalitarianism— public opinion surveys, labor force reports, analyses of "expert" comments, and studies of task allocation in the family. He focuses attention on Western nations, and documents in detail both the substantial improvements that seem to be taking place *and* the slow pace of other changes. By emphasizing both the ideological factors and the actual changes in work (which give the woman an objectively firmer basis for independence), we see how each interacts with the other. Very likely, a change in ideology, in the social definition of women, cannot go far in any one direction without changes in the economic and political realities. Men and women cannot change their opinions about women much, unless women are given new options, achieve high positions, succeed financially, and gain political power. But with each step in ideological egalitarianism, other changes are more likely; and with each occupational or political improvement, opinions and ideologies about women are likely to become more favorable toward women's equality.

THE STATUS OF WOMEN IN
MODERN PATTERNS OF CULTURE

by Jessie Bernard

In discussing changes over time, it is important to remind ourselves of the enormous stability of social forms. The modal or typical segments of a population show great inertia; they change slowly. The modal or typical college girl today is not astonishingly different from her counterpart of the 1940s—or even the 1930s or 1920s. What does change, and rapidly, is the form which the nontypical takes. It is the nontypical which *characterizes* a given time: that is, the *typical*, which tends to be stable, has to be distinguished from the *characteristic* or characterizing, which tends to be fluctuating. When we speak of "the silent generation" or "the beat generation" or the "antiestablishment generation" we are not referring to the typical member of any generation but to those who are not typical. To say, therefore, that the characteristic issues for young women of the 1960s are rights to privacy, to contraception, or to greater sexual freedom is not the same as saying that the typical young woman actively espouses these issues.

Technological Culture and the Status of Women

The term "culture" as popularly used has, like "status of women," only an imprecise referent which most people feel they understand until they try to define it. Actually, the norms which define the status of women constitute a considerable segment of any culture. They *are* major components of the culture—nonmaterial aspects, to be sure, but no less real for that. They act upon the material, especially the technological, aspects, as well as being themselves acted upon by them. If the mores had forbidden women to follow their work into the mills and factories, the technologies which depended on their work would

From Jessie Bernard, "The Status of Women in Modern Patterns of Culture," The Annals, 375 (1968): 6–14. *Reprinted by permission of the author.*

have been retarded. But if the technology had not created the wage-paying jobs for them, the status of women would have continued to be one of universal dependence. It is a nice theoretical point to determine, in any one case, which way the influence operates. The emphasis for the most part has tended to be on the effect of material culture on the status of women rather than the other way round. And the effect, it has been found, has been great.

A generation ago, a team of cultural anthropologists surveyed the literature on the material culture of "the simpler peoples" to see how it related to their institutions. So far as the position of women was concerned, they concluded that it was "not favorable as judged by modern standards." [1] It was a little worse among pastoral peoples than among hunting or agricultural peoples and worse in some areas of the world than in others, but "the preponderance of the negative type holds throughout." [2]

Not so among industrialized cultures. Among them, the status of women goes up along with that of the other formerly disadvantaged. With industrialization and urbanization, families everywhere tend to converge on the so-called conjugal system, a system which favors women:

> Everywhere the ideology of the conjugal family is spreading, even though a majority does not accept it. It appeals to the dis-advantaged, to the young, to women, and to the educated. It promises freedom and new alternatives as against the rigidities and controls of traditional systems. It is as effective as the appeal of freedom or land redistribution or an attack on the existing stratification system. It is radical, and is arousing support [even] in many areas where the rate of industrialization is very slight.[3]

The "material culture" which we call industrialism is the first, Goode reminds us, which permits women to hold independent jobs, to control the money they earn—a fact which greatly improves their bargaining position within the family—and to assert their rights and wishes within that group. In addition, the new system gives women allies in the outside world, third-party support for their demands within as well as outside the family.

[1] L. T. Hobhouse, G. C. Wheeler, and M. Ginsberg. *The Material Culture and Social Institutions of the Simpler Peoples* (London: Chapman and Hall, 1915), p. 173.

[2] Ibid., p. 174.

[3] W. J. Goode, *World Revolution and Family Patterns* (New York: Fress Press, 1963), p. 369.

Although there is nothing in the material culture of industrialized societies which precludes full equality for women, the actual prospects for full equality are not bright:

> . . . we do not believe that any . . . system now in operation, or likely to emerge in the next generation, will grant full equality to women, although throughout the world the general position of women will improve greatly. The revolutionary philosophies which have accompanied the shifts in power in Communist countries or in the Israel *kibbutzim* have asserted equality, and a significant stream of philosophic thought in the West has asserted the right to equality, but no society has yet granted it. Nor does the movement in Western countries, including the Communist countries, suggest that the future will be greatly different. We believe that it is possible to develop a society in which this would happen, but not without a radical reorganization of the social structure.[4]

Two Roadblocks to Equality

Two roadblocks, Goode finds, stand in the way of this radical reorganization of the social structure, essential for full equality:

> (1) The family base upon which all societies rest at present requires that much of the daily work of the house and children be handed over to women. Doubtless, men can do this nearly as well, but they have shown no eagerness to assume these tasks, and (2) families continue to rear their daughters to take only a modest degree of interest in full-time careers in which they would have equal responsibilities with men.[5]

With respect to the care of the home, modern technology has reduced the time and effort required to a very moderate level.[6] And whether or not men show any eagerness to assume household tasks, they do show at least willingness to assume them, as studies of the marriages of working women show.[7] In any event, no radical reorgani-

---

[4] Ibid., p. 373.

[5] Ibid., p. 373.

[6] Robert W. Smuts, *Women and Work in America* (New York: Columbia University Press, 1959), p. 26; W. F. Ogburn and M. F. Nimkoff, *Technology and the Changing Family* (New York: Houghton Mifflin, 1955), passim.

[7] The research literature is summarized in F. Ivan Nye and Lois W. Hoffman, eds., *The Employed Mother in America* (Chicago: Rand McNally, 1963), chap. xv.

zation of the social structure would be called for if care of the house were the only roadblock in the path of equality.

The care of children is a more difficult one to deal with. The President's Commission on the Status of Women recognized the need for services to help mothers carry their responsibilities. They recommended a wide array of such services, including child-care services, health services, and services related to the home, as well as services related to employment.[8] And they placed the responsibility for providing these services on the local community, on voluntary organizations, on professional associations, and on federal and state governments.[9] These are among the new rights women ask for in the drive for equality.

Even without them, the care of children, though difficult, is manageable when we are dealing with, let us say, two children, whose intensive care takes only about ten years of a woman's life. But it becomes formidable when we are dealing with four, five, or six children, whose care covers a span long enough to preclude other life options.

Motherhood and the Status of Women

Although the existence of abortion and infanticide in many past societies shows that motherhood *per se* is no guarantee of high status for women, still in many societies, both Oriental and Western, there has been a strong tendency to honor and encourage motherhood. "Facts about the desirability of offspring should [therefore] always be noted in a study of the status of mother and wife." [10] Actually, there has always been a reverse relationship between the birth rate and status as measured by such indexes as income, education, and occupation. This inverse relationship was, in fact, often invoked in the nineteenth century

[8] U.S., President (Kennedy), Commission of the Status of Women, *Report of the Committee on Home and Community,* October 1963, passim.

[9] No mention was made by the Commission of the responsibility of employers to supply help except in respect to paid maternity leave. For a discussion of employers' attitudes, see Nye and Hoffman, eds., loc. cit., chap. xxvi. Yet the question may well be raised with respect to motherhood: why should women have to pay the entire cost? When mechanization and automation began to deprive workers of their jobs, the same question was raised: why should one set of workers have to pay, with their unemployment, the entire cost of technological progress? Severance pay, retraining, and other devices were introduced to spread the costs. Perhaps the "right" of women to part-time jobs and to other concessions by industry to their peculiar career needs may be just around the corner. They may, in fact, constitute the radical reorganization of the social structure to which Goode referred.

[10] Elsie Clews Parsons, *The Family* (New York: G. P. Putnam's Sons, 1906), p. 229. Mary Wollstonecraft argued for the emancipation of women on the grounds of impaired maternity.

as an argument against the emancipation of women. Legal independence would create instability in marriage; economic independence would detract from motherhood or, worse still, lead to "race-suicide." [11] Such logic underlies the *Kirche, Küche, und Kinder* policy with respect to the status of women. Still, despite the jeremiads, the birth rate did go down and the status of women as measured in terms of political, legal, and economic rights did go up until well into the twentieth century.

Only a Modest Degree of Interest in Equal Responsibilities

Goode's second major roadblock to equality—lack of interest on the part of women in assuming equal responsibilities—can be documented by a respectable research literature[12] which suggests that most women would reject any radical reorganization of the social structure required for the achievement of full equality. Under the impact of the pressures of sympathetic men and activist women, much-publicized campaigns are inaugurated to find women for top positions in the federal government; administrators are hounded by the White House to upgrade women staff members; honors are bestowed on top-level women; a President's Commission is appointed and labors long and industriously to improve the status of women—all with less than spectacular success.

Thoughtful leaders look with a jaundiced eye on the refusal or unwillingness of women to take full advantage of their opportunities.[13] They have little patience with the regression of women into maternity. Hear Margaret Mead:

> We may well ask, in these days of great freedom, when education is as open to women as men, when the great professions of medicine and law, teaching and scientific research are open to women, how do we stand?
>
> The answer is very simple; we stand very badly indeed. . . . And we may well ask why. Why have we returned, for all our great advances in technology, to the Stone Age arrangement in which women's main ambition is to acquire and hold a mate, to produce or adopt children who are to be the exclusive delight and concern of a single married pair, and which work outside

[11] Ibid., p. 357.

[12] Dael Wolfle, *America's Resources of Specialized Talent* (New York: Harper, 1954), pp. 234–36; Jessie Bernard, *Academic Women* (University Park: Pennsylvania State University Press, 1964), chap. xii.

[13] Margaret Mead, Introduction to B. B. Cassara, ed. [*American Women: The Changing Image* (Boston: Beacon Press, 1962),] pp. xi–xii.

the home . . . holds no attraction in itself, unless it is subservient to the demands of an individual household. . . . Woman has returned, each to her separate cave . . . almost totally unaware of any life outside her door.[14]

Pearl Buck observes that men have changed but women have not:

The door of the house is wide open for women to walk through and into the world, but the stupendous scene beyond terrifies her. She slams the door shut and pulls down the shades. She is so terrified that she sometimes even rails against the exceptional woman, the daring individual who accepts the invitation of the open door and enters into wider opportunity and assumes the new responsibility. . . . Old prejudices are fading, intelligent men are eagerly seeking intelligence whenever it can be found and they are impatient when intelligent women continue to live in narrow ways, apart from the world's problems and dangers. . . . The question which faces every woman is no longer, "Do I want to?" or "How can I?" The answer is simple. "You must!"[15]

And Agnes E. Meyer says sternly: "I feel very strongly that the educated women of America are not taking their responsibility to the nation's strength and welfare seriously enough."[16] Ethel J. Alpenfels documents the recession of women from the professional world, noting the decline of women in the professions from one half in 1930 to about one third in the 1960s.[17] "The status of women deteriorates," she notes, "even while the administrative heads of their universities and colleges ponder the ways and means of salvaging lost talent."[18]

Even when women are themselves held responsible for their inferior status, men are often blamed for making women what they are. Thus, Marya Mannes: "Women are not by nature denied the ability to think creatively and abstractly. It is rather that this ability is unpopular with women because it is unpopular with men."[19] Or culture in the form of

[14] Ibid.
[15] Pearl Buck, "Changing Relationships between Men and Women," Cassara, ed., loc. cit., pp. 8–9.
[16] Agnes E. Meyer, "Leadership Responsibilities of American Women," Cassara, ed., loc. cit., p. 11.
[17] Ethel J. Alpenfels, "Women in the Professional World," in Cassara, ed., loc. cit., pp. 78–79.
[18] Ibid., p. 79.
[19] Marya Mannes, "Female Intelligence—Who Wants It?," *New York Times Magazine,* January 3, 1960 (Cassara, ed., loc. cit., pp. 78–79).

a "climate of opinion" is blamed. "It is not the individual young girl, or young wife or older woman who is to blame; it is the climate of opinion that has developed in this country." [20] The most vitriolic attack on the refusal of women to take advantage of their opportunities, by what might be called the men-by-way-of-women approach, was that of Betty Friedan, whose excoriation of the feminine mystique, or what Margaret Mead had called a "retreat into fecundity," [21] precipitated one of the most heated controversies of the decade. Miss Friedan pointed an accusing finger at everyone responsible for glorifying the exaggerated maternity of the postwar period—psychoanalysts, educators, advertisers, industry—and at women for succumbing.[22] Though she blamed men, she put millions of women on the defensive. Their lives *did* begin to look trivial under her unsympathetic eye; they *were* able-bodied; they *did* have little to do around the house; the children *did* resent too much meddling in their lives.

As frequently happens, the trends here attacked had already begun to moderate by the time they had been widely recognized and bemoaned. Five years before Betty Friedan's book appeared, women were already beginning to delay marriage,[23] return to college,[24] go on for graduate study,[25] as well as reduce the number of babies they bore.[26] Whether they would also now be willing to undertake full-time careers and assume equal responsibilities with men was still a question. It is too early as yet to discern trends. But the indications are that neither a full-time career nor unbridled motherhood will be the characteristic option. For even during the period that was dominated by the feminine mystique, there was almost a stampede of mothers back into the labor force; the feminine mystique did not keep millions of mothers from wanting jobs[27] not, however, at the higher, more responsible levels. A

[20] Mead, Introduction, Cassara, ed., loc. cit., p. xiii.

[21] Ibid., p. xii.

[22] Friedan [*The Feminine Mystique* (New York: W. W. Norton, 1963)], passim.

[23] The age at first marriage: 1940 (21.5); 1947 (20.5); 1955 (20.2); 1960 (20.3); 1963 (20.5); 1965 (20.6); 1966 (20.5).

[24] Percentage of high school graduates who were first-time college enrollees: 1950 (31.3); 1954 (36.9); 1958 (40.0); 1962 (44.4); 1964 (45.0).

[25] Proportion of all Master's and other second-level degrees granted to woman: 1940 (38.2); 1950 (29.2); 1960 (31.6); 1964 (31.8). Proportion of doctorate and equivalent degrees granted to women: 1940 (13.0); 1950 (9.6); 1960 (10.5); 1964 (10.6).

[26] The rate of third births declined from 33 per 1,000 in 1957 to 24.4 per 1,000 in 1965; of fourth births, from 21 per 1,000 in 1961 to 15.7 in 1965; of fifth babies, from 12 per 1,000 in 1959–1962 to 9.3 in 1965. See "Baby Boom Ends," *Statistical Bulletin* of the Metropolitan Life Insurance Company, xliv (October 1966), 1.

[27] Nye and Hoffman, eds., loc. cit.

job, not a career, was the trade-off in their dilemma. And even this compromise was far from achieving universal acceptance. Despite the urgent efforts of educators, counselors, and leaders, girls—and boys— are still unaware of the pattern of women's lives in this day and age. They "hold traditional attitudes about the place of women in modern society," and, as a result, "most of the girls will finish their education either unprepared or poorly prepared to take a place in society in which they will feel satisfied and fulfilled." [28] Goode's second roadblock stands firm.

Sexuality and the Status of Women

It was a standard argument against woman's rights in the nineteenth century that suffrage and political activity would "unsex" women. The converse was not usually articulated, namely, that emphasizing female sexuality would detract from serious participation in the outside world. But Agnes Meyer was making precisely this charge in the 1960s:

> It seems tragic that just when the challenge to women and their opportunities for service are greatest, the younger ones are so profoundly influenced by the overemphasis on sex now so prevalent in our whole culture that they are reverting to female rather than to womanly ideals. [29]

And Marya Mannes and Margaret Calkin Banning concurred. Miss Mannes noted that it was the *Playboy* Bunny and the whole *Playboy* psychology that degraded women;[30] and Mrs. Banning, that the emphasis on glamour tended to demote women.[31]

The men did not agree. They defended the idea of "an impossibly attractive, charming . . . woman" as an ideal.[32] And even from the Soviet Union came word that feminine beauty was a worthy goal.

Soviet women were advised to pay more attention to their looks and charm. Men were told to look upon them as something more than a

---

[28] Kenneth K. Kern, "High School Freshmen and Seniors View the Role of Women in Modern Society," *The Bulletin on Family Development* (of the Family Study Center, University of Missouri, Kansas City, Mo.), V (Winter 1965), 11, 12.

[29] Agnes Meyer, in Cassara, ed., loc. cit., p. 11.

[30] "Portrayal of Women by the Mass Media." *Report of the President's Commission on the Status of Women,* p. 22.

[31] Ibid.

[32] Ibid.

comrade worker. "We need an art which educates young boys to admire the miracle of beauty in women and young girls to aspire to imitate the examples of such beauty," said *Literaturnaya Gazeta* (Literary Gazette).

"Along with the full equality of women we need a cult of women's charm." The publication complained that Soviet women often are negligent about their appearance. There has been a tendency under communism to regard attention to clothes, cosmetics, and hairdo as a waste of time. But "the esthetics of woman's beauty is needed by the whole population, both men and women," the article contended. It was written by 68-year-old Ilya Selvinsky, a poet. A common theme, repeated by Selvinsky, is that legal equality does not mean that the sexes should behave and be treated exactly alike. The article urged not only that women become more feminine, but that they be idealized. "For a barbarian a woman is simply a person of the opposite sex," Selvinsky said. "But art teaches men to idealize women. This distinguishes civilized people from primitive ones." [33]

To be sure, Agnes Meyer, Marya Mannes, and Mrs. Banning are not talking to the same issue as is the Soviet poet, Selvinsky. But in his plea for feminine glamour there are reverberations of the nineteenth-century lady-on-a-pedestal, adored at a distance, and not permitted to demean herself by entrance into the male world. And, as the women sense, "to be looked up to" is not a substitute for equality.

A Zero-Sum Game?

There are even profounder aspects to the relationship between sexuality and the status of women. For women, the relevant problems have to do with the implications of sexuality for equality; for men, with the implications of equality for sexuality.

Some of the rights which women demanded in their movement for emancipation did not have the effect of seriously depriving men of their rights. Giving women the vote did not deprive men of theirs.[34] But granting other rights to women did deprive men. In such cases, it was a zero-sum situation. Laws, for example, which gave property rights took rights away from men. And laws which forbade discrimination in employment deprived men of an advantage in certain kinds of

---

[33] "Charm Comes to Comrade Olga: Will She Ogle Back?," *Washington Post,* April 13, 1967.

[34] Alan P. Grimes, *The Puritan Ethic and Woman Suffrage* (New York: Oxford University Press, 1967).

jobs. In a sense, any attempt to equalize unequal statuses can raise one by lowering the other. In this sense, sexual equality is paid for by men.

In the past, when the drive toward equality of the sexes dealt with a single standard, it was the feminine standard that was sought; in recent years, the male standard. A cultural pattern inherited from Victorian times prescribing a passive, recipient, nondemanding role for women in the sexual encounter was transmuted into one which, at least in some circles, called for active, even aggressive, sexual behavior on their part. There was to be no double standard so far as sexual satisfaction was concerned. Orgasm became almost a civil right. Women had sexual rights as well as men (whether they wanted them or not).

We have been so amazed at these phenomena, so concentrated on the changes in female sexuality, that until now we have not noticed the effect they were having on men. Recently, however, the psychological costs to men have received attention. It now appears that granting women the privilege of sexual initiative, not to mention aggressiveness, can have a sexually depressing effect on men. A growing literature alerts us to the "masculinity crisis" of modern men.[35] It raises the question: How much equality can the sexes stand? Women who prize male sexuality may be willing to pay a price to protect it; they will guard Goode's second roadblock; they will settle for less than complete equality. But others will want to know: Why should we?

There are certainly no easy answers.

[35] See, for example, Myron Brenton, *The American Male: A Penetrating Look at the Masculinity Crisis* (New York: Coward-McCann, 1966); Hendrik M. Ruitenbeck, *The Male Myth* (New York: Dell, 1967).

CIVIL AND SOCIAL RIGHTS OF WOMEN

by William J. Goode

Perhaps the most striking change in the movement towards equal rights may be found in a legal datum: in 1900, two generations ago, women were permitted to vote only in New Zealand, and in four states of the United States. By 1954, they obtained the right to vote in sixty countries (including non-Western nations), and only seventeen independent countries denied them the vote. Women have been permitted to occupy high supervisory positions, and seats in national legislatures. They hold posts in the national cabinets of many countries; they may become ambassadors. Although perhaps the Communist countries are in many respects ahead of the non-Communist ones, most Western countries have permitted women a wide range of freedoms once denied to them: entrance into universities, the ownership of property, making independent contracts under certain conditions, equal inheritance with brothers, and many others. It is no accident, of course, that many of women's rights are to be found in the area of economic freedom, but these in turn are determined by changing attitudes and values.

The West is the first major civilization to give such equality to its women. Even the period of great license of imperial Rome during its decline did not give women a similar position. In Rome, women had great freedom with repect to sexual behavior and divorce, but no range of important tasks was defined as open to them. Indeed, we may perhaps speculate that had Rome put its women to work, the society might not have fallen. Yet neither Rome nor any other society prior to our epoch has ever attempted this solution of its social and economic problems. Why is the West different?

"Machine technology" has been offered as a simple explanation to the question of why women were permitted to earn a living outside the home. Under the processes developed by Western technology, tasks are

From William J. Goode, World Revolution and Family Patterns *(New York: Free Press of Glencoe, 1963), pp. 55–66. Revised by the author for this edition. Reprinted by permission of The Macmillan Company.*

broken down into small parts with machines carrying out segments of the work. Thus, women and children, or unskilled men, may supervise machines although they lack the strength or skill to carry out alone the task performed by the machines they attend.

But such an explanation is unsophisticated. Few tasks, even in ancient Rome, required great strength, and women can learn—and in our society have learned—any skill whatsoever, from writing novels of the first rank to performing surgery, from driving an automobile to operating a giant computer. (Millions of brain-hours devoted to the task of isolating and demonstrating *specifically* male skills and talents, motivated in part by a male desire to prove his own innate superiority, have established no conclusions of this kind.) Differences there are, and we owe much of both our sorrow and joy to them, but they apparently do not lie in the realm of those innate abilities which can be trained into skills. With a different set of cultural values and social structure, many of Rome's factories could have been run by women, and its immense bureaucracy of colonial administrators could also have utilized women. Apparently the Romans, the forebears of our Western civilization, saw eye to eye with their descendants in the Western Middle Ages on this point: women were not to be permitted to do important tasks outside the home.

One cannot, then, make a defensible case for the thesis that it is modern technology, with its division of labor, that creates the statistically unusual status of women. Nor can we find any better proof for the notion that it was the desire for economic profit that made woman useful to the West and thus gave her a new position. In all great civilizations, women could have discharged most jobs adequately, had they been trained for them, and all civilizations would have been wealthier had they done so. However, those tasks were culturally defined as impossible for women. I believe that the crucial crystallizing variable—i.e., the necessary but not sufficient cause of the betterment of the Western woman's position—was *ideological:* the gradual, logical, philosophical extension to women of originally Protestant notions about the rights and responsibilities of the *individual* undermined the traditional idea of "woman's proper place."

I do not see at present how such a thesis can be demonstrated, though it would be easy to make a *plausible* case for the idea. Unquestionably, in the Communist nations of Europe, the immediate impulse has been ideological.

It appears more certain, however, that the social *implementation* of this change in values—and all great changes in values must be supported (when they are not caused) by changes in the social structure—

was the development of a free labor market, in which the individual was hired for his own skill, with little or decreasing regard for his family position. Using Parsonian terminology, this is a change from ascription to achievement, from quality to performance; or, in Sir Henry Maine's terminology, a change from status to contract. The woman, like the child, no longer needed to depend on her family elders or males when she wanted to work. Consequently, she achieved an independent basis for her own existence, so that she could, in the larger society as well as within the family, drive a better "role bargain." That is, she could achieve a better set of rights and obligations with respect to other statuses.

Men have not, however, yielded their ancient prerogatives willingly. After all, no ruling status group readily relinquishes its powers. We have only to view the battle of colonial peoples for independence over the past few generations, or the attempt by ethnic groups within European countries to gain equal rights, to understand how strong are the resistances to equalitarianism. Journalistic accounts of the position of women in Western nations typically exaggerate their equality, but precisely because this is new and thus worthy of notice. We should, therefore, take a serious look at the extent to which this movement has not yet been fully accomplished in *any* Western nation, Communist or non-Communist.

Perhaps a useful point of departure would be an analysis of the implicit values, even of "family experts" in the West. Let us focus on France, since this country seems to fall between the ideologically rather conservative Latin countries (Italy, Brazil, etc.) and the more liberal Communist countries.

The best summary of this position can be found in Andrée Michel's qualitative content analysis of much of the current family literature. She points out that their implicit *value* judgments, often *expressed* as empirical judgments, contain three important themes: (1) the notion of the emancipation of both women and children is seen to be identical with the idea of a "destructive evolution" or "disintegration" of the family; (2) the concept of "strength" or "solidarity" of the family is viewed as identical with the authority of the father; (3) the "unity" of the family is identified with the prerogatives of the husband and father. Let us consider each of these briefly.

The "menace" of disintegration, destruction, and individualism seems to be equivalent, in the minds of many French writers, to the loss of masculine privileges. Such a menace seems to be found wherever liberal legislation is proposed to grant woman her own voice in such matters as maternity and the choice or exercise of a profession. Secondly, whenever the authority of the male seems to diminish, many of these experts seem to suppose that thereby the family itself has been weakened. Indeed, Rouast seems to be pleased that the French laws of 1938 and 1942, which emancipated the French woman somewhat further, were in fact no more than verbal formalisms which left intact the prerogatives of the husband within the household.

Third, the notion of a family hierarchy in which the male is the final authority is viewed as necessary for the unity of the family; the husband should have the right to decide the place of residence, to give his name to the woman, and to decide on the education of the children. That is, the law is viewed as correct in giving the power of decision to the man with respect to all the affairs of the common conjugal life.

As Michel properly notes, such opinions rest upon myths, and frequently upon debatable or erroneous facts and logic. Here, however, we are not concerned with the *correctness* of these ideas. After all, they are value judgments, and cannot be proved or disproved empirically. For our purposes, they are data. They are especially interesting because they demonstrate that even among an intellectually emancipated group, whose field of interest is the analysis of the modern family, much of the movement to give equality to the woman is interpreted as disorganizing.

We have not located a comparable analysis for other Western countries, but we believe that such an analysis in the United States would locate a substantial number of family experts who would similarly identify women's rights with "the modern distintegration of the family." American experts would less frequently express their own philosophy about the family, and a smaller percentage would accept the French value position just noted.

In a study of relatively well-educated Belgian (French-speaking) adult men, excluding the clergy, it was found that their answers conformed to the values expressed by the experts already noted. For example: 32 percent thought it perfectly all right for a woman with a school-aged child to work away from home, and 42 percent said it was good that women were allowed to follow all the university courses of instruction, including those of lawyer, surgeon, and engineer. But 26 percent thought that men should never be under women's supervision as, for example, in an office. Only 25 percent thought that women would be as capable as men in occupying all higher management posts in industry, finance, and the state, and only 12 percent said that a husband should not have more authority over his wife than she over him. Ten percent thought a woman should be less educated and cultivated than her husband, and 10 percent said that a woman could never become a great scientific genius like Pasteur or Einstein, and 29 percent thought it contrary to nature for a young woman to take the initiative in openly declaring her love to a young man.

In the actual study, women form about half the sample. Here, I include only the opinions of men, which are more strongly antifeminist than those of the women. The answers are scaled items. I have reported only those percentages agreeing to the most extreme antifeminist responses.

In general, the answers of women are more strongly in favor of giving greater respect or equality to women than are those of the men. The answers given by respondents having a university education are also more strongly favorable. The young are more favorable than the old, but here the study, without being able to make exactly the same comparison, at least suggests the general conclusion of Kirkpatrick a generation ago: that though the young are more favorable toward the woman's position than the old, when *education* is held constant the difference is *not* significant. That is, the differences among the age groups are not great in this Belgian sample. Nevertheless, what concerns us primarily is the simple fact that in spite of the general belief that women have indeed achieved equality, it is clear that even among those who supposedly form the vanguard of opinion, this equality has not been conceded.

Since the attitudes are even less favorable to the equality of women in less educated strata one might interpret all such values as remnants of an outmoded philosophical position, which will eventually disappear along with racist and other similar attitudes. After all, a man may be unwilling to concede equality to a woman, but if she is the manager of his office, he must obey her instructions just the same. Or a university professor might well prefer that his wife stay at home, but she may nevertheless hold a job. Consequently, it might be held that the more important datum would be the extent to which women have come to occupy *important* positions in the occupational sphere, *independently* of men, so that eventually their greater scope of freedom will be conceded in value patterns as it is in behavior.

At first glance, indeed, such a view seems tenable. Certainly women now hold many more high posts in government and industry than they did sixty years ago. And, within the highly industrialized nations, women form a large part of the labor force.

However, the change seems to be more qualitative than quantitative, and perhaps in this fact is to be seen the portent of the future. Women have always worked, in the field and in the home. Even in the cities, only a tiny minority of women were allowed to avoid work. In Western countries that were extremely poor, such as Italy, a high proportion of lower-class women also engaged in *paid* employment, and thus by technical definition were part of "labor force," i.e., formed part of the economically active population. On the other hand, most of these women were engaged in domestic employment or in agricultural work, and in both types of work they were under the supervision of men. Even more important, their jobs were obtained through male kinsmen. If we consider only the 1910–1950 period, most Western countries did experience an increase in the percentage of all females engaged in such "economically active" work.

Few countries, however, show much of an increase. Most increases are less than 4 percent. Indeed, one must conclude that the work participation rate tended to rise in countries where it had been low, and to fall or remain stable where initially it had been high. If we look only at the nonagricultural work force, the picture is complex. Table 1 shows that for the 1900–1950 period in some Western countries, although female participation did increase, at most it increased very little; and in Switzerland, the Netherlands, Portugal, Norway, France, and Italy there was a decrease. Of course, the exact percentages are influenced by various technicalities of labor force definitions. In sheer quantitative terms, the changes have not been spectacular.

For example, in Italy at the turn of the century, there were many women engaged in paid employment in agriculture, and the majority of workers employed by the textile industry probably were female. However, there has always been a labor glut in Italy with accompanying unemployment. The small expansion of Italian industry has not kept pace with the decline of female employment in agriculture or in

TABLE 1. PERCENT OF WOMEN IN THE TOTAL NON-AGRICULTURAL LABOR FORCE, 1900–1950*

	About 1900	About 1930	About 1950	About 1960
Germany†	(1907) 27	(1933) 30	(1950) 33	36.7‡
Belgium	(1900) 32	(1930) 27	(1947) 25	(1963) 31.6
France	(1906) 37	(1931) 34	(1954) 35	(1963) 33.3
Great Britain	(1901) 32	(1931) 31	(1951) 32	(1962) 34.4
Italy	(1901) 32	(1931) 30	(1951) 28	(1963) 28.8
United States	(1900) 23	(1930) 26	(1950) 30	(1968) 37

* Adapted from Jean Dirac. "Quelques vues sur le travail feminin non agricole en divers pays" *Population*, XIII (January–March, 1958), 72.
† East and West combined.
‡ West only.

domestic industries of a relatively unskilled type. The resistance of Italian males to their women working away from home has been strong and until recently there was official Catholic Church opposition to female labor outside the home. Even the numerous laws to "protect" women have worked against their employment: since male labor was so cheap, and laws designed to improve women's working conditions increased the cost of hiring them, it has not been generally cheaper to hire women. Consequently, the female participation in Italy's labor force has dropped slightly since the turn of the century. . . .

The changes that have occurred in the United States may be noted briefly:

1. In 1890 women in paid employment accounted for about one sixth of the working population; in 1961 they comprised over one third of the labor force.

2. At the end of the nineteenth century, about half of the adult women never entered paid employment; now at least nine out of ten women work outside the home at some time in the course of their lives.

3. Women who reached adulthood about the turn of the century participated in paid employment on the average for 11 years during their lives; today's school girls are likely to spend 25 years or more at a job outside the home, over their lifetime.

4. About two out of every five mothers whose children are of school age are now in the labor force. Over eight out of ten employed women not working on farms in 1890 were in domestic or personal service, teaching, or in the clothing and textile industry; now less than one out of ten employed women are in domestic service, 29 percent are in clerical work, 17 percent are semi-skilled operators, 11 percent are professional and semi-professional workers, and 8 percent are in sales occupations.

5. The most striking increase in employment has been among married and older women; today the peak participation in paid employment occurs at ages 18–19 years and the proportion working then declines until after age 30, when the percentage of women in the labor force rises for each successive age group. Now, the chances of a woman of 60 working are as high as one of 40.

These changes are not, however, to be found in all other countries, though perhaps they can be found in most countries in which there has been a decline in domestic service, in home and handicraft industries, and in agriculture. We would suppose, even without being able to obtain adequate data at this time, that these changes would be parallel in the European Communist countries. On the other hand, the employment of married women has actually declined in Norway, and in the 1950s it was only 3.5 to 5.6 percent for the age groups under 60.

Sociologically, it would be much more interesting to compare the percentage of *higher*-level jobs occupied by women over the past half-century. We have not found such a comparison, and believe that existing data would permit only spotty comparisons, since most earlier employment data give employment by type of industry but not by *level* of job. Even in Italy and Spain such a comparison probably would show a marked increase in the percentage of women who hold higher-level positions in most types of occupations. Such a comparison can be made, for example, among French teachers, where the number of women per hundred men in the higher levels has increased markedly since 1900. At that time there were twenty-one women to one hundred men teaching in secondary schools; in superior schools the ratio was ten women for every hundred men. In 1930, secondary school teachers were 44 percent women; in technical and superior schools the percentage of female teachers was 25 and 28 respectively. And finally, in 1954–1955, the percentages of women teaching in secondary, technical, and superior schools had risen to 95, 56, and 56 respectively.

In the Soviet Union the reported proportion of women professionals to all professionals was 53 percent in 1959 as compared with 23 percent in 1928. One might question the reliability of the data here since even 23 percent is a surprisingly high figure for as early as 1928, before far-reaching changes had been effected in revolutionary Russia's social system. It is also true that this figure is largely made up of people listed as physicians, and women constitute 75.5 percent of the medical profession. However, even though women appear to dominate medicine it might be assumed that this number includes medical practitioners at lower levels of competence than we in the United States normally consider qualified as physicians. That is, the figure may include such lower-ranking occupations as medical technicians.

Women in the Soviet Union also seem to comprise a greater proportion of the traditionally male professions than in other Western countries (although, again, caution must be exercised in appraising the percentages). Available figures show that in 1959, 29.6 percent of engineers, and 32.1 percent of jurists were women. Even allowing for imprecision in the categories and the possibility of exaggeration in the percentages, there is no doubt that in the Soviet Union and other Communist nations, there are increasing percentages of women in the prestige occupation.

About one in four graduate students at Polish universities is a woman and, according to the 1959 Soviet Census, out of 3,778,000 people who completed higher or university educations, 49 percent were women.

State encouragement and support of higher education for women, the availability of child-care centers and institutions, and the still unrecovered loss of manpower suffered as a result of World War II, all contribute to the situation of women in the Communist world as a special case within the West.

One might hypothesize that where women have been in a socially and economically underprivileged position, and where men are unable to provide for them at a level viewed as adequate, they are willing, like the young men with few opportunities in tribal life, to seize new career opportunities. Women in Communist China, for example, have had less to lose and relatively more to gain from work than Western middle-class women who expect to be provided for. Western women receive support and encouragement for *not* assuming a career and have a substantial investment in the *status quo;* the women in Communist nations receive propagandistic encouragement at the least, and often material benefits in addition.

Without doubt, the direction of change toward women assuming a place in the professions can be paralleled in every Western country. We must not, however, exaggerate the differences. The percentage of women professionals in the United States has increased substantially over the past eighty years, but the percentage of women in the professions of highest prestige, such as medicine and law, has increased hardly at all. In fact, the percentage of female college graduates who go into the professions is probably lower now than half a century ago, since at that time almost *all* women who went through college went into serious work. In every occupation, even that of social work (which is predominantly female), the percentage of women decreases as one moves up in the administrative hierarchy.

Such an observation can be made throughout the Western world. Although, as has been noted, a majority of Soviet physicians are female, as one moves up through the levels of training and prestige of university and hospital staff appointments, the percentage of women declines. It is likely that this broad pattern—i.e., the higher the level of the post, the higher the percentage of posts in the hands of men—will not change in the coming generations. What has changed, and what will continue to change, is the *proportion* of women in such higher level positions.

It cannot be supposed that all the resistance to these changes comes from the "prejudices of men." Most studies of employment show that women are somewhat less committed to their jobs, and, of course, are generally less well trained. The resistance to equalitarianism may be seen especially in the social assumption that whatever job the woman takes, she should nevertheless continue her responsibility for homemaking tasks. Her husband may help somewhat, but the prime obligation is hers. No one assumes that by taking a job a man is "neglecting" his homemaking tasks. No alternative arrangements or services are available, except to the very rich. Consequently, the burden a working wife assumes is great, and her motivation to continue working is reduced. Possibly, if alternative services were available, more women would express a desire to work, and would feel free to develop career-oriented attitudes.

With reference to women's lack of commitment, even in the United States the young man is much more likely to receive a university education than is the young woman. Of course, the American woman's chances have increased over the past generation, by contrast with Great Britain where the percentage of women among full-time university students has not changed since 1921–1922. More important, a substantial proportion of both women and men prefer that the woman stay at home and not follow an occupation. Norway may be viewed as one of the more equalitarian nations, but three quarters of Norwegian housewives in one sample preferred to stay home rather than work at a paid job. . . .

Many variables enter into these opinions. Since women are expected to continue to discharge their domestic duties even when they work— and this is true in Russia as well—a woman who works takes on a great burden. As the studies of time budgets have shown, the working woman has to work more hours per week than one who stays home. For example, in a careful study of time budgets of French wives, it was found that the married woman with a job had to work from six to well over twenty hours per week longer than the married woman without a job. . . .

This change in the definition of appropriate wifely behavior, and its emphasis upon establishing the home through the additional earnings of the wife, means that the wives of lower-class husbands are much more likely to be in the labor force than wives of husbands in higher social strata. On the other hand, it seems likely that the middle- or upper-class wives more frequently *prefer* to work than do lower-class wives, which would tend to support my earlier speculation about the influence of economic factors on women's attitudes toward work. . . .

A few comments on these points will attempt to sharpen some of the issues involved in this area of change. First, it seems possible that there is some relationship between the drop in age at marriage in many Western countries, and the extent to which young or older women have entered the nonagricultural labor force. Secondly, unquestionably a higher proportion of the upper-level jobs in most occupational sectors of Western countries can be attained by women, as compared with fifty years ago. This change is most striking in the Communist and Anglo-Saxon countries, although it is apparent in all. Of course, such changes are to be found in the *intermediate* levels of competence and supervision as well. Thirdly, women have not, on the other hand, moved very rapidly into the upper levels of jobs over the past generations, certainly far less quickly than should have been supposed from their movement into universities, the opening of curricula and training opportunities, and the seemingly strong feminist movement of a half-century ago. For example, though it is true that some women have become physicians in the United States, over the past half-century women have not *increased* their share of this highly prestigious profession. They have, of course, come to occupy many quasi-professional jobs such as laboratory technicians. Even when they have become medical specialists, their specialties have primarily been the "female" specialties, those associated with traditional womanly activities like psychiatry, pediatrics, and gynecology.

Fourth, in most Western countries, women can now obtain training, and can, under some handicaps, enter almost any occupation, including those traditionally open only to men. But, fifth, their *motivation* to do so is undermined initially by a socialization that still emphasizes that certain jobs are *male* tasks, and that a woman should not take a career seriously. In addition, their motivation is continually undermined by the acceptance in all Western countries of the idea that a woman must choose between two exclusive alternatives—work *or* home—an idea demonstrated best by the fact that the married working woman is still expected to carry on all her domestic duties, regardless of job demands. By contrast, a man's motivation to work is never undermined by such a choice: he *has* no choice. Even in Communist countries, it must be remembered, women can stay at home and much propaganda is devoted to persuading women to take outside jobs.

Finally, in spite of the great percentage of women working in the United States and in some other Western countries, it can be supposed that only a small fraction of adult women have a serious career orientation. This lack of career-mindedness is not necessarily sex specific, however. Many men, as well, have only a modest interest in their jobs:

in a Detroit area survey, although 83 percent of the men and 66 percent of the women said that they would work even if they did not have to do so, three fourths of those men gave "negative reasons" for working, and in addition, 17 percent of the entire male sample said that they would not work if they did not have to do so. Every study of men's satisfaction with their work shows that the percentage who like their work increases with the level of challenge, prestige, and income, and we can suppose the same pattern applies to women. Thus, the lower-class woman is much more likely to have to work, but is much more willing to stay home if the man's income rises sufficiently to permit her to give up her job.

2

PERSPECTIVES: BIOLOGY, PSYCHOLOGY, THE ARTS AND WOMEN'S DESTINY

"Biology is Destiny!" has long been the cry of those who reasoned that women's unequal position in society rested on the innate physiological differences between men and women. Certainly the view of the man on the street, as well as of many of his professional brethren, is that women's biology limits them in developing skills and analytical ability and prevents them from full participation in economically productive work and decision-making at the upper levels. Only a minority, but, of course, it is growing, have argued that sex differences are of little real significance in determining intellectual capacities.

Industrialization had important consequences for women's destiny because it removed most of the sex-linked biological criteria for work. As machines took on the physical tasks that man's muscles did before, the weak as well as the strong could engage in production on a fairly equal basis. Physical strength became irrelevant, especially for work done at the highest strata of the occupational scale. Industrialization also drew increasing numbers of women into the labor force, which, at least potentially, made them economically independent of men, and which also engaged them in work that only men had done before.

Not only physical strength stood between women and opportunity. The belief in wide differences between the sexes reinforces their segregation into certain spheres of work. Since men have traditionally been the gatekeepers, their views of women have been more important than woman's views of men. Whether men saw the differences between themselves and women as delightful or unfortunate, they saw themselves as ordinary and normal and women as curious or discrepant. In either case, these inborn differences seemed to be adequate justification, if any was needed, for the sexual division of labor: hearth or hunt, children or war, weaving or quarrying.

The development of technology does not necessarily increase the level of man's rational objectivity. The suitability of the male's physiology for different kinds of work has never been explored other than in the grossest way. Although we know men can carry weights or engage in physically taxing occupations more easily than women, we have not sufficiently determined what long-range effects this has on their general health and longevity. We know today that women have a greater life expectancy, partially because men are subject to a range of anxiety-producing and physically depleting activities. This means that the physiology of men does impose limits that are not recognized as such in the cultural definition of the appropriateness of his work. Perhaps the focus on women's physical limits stems from the fact that they are more obvious, as with pregnancy. But though many women suffer considerable discomfort during pregnancy, others feel fine and continue to work throughout—particularly those who hold responsible, well-paying jobs. There seems to be a connection between physical distress and dissatisfaction with one's work.

One may also consider the reverse of the physical strength argument. Men suffer *no* physical limitations that would prevent them from doing much of the work of the home: knitting, mopping floors, caring for children, or cooking. Even emotionally, many men are, no doubt, better equipped to handle children than are their wives; and many men exhibit more talent and interest in cooking than women do, gaining international fame as chefs.

Centrally, the debate is a problem in data *and* logic. First, the psychological or biological mapping of the sexes is incomplete; we do not know enough. Second, the problem of logic intrudes, since we may not be able to reason from the biological trait to the sex-role duties imposed by the society. If, as some biologists believe, women's bodies produce some kind of "mothering hormone" at the time of birth, it is important to know how long that continues (a problem of *fact*); but in strict logic we cannot argue that women *should* mother their own or any other children, simply because the hormone is produced. Nor does it explain why some men are more tender and nurturant to their children than their wives. If women are on the average weaker physically, this does not, in strict logic, then infer that men should be their protectors.

Equally important, however, is another problem in logic. Even if the biological differences *are* important in determining whether women or men would be better suited to engage in certain activities, from cooking to navigation, it is obvious that *some* men are weaker, less skilled and talented, and less able to direct a corporation, than *some* women. Consequently, the imposition by the society of such a discrimination pattern would remain illogical. The biological differences, if they are relevant for task allocation, do not prove that we use a *less* competent person because he or she is of the "right" sex.

The discussions of biology and capacity rage on, often at high emotion, typically between the defenders and the opponents of the determinism of *women's* biology. Often the discussions become debates, with the participants forced into polar positions in which the complexity of the situation becomes obscured.

Jessie Bernard is one social scientist who adds to our understanding of that complexity and contributes some thoughts about man's biology. She wonders, for example, whether the exposure of men's genitalia to external stimulation, often creating a heightened sexual arousal, may affect his behavior. Although it has been suggested that the hormonal changes during menstruation may affect women's ability to make decisions in that transition, few have speculated about the effect of feeling a loss of potency on men's capacity to make decisions, administer prudently, or exercise wise judgments.

Florence Ruderman contributes to the debate by arguing that women do have a different "interior climate" than men; their psychological predispositions are oriented toward familial and emotional activities. Moreover, she asserts (with many other analysts) that men are psychologically vulnerable and would be damaged considerably if women ceased being supportive and submissive. In her view, men "need" to be in power if they are to function well.

Lionel Tiger focuses on a different phenomenon—the male society or male "bond," the result of a long evolutionary process, which, in his view, is the basis for the effective association of men toward political, economic, and military objectives. If women participate in these male spheres, the bond is disrupted or weakened. Those societies, he argues, that kept women subordinate and excluded survived best.

Tiger does not evaluate the decisions reached by men in such bonds other than on the basis of this expediency. Since all societies do keep their women subordinate, we cannot know whether, in fact, their participation in male-bonded groups would be disruptive or useful. Some groups of men are more successful than others, while all presumably exhibit this bonding. However, his analysis does alert us to the importance of examining certain social *structures* or bonds, and thus to the question of how contemporary societies might be changed.

Some radical feminist leaders today argue that the structure of society is not simply the outgrowth of physiological forces, but may betray our sense perception of physiology, persuading us to accept untrue "facts" about it. Their discussion of the vaginal orgasm for example, is part of a political creed and condemns sexual intercourse as an instrument of oppression against women.

The reader may view this analysis as wildly deviant or radical or he might argue that one half of the world (the women) should be submissive so that the other half (the men) can function more effectively. But rarely is any attention given to the damage imposed on those who play the submissive role.

Indeed, it may be wise to ponder how many of the arguments regarding the abilities of *any* segment of human beings—women and men, blacks and whites, different nations—are generated by the need for rationalizations or legitimations of political opinions. The analyses presented in this section provide some materials for thinking about this problem, as well as about the problem of inborn differences between the sexes.

Whatever biological forces contribute to the different ways men and women behave, we know that the messages and models that society provides also shape these differences substantially, since the ideals for masculinity and femininity *vary* from one social group or society to another.

Some of these social messages are direct. Parents, teachers, and schoolmates tell children how to act; they also punish for failing to meet expectations, and reward for doing the right thing. A boys is ridiculed in our society for "being a sissy," encouraged to fight back, jeered at if he plays with dolls, and praised if he is good at sports and machines. A girls is scolded if she is boisterous and rough, chided if she wants to play football or fails to exhibit docility and sweetness.

Social scientists and laymen have argued for decades about another set of messages and models—those presented in our magazines, television, movies, and billboards, and the images of men and women encountered in literature. As early as Plato, philosophers argued that the arts shape men's minds and that the lessons we learn in school determine our behavior later when we direct adult enterprises. On the other hand, many have responded that such models only *express* what is already in the culture. That is, we are moved by films, poems, or novels, simply because they embody what we already believe.

With respect to any specific medium, such as television, it is difficult to prove that what is presented there will have much effect on the ideals men and women accept concerning how they should act or feel. It seems clear, however, that the *total* set of experiences from all such sources—sermons and soap operas, magazine articles and movies, novels and billboards—will shape people's attitudes and responses, since they constitute much of our daily experience.

Thus, although movies themselves do not make up much of our experience, if what we learn and are moved by in films supports what we live through in literature and the arts, television, and sermons, the cumulative impact must be considerable. In this chapter, Sandra Shevey focuses on the models and messages presented to us in motion pictures. The movie hero is active, physically strong, direct, and successful; he is rarely shown as a sensitive artist. Even if he does not win a conflict, his spirit remains autonomous. He makes his own choices.

By contrast, heroines are weak and need to be saved; the solutions proposed for escaping come from men, not women. If heroines have initiative and competence, it is also indicated that they lack more feminine qualities. They become whole people only by finding true love, by giving in to a man, or by having a child. They are not doers of heroic deeds, but they are supposed to wait for their men to return from the war or the office. They can be sex objects or good wives and mothers, and if they are "good" they should put aside their jobs or careers for domestic duties.

True enough, the simplistic portraits painted by Hollywood and the radio or TV serial have become more complex in recent times. The hero may now be an anti-hero, a tortured spirit, an old man, or a cripple. The heroine may leave one man for another—note, however, that she does not leave a man for her work. Nevertheless, it is too early to claim that the movies that most people see are changing greatly. Shevey expresses the hope that pictures of women who are independent creatures, with minds of their own, may be created by modern independent producers who are not afraid to smash old idols and thus risk box-office failure.

Shevey's muted optimism may seem unfounded, if we consider Kate Millett's searing critique of modern writers. Both in style and ideas such men as Henry Miller and Norman Mailer have sneered at the past and its hoary traditions; they are part of the avant-garde of current literature. But far from providing us with richer, more perceptive images of women, or suggesting that relations between men and women might be based on reciprocal gratification, intellectually as well as sexually, these writers (each in his own distinctive style) suggest that the "emancipated" man may simply use women (or men) in cruel and callous sexual exploits. The sexual act and the sexual relationship is a microcosm of society, Millett argues, exhibiting the universal oppression of women.

What of the information we get from the *social sciences* about how men and women differ? It has been alleged that even political leaders who do not take seriously the opinions of professors are likely to believe the economic theories they learned in their sophomore year at college. Since the problem of why men and women behave as they do has fascinated psychologists and sociologists for generations, the literature is vast. Few can escape reading some of it, since it appears not only in sober scholarly tomes, but has also been popularized in magazine articles, television programs, and the radio.

Even the work of psychologists, anthropologists, and sociologists has been criticized on the basis of their cultural biases, since they have drawn some conclusions about the proper role behavior of women that may not be fully supported by available data. Any careful examination of supposedly scholarly writings on this topic will uncover many sexual stereotypes and prejudices. The reader might look at the more "objective" pieces in this volume to see whether or not they harbor hidden sterotypes.

WHAT DO YOU MEAN "THE SEXES"?

by Jessie Bernard

Those who accept sex differences as more than cultural artifacts, as more than figments of our culturally created imagination, are not convinced by the evidence marshaled to rebut this view. They wonder, for example, about the fact that the feminine. Arapesh recently had been headhunters and constantly on the verge of fighting one another. Or the fact that the masculine Tchambouli women devoted themselves so happily and efficiently to the care and feeding of children. Or that their cheerful working together to prepare a feast would fit equally well a group of women preparing a church social in the Middle West. Or the fact that the Arapesh men and the Tchambouli men, both presumably feminine, were so different—the Arapesh being gentle, unacquisitive, and cooperative and the Tchambouli quarrelsome, bickering, strained, and catty. Or the fact that the Mundugumor and the Tchambouli women, both presumably masculine, were also so different, the first nursing their babies willingly and generously, the second, grudgingly. Or why, if as Margaret Mead said, the Arapesh and the Mundugumor did not differentiate the sexes temperamentally, the women differed from the men. Or why the Mundugumor made little girls desirable to others, dressed them up and decorated them, protected them from hazing, did not use them for hostages. Or why married women had fewer affairs than men. Or more to the point perhaps, why recent anthropological and social-psychological research with more refined techniques arrives at different conclusions. Why a number of studies find that by and large, among peoples as diverse as the lowly Pygmies of Africa and the highly literate Israeli in their kibbutzim, boys value aggression, competition, and dominance more than girls do, while girls value nurturance, stability, and order more than boys do.

They are willing to concede that a great deal that goes under the

From Jessie Bernard, The Sex Game (*Englewood Cliffs, N.J.: Prentice-Hall, Inc.,* 1968), *pp. 46–52, 64–67. Copyright © 1968 by Jessie Bernard. Reprinted by permission of the author and Prentice-Hall, Inc.*

rubric of masculinity or femininity is indeed a cultural invention. Curls, ruffles, and lace were not considered unmasculine in the eighteenth century, as portraits, even of our own founding fathers, show. No one would dream of calling them effeminate. Nor are the cleverly tailored pants that women wear today masculine. The symbols of masculinity and femininity can change from age to age. They are by no means trivial, of course, for this reason. For to say that something is *only* cultural in no way denigrates its importance. It is sometimes easier to modify a biological trait than a cultural one.

But to concede that some masculine and feminine traits are cultural artifacts is not the same as saying that all are. Those who accept sex differences as something more than masculinity or femininity are not willing to write off all the evidence. They do not believe that the sexes are mere figments.

The effect a women has on a man is different from the effect she has on a woman; and the effect a man has on a woman is different from the effect he has on a man. An ancient literary device is one in which an imposter of one sex masquerades as a member of the other. When he or she is unmasked, the whole situation is transformed. Everyone's relationship to the revealed character depends on his or her sex. If an ambi-sex name is misinterpreted and a receiver learns he has been communicating with a woman rather than, as he had supposed, with a man, their relationship changes. It can be argued that the change is a derivative one, based on role rather than on sex per se. This cannot be denied, but neither can it be denied that, quite aside from role, a pretty girl affects a young man in a way that her brother does not. And whether one labels it biological, psychological, or cultural, this difference in the effect each sex has on the other is itself a sex difference.

It is, then, impossible for either sex to have the same experiences as those the other has. No matter what a culture may prescribe, the sexes are not reacted to the same way. They are rejected differently; they are accepted differently; they are ignored differently. They are deprived differently; they are indulged differently. These are social phenomena and independent of culture. No culture can provide identical experiences to both collectivities. The timid man is treated differently from the way the timid woman is treated, the aggressive man from the aggressive woman. Since minds and hearts are shaped and formed by experiences, people with such different experiences have to be different.

Not all differences between the sexes are relevant for communication between or among them, so that they do not seriously influence relationships. Some *are* relevant, though even these may not have much influence on communication, or at most only minimal influence.

A linguist has noted that when people of different cultural backgrounds fail to understand one another, each tends to blame the other for his stupidity. And so, often do people of different sex. What seems so clear and obvious to women may be unintelligible to men, and of course vice versa.

Psychologists have accumulated a vast literature documenting sex differences in a wide variety of areas. But in the area of intelligence they have found very little. When they first set up mental tests they started with the extraordinary assumption that the IQ of boys and girls must be equal. If any test gave an advantage to boys, it was discarded or compensated for by a test that gave an equivalent advantage to the girls and vice versa. The average IQ had to end up at one hundred for both sexes.

Actually, boys tend to do better in mathematical and mechanical tests. Girls tend to do better in verbal tests, a fact that may or may not be relevant for verbal communication between the sexes. Some researchers are of the opinion that these verbal sex differences are cultural in origin, resulting from differences in socialization and that they are declining as a result of changes in the way children are reared nowadays, underplaying, as it does, sex differences. Yet in one recent study, girls still had surpassed the boys, certainly up to the age of eight.

Some—puzzled Parallelists, perhaps, and nonplussed Assimilationists —fall back on differences in the way the sexes use their intelligence to explain differences. Margaret Mead has supplied them with support in her conclusion that women actually think differently from the way men think. Yet in one study attempting to pin down the nature of this difference, the results were by no means convincing. The researcher, for example, had forty groups of four members each with varying sex composition discuss given topics, tape-recording what they had to say. When the records were transcribed, judges could identify the correct sex of the speakers at a level of accuracy just barely above chance, and this slight margin of accuracy could often be explained on the basis of kinds of words used and style of participation.

To the extent that there really are differences in the way women think, they may be due to the fact that, having different muscles and glands at the disposal of their brains, they have different kinds of experiences. The major differences may also be intrinsic but social in the sense that they lie in the effect each sex has on others. Women are different in part because they affect others differently than men do. Therefore, they have different experiences to supply their minds. This difference is not always cultural, but it is social.

The *What*-difference? school emphasized the fact that many scientifically documented sex differences were merely differences in the distribution of traits common to both sexes. Here the distinction between traits that are typical and those that are characteristic is relevant. Both sexes may be quite alike in a given trait but when or if they do differ, men differ in one direction and women in another. Thus, for example, one study of thirteen hundred subjects hypothesized that (1) masculine thinking was a less intense modification of feminine thinking; (2) masculine thinking was oriented more in terms of the self, while feminine thinking was oriented more toward the environment; (3) masculine thinking anticipated rewards and punishments as a result of the adequacy or inadequacy of the self, whereas feminine thinking anticipated rewards and punishments as a result of the friendship, love, or hostility of the environment; (4) masculine thinking was associated more with a desire for personal achievement and accomplishment, while feminine thinking was associated more with a desire for love and friendship; and (5) masculine thinking found value more in malevolent and hostile actions against a competitive society, while feminine thinking found value more in freedom from restraint in a friendly and pleasant environment. After long, involved, and technical testing of these hypotheses, the authors concluded that "the basic factor which cannot be ignored is the extreme similarity between masculine and feminine thinking, with the feminine modes dominant for both groups. For men these modes are only partially overlaid by the jungle-like orientation." The so-called feminine mode of thinking, in other words, was typical of both male and female subjects. But when they did differ it was in a certain characteristic way.

In any event, though, whatever the nature of sex differences in mentality may be, they are not great enough in and of themselves to interfere with communication between the sexes. If or when the sexes do not succeed in communicating with one another, the failure cannot be attributed to lack of the requisite intelligence. Whether or not it is true that women do, in fact, think differently from men, it is a strategic advantage to have men think they do.

Because of the common species heredity and the common body systems, especially the sensory systems, we can assume that all of us, regardless of sex, experience red when stimulated by the proper wave length, hear high C when the proper note is struck, taste sweetness when we eat sugar, smell fragrance in a rose garden, feel softness when touching silk. The same confidence in assuming similarity in all sensory experience, however, is not warranted, for some differences between the sexes in relevant areas of experience can influence communication and therefore the relations between them. Some of these differences are physiological, some anatomical. Some are culturally induced. And some are bio-socio-cultural.

Certainly, as to within-body sensory experience, physiology and anatomy contribute to differences. At any one time about 8½ percent of all females in the United States between ten and fifty are pregnant (as of 1960), and of the rest, a fourth, say, of those not breast-feeding their babies are menstruating. Perhaps another 10 percent are experiencing premenstrual symptoms of one kind or another. About half, in brief, and perhaps even more, are reacting in some way or other to stimuli not present in the male body at all. The young man can only observe from the outside the young woman's submission to the inner calendar which so profoundly influences her moods and her responsiveness to him. As to young males, most probably woke up with an erection and have been aware of sensations emanating from their organ off and on most of the day. The two sexes are thus constantly exposed to differing internal stimulation. Each sex is immersed in its own part of the sexual gestalt.

Anatomy makes for differences in kinesthetic experience. A heavy wet cape whose weight is carried by the shoulders feels different from a heavy wet skirt whose weight is borne by the hips. The relative distribution of weight by the male and female frames must similarly generate differing kinesthetic experiences. What effect such differences have on general kinesthetic sensations of women and of men is indeterminable since there are no people who have experienced both.

Erik Erikson has spoken of inner and outer space as related to boys and girls, boys tending to think in terms of open, and girls in terms of closed, space. If it were possible to think in terms of internal body sensations, might we also find sex differences? Quite aside from the fact that there are different organs present, do women experience different body sensations from men? Are they more aware of inner body sensations and is that why they seem to men to be fussier about their bodies? The constant attention which the bodies of women seem to need has been called narcissism. The aspect that has to do with adornment and exhibition women share with men, for males as well as females "on a public beach . . . receive some sexual gratification from displaying their anatomy. [But] in numerous instances the display is not a form of solicitation—they are not seeking sexual activity. . . . [They just] wish to enjoy the knowledge that they are sexually desirable." But there seems—to men, at least—to be an increment which is beyond mere adornment or sex appeal and has to do with the serious care of the body.

The remarks of a group of young men during an informal discussion not too long ago went something like this: "The bodies of women seem always to require attention. They are always too hot or their feet hurt or they are cold. They are always aware of little aches and pains. They have a headache or they are hungry or thirsty or tired." In addition to these constraints, they included some narcissistic items in their bill of particulars which culture adds to biology: hairdo, makeup, stockings, heels, brassiere, girdle, hemline, and all the other accoutrements of the female body.

> They have to fix their hair—always their hair—or their make-up. They have to stop to straighten the seams of their stockings. They say they look awful. Not the same girls for all these things. But all of them for some. They seem never to forget their body sensations. The excitement is out there, but when you want to run out to meet it, they pull at your sleeve to keep you back because their shoes hurt or they have to put on more eye shadow or powder their nose. Their bodies get in the way. They don't seem to enjoy movement for its own sake. You hate it when they are like that. But the girls who aren't like that aren't the kind you care for either. . . .

It did not occur to these young men to wonder how it feels to carry around those encumbering breasts or to run with such awkward hips.

Each sex views the other from behind a wall of quite different kinesthetic experience. If each sees itself in the other, it will often see wrong. Each sends the kind of message it is equipped to send; each receives the kind of message it is equipped to receive. They may pass wide of the mark.

Kinsey and his associates documented less speculative and more demonstrable sensory sex differences which may influence communication between men and women. They have to do not with sensations originating from stimuli within the body but with those originating outside the body, and specifically with stimuli which produce sexual arousal. They reported, for example, that women were less stimulable sexually than men. In only three areas of stimulation—watching motion pictures, reading romantic literature, and being bitten—did their female subjects approach or exceed males in stimulability. In twenty-nine out of thirty-three categories of outside stimuli, fewer females than males were sexually aroused.

Both internal stimulation and constant stimulation from the outside world combine to keep the vulnerable young man at a fairly high level of sexual restlessness. If he does not find release in one outlet or another, he will be uncomfortable. Not so the young woman. The tensions that build up in her body have to do with ovulation, a process so little felt that she does not even know when it occurs. . . .

But if the dependence of sexual relations on male arousal forces a humiliating and subservient role on women, it has equally great impact on men. It puts them to a test—sometimes agonizing. A woman can pretend and deceive; an erection cannot be pretended. She can be unengaged and still participate; he must remain erotically stimulated in order to sustain the erection. Her success or failure is not, or need not be, observable; his, especially his failure, is highly visible, and according to one psychiatrist, highly publicized also.

> . . . modern man literally lives in a sexual goldfish bowl, where he is constantly up for appraisal. His girlfriend has usually read the latest psychiatric book on sexual behavior, in which practically anything he does is called "infantile"; his friends openly discuss frequency and duration of the sexual act; his family ridicules him if he escorts an unattractive female; and for years, he has heard the older females mocking the sexual prowess of their husbands. There is a constant aura of jokes about male sexual inadequacy in the atmosphere. Haunted by his dwindling stature, he may look for help to the marriage manuals, where he is reminded once again, that it is his responsibility to satisfy his wife.

It was different in the past, in the days when sexuality was the prerogative of males, when women were pure, not only undemanding sexually but positively rejecting. It was the resexualization of the female body and the consequent demands by women for sexual "parity" which highlighted the dependence of sexual relations on male readiness.

The resexualization, or transformation, of the female body constitutes one of the major revolutions of this century. No one seemed to think of it as epochal or world-shaking when it came. The suffragettes were not the leaders in this revolution, nor even the great feminists. The women who spoke for free love may have had it in mind, but their target was primarily legal and other institutional controls which constrained the relations of the sexes. The real torchbearers were the marriage-manual writers and the schools of thought which they pioneered. Under their tutelage the responsiveness of the female body became the responsibility of men. In the early years of the century, the relationship was still that of a benign master conferring a grace on a subservient. Sex was still a man's game. But little by little the news got around. Women could be sexually responsive. Even White Maidens. Later on it was bruited about that, further, she could experience orgasm. It seemed incredible. A spate of research studies confirmed the fact. In one generation—Kinsey and his associates pinpoint it in the 1920s—the sexually involved population potentially doubled.

As if this were not enough, it was now learned not only that the female body was capable of experiencing orgasm, but also that because of shorter refractory time, it had even greater orgasmic capacity than the male body. Women could outperform men. The fifteenth century had known this. Imperial Rome had undoubtedly known. Contributors to the great Hebrew library had known. But the nineteenth century had not known. Now the twentieth century did. The female body could tolerate abstinence better than the male body could; it could also outperform him. At both ends of the scale it did better. There was the added humiliation to men that the do-it-yourself female climax was quicker and physiologically more intense than the one he cooperated in. . . .

All of this, conceivably, could have been absorbed without too much trauma, but, the twentieth century being what it is, the combination of resexualized bodies and an ambience of equality, there developed a veritable cult of orgasm. Women came to expect, even demand, sexual gratification on equal terms. It became practically a civil right.

Most western societies tend to give lip service to a single standard of sexual behavior: no sexual relations outside of marriage. In actual practice, however, they tend to be less permissive toward women than toward men and to give men the prerogative of initiating relations. A variety of reasons may be invoked to justify this double standard. Whatever they may be, whether valid or not, the double standard has the actual effect of protecting men against the greater potential sexuality which an emancipated female sex could demand. Just as marriage, however much men may rail against it, is a man's best friend (the man protected by marriage shows up better than his unmarried brother on almost every index), so also, in fact, is the double standard. The men of the nineteenth century put women in a pumpkin shell and there they kept them very well while they went about building empires and industrializing their world and otherwise tending to the really important things. It was useful to have women out of the way or at least in their place in order to free men to do these things. It also kept them from making undue sexual demands on men.

"I just don't get it," a boy from Seattle is quoted as saying. "I've shown this girl Audrey in every way that I'm not interested, but she still chases after me. Man, she must be sick!" And the counselor replies for the benefit of the girls that "teen-age boys find boy-chasing girls unfeminine—in fact, frightening." And a psychiatrist finds the increasing assertiveness and sexual demandingness of women "horrifying, a danger to the future of the human race."

The aggressive cult of orgasm in women placed great burdens on men. When men had had the final decision about sexual relations and women had bodies trained for frigidity, there had been no occasion to measure either the quantity or the quality of their sexual capacities. If men were poor sex partners, no one was the wiser, not even the men themselves. The women expected little and that was what they got. With the inflation of women's demands, the sexual performance of men came to be measured by very exacting standards. Worst of all, it was the wife who did the measuring. Since the books taught that the entire responsibility for female responsiveness was his, any failure was attributed to him.

SEX DIFFERENCES: BIOLOGICAL, CULTURAL, SOCIETAL IMPLICATIONS

by Florence A. Ruderman

Biological Considerations

Have women simply been "discriminated against," oppressed, exploited? Is there any reason to think that differential treatment ("discrimination," if you will), including a restricted range of roles, exclusion from certain spheres, lesser pay for the same job, lesser likelihood of promotion, etc., is anything other than prejudice, or a result of men's greater strength and mobility? The usual answer here is that anatomical differences, and asymetrical roles in regard to reproduction, have provided the traditional basis for allotting "outside" roles—the instrumental and leadership roles of society—to males, and for restricting females essentially to the domestic sphere. It is women who conceive, carry, bear, and nurse the young, and they who are primarily concerned with their care and upbringing. By extension, then, women are assigned the "nurturant" functions, for the aged, the weak, for society generally.

If this were all, we would still be justified in attributing some degree of inevitability, or inescapability, to the division of labor and associated "discrimination" by sex, with its implications of female inferiority. But we might also be tempted to ask whether the different involvement in reproduction is not rapidly becoming an outdated determinant of social ascription. Today women can choose whether or not to become pregnant. The risks and disabilities associated with pregnancy and childbirth are not as great as they once were. Nursing need no longer tie a woman to the house. Families are small, and a much smaller part of a woman's life today is occupied by pregnancy, nursing, and

From Florence A. Ruderman, "Our Species Learns to Be Human," paper read at the New York Academy of Sciences Workshop on the Impact of Fertility Limitation on Women's Life-Career and Personality, 1970. Published in the Annals of the New York Academy of Sciences, Vol. 175 (October 30, 1970). Reprinted by permission of the author.

childcare. We are even being told that test-tube babies are in the offing. And at the same time, the male's greater strength and motor capacity are steadily losing their social significance, as neither work nor mobility are now primarily dependent on physical attributes. All of this means that, superficially, sex might seem to be an increasingly irrelevant factor in assigning social roles, socializing to patterns of behavior, and so on. But we should also consider that the sex differences which are manifest—both anatomically and in reproduction—are only, so to speak, the top of the iceberg: that far more pervasive "inner" differences of mentality, temperament, drive, innovativeness, are associated with these "external" sex differences. Sexuality is more basic and more diffuse than sex: it works through a complicated endocrinological system, a hormone structure, that makes male and female not simply the identical thing packaged differently (with the differences in structure and reproductive functioning largely "incidental"); rather, it makes them, in their nature, in their very being, unlike yet unalike—to some small but critical degree, essentially, qualitatively, different.

This is not a field in which we know very much as yet, although it is an area of vast social significance. But some facts are known, and are relevant here. To review only some of these: Sex is a crucial element of differentiation throughout the animal kingdom. In human life, a difference in the nature of "maleness" and "femaleness" is manifest on the level of sperm: e.g., in the highly disproportionate production of male cells; it continues through the greater frequency of conception of males, the greater vulnerability of the male fetus, male neonate, and so on. And from birth (if not before) differences in behavior in response to inner and outer stimuli, are marked. Male babies sleep less, are more restless, cry more, demand more attention, are more "unconsolable," and so on. Female neonates, despite greater tactile sensitivity, show greater placidity and contentedness. Recent discussions of the apparent relationship between the "XXY" chromosome pattern and a propensity to crime point to the "Y"—male—chromosome as a factor in aggressiveness, violence. Our increasing (although still very limited) knowledge of drugs which affect mental and emotional state (hormones are used, for example, in tranquilizers and other psychopharmacological preparations) similarly suggest that sex-related substances affect us, however subtly, on many levels of feeling, perceiving, behaving.

We can trace further differences. Very early in life, differences between the sexes appear in verbal ability (usually greater and developed earlier in girls), in social skills, in passivity and docility; in abstract conceptual and spatial thinking (greater in males, and manifested in ways apparently "uncontaminated" by cultural or social influences);

in drive and persistence; in objectivity, innovativeness, in intellectual creativity. There seems to be a far greater inner pressure, a creative tension, driving males. This is found over and over again: in tests and observations of schoolchildren, in comparisons of productivity and "scope" of male and female professionals, etc. In short, before we ascribe everything to oppression and exploitation, to convention and socialization—or even to the unequal burdens of reproduction and childcare—we should consider that more basic, intrinsic differences— inescapably bound up with life itself—may provide males and females, typically, with a *different interior climate*. To put this as strongly as I can, I think a scientific attitude itself requires, if not actually the belief, then at least recognition of the possibility, that as universal a distinction—through virtually all forms of life, through aeons of evolution—as that of sex cannot be simply a limited, "functionally-specific" difference, affecting only reproduction in a narrow sense and completely independent of the rest of our feeling and behavior; that it must, particularly in as complex a creature as man, be associated with subtle and far-ranging differences, from the level of biological functioning to that of personality and mental organization.

I do not mean to suggest that any limitations should be placed on men—or women—in choosing their fields of endeavor or styles of life. It should also be clear that there is within each sex a wide and overlapping range of abilities, potentialities, etc. But I do mean to suggest that there are *general* differences, and that these may be more basic and more pervasive than we are likely, in the present climate, to be willing to grant. Perhaps we should consider, too, that just as the male seems to have greater physical vulnerabilities than the female—from conception on—so too there may also be greater psychological vulnerability. This is suggested not only by the above-cited facts, but also by such well-established facts as the greater proneness of males to crime, suicide, and many forms of personal and social disorganization. I would like to suggest that perhaps assuring, structurally and ideationally, a special place or significance to maleness itself is an essential component of social organization, i.e., of society. In any case, if indeed there are, on a biological basis, differences associated with sex and affecting inner state, mental and emotional drive, etc., on the average, or in the aggregate, then it is probably unavoidable that societies will take account of this, building it into cultural definitions and institutionalizing it in norms and social structures.

Before leaving this section, I want to point to a few other relevant facts. Certain differences in behavior and basic needs (again in general), such as the greater importance to males of initiative—including an initiating role in sex—may also have deep biological sources. The male's greater need to be, or at least feel himself to be, the initiator in sexual encounters seems to be deeply ingrained, biologically. In animal species in which the female may be as powerful or as aggressive as the male, she nevertheless becomes docile and passive during the rutting season; in silver foxes it has recently been found that there is a genetic relationship between multiple periods of heat and docility. In some species, ritualized gestures of submissiveness—assurance of absence of threat—on the part of the female is a necessary prelude to copulation. And in our own species, the sudden increase of female sexual demandingness, generally associated with "the pill" but probably having more complex social causes, has been creating problems of male resentment, and even a rise in clinical impotence. Certain other differences in behavior and basic needs—again in general—such as the male's greater need for dominance, for recognition, for achievement, probably also have profound (if obscure) biological bases. So deep may these roots be that it may be a social threat, i.e., a threat to the stability and strength of a society, to block the need for achievement, recognition, a place in the "outer" world, on the part of males; while such a threat does not exist when such needs—on the whole much weaker, and often nonexistent—are blocked for females. Again, I suggest that "learning to be human" may mean learning to understand and accept such differences. It may mean learning to recognize and accept our own potentialities and limitations, and learning to accept and adapt to the special needs and vulnerabilities of others, and in particular, others in our own families—husbands, children. For many reasons, a greater adaptiveness must come from us—not from them.

Cultural Considerations

If we now leave aside biological differences or those aspects of behavior which can be traced to a biological basis, we have still the elements of culture to deal with. Of course, cultural forms are themselves to a considerable extent elaborations on the ideational plane of observed—or assumed—biological facts; but the cultural elements can have a life of their own—indeed, this is inevitable, and this, too, corresponds to something "human." We need to have beliefs, ideas, a sense of meaning, about who we are and what we are. All cultures have elaborate beliefs about sexual differences, about appropriate sex and family roles, and so on. Certainly cultures can and do change; and I have already suggested that I do not, by any means, consider all cultural forms, all beliefs, ideas, etc., equally valid or sound. But we may ask whether a *universal* of human cultures—I refer to all of the beliefs, religions, philosophical, or whatever, that assign not only different roles but an essentially different nature or character to men and women—can be readily overcome, or simply dismissed as mythology. We are sometimes told that there have been matriarchal societies, societies where the men are the babytenders and housekeepers, while the women are the leaders or rulers. In fact, there have *not* been. It is instructive to look at those modern societies where allegedly the greatest strides have been made toward equality of the sexes, freeing women of the burdens of the family, etc. If we look at these societies, we see that the departures have been more apparent than real. England has long had a tradition of the strong-willed eccentric (and wealthy) lady—but it is a male-dominated society to an extraordinary extent. The same is true in Scandinavian countries. The situation in countries with a revolutionary background is even more revealing. In Russia, women overwhelmingly work, and are represented in fields we tend to think of as male (this includes not only professions such as medicine and dentistry, but also heavy physical labor); yet in all fields they are concentrated on lower levels and in subordinate positions. Perhaps even more to the point, while Russian women—married women, mothers— are pressed, both by official doctrine and economic hardship to work outside the home, all aspects of domestic work remain theirs as before, including the cooking and cleaning, the long hours of waiting in line to buy food, and so on. In other words, Russian women are working more and harder than ever, but the inequality in status and in domestic burdens remains. And the cultural ideals of the revolution—of complete equality of the sexes, of the freeing of the bonds of family life, of the state taking over domestic and childrearing functions—have been quietly laid aside. The Israeli kibbutz is a fascinating and in many respects successful experiment, but here, too, there are points which must not be overlooked. It is only a small minority of the Israeli population that lives in kibbutzim; and, despite the early ideology of supplanting the family, the kibbutz succeeded precisely because—whatever the verbalizations may have been—crucial elements of the cultural background of the members proved stronger than the Marxist ideals; the kibbutz clung, in the last analysis, to a strong morality and ethnic, including a "puritanical" sex and family ethic. In recent years, even those elements of traditional family life and sexual differentiation that had been weakened have reappeared or been reinforced: kibbutz children now spend more time with their parents and in some kibbutzim may sleep in their rooms; and the kibbutz now typically assigns men and women to different roles on the basis of sex. It is the women who work in the kitchens, the laundries; it is they who are the children's nurses and teachers. In fact, so strong is—apparently—the hold of cultural elements that define certain spheres of life, as well as certain ways of acting, feeling, etc., as essentially "male" or "female," that we may venture the prediction that no matter how revolutionary the society, no matter what its attitude toward the family, it will sooner or later revert to cultural differentiation and some degree of social ascription on the basis of sex. These cultural elements, too, are facts of life—part of being "human." We may even wonder if they do not correspond to a basic "human need," and whether a culture which did not elaborate differences by sex—one of the most fundamental ways of providing meaning, identity, and channelizing aspirations and longing—could possibly be maintained, in any society, for long.

Societal Considerations

All societies require that certain functions—certain roles—be fulfilled. Even the most primitive societies have a division of labor—even such primitive societies as hippie "communes." These essential functions include both so-called integrative, expressive functions—including those concerned with physical care, emotional support, socialization—and instrumental functions: leadership, control, defense, production, etc. We are increasingly being told that women can fill the latter roles as well as men (or at least, that they *could*, if they were brought up to believe they could); and that men can and indeed are eager to assume housekeeping and childrearing roles. I know of absolutely no evidence for these assertions, or even of anything to suggest the possibility of this, on anything like a mass scale and an enduring basis. I think such statements, especially when they come in the guise of scholarly or scientific knowledge—unsubstantiated and, apparently, rarely challenged—are misleading and irresponsible. I repeat, I know of no evidence that, on a large scale, women could (or even want to) assume roles or primary responsibility in the economy, government, etc., or that any substantial numbers of men want to become fulltime babytenders and housekeepers. I do know of considerable evidence to the contrary. In my own research, for example, I found that situations in which fathers are the major childcare agents for working mothers are generally unhappy situations (for all); that men in such roles tend to be embittered and resentful—and also, not irrelevantly, to perform poorly. And in those situations in which father does not work, while mother does—i.e., where there is a virtually complete reversal of roles—there is almost always a high level of tension and conflict. And, on the other hand, I found that while many women are genuinely committed—dedicated—to their outside occupations, many more simply enjoy the change in routine, being "out," and so forth. The general level of commitment to work is quite low and undependable. In short, the prospects that we can—or should—attempt, in the foreseeable future, any mass reversal or even statistical "equalization" of roles of men and women seems to me highly illusory. Perhaps, instead, we should reconsider the possibility that the traditional division of labor may be—certainly not in all cases, but in the aggregate—not the result of injustice and alienation, but the result of an interaction of societal needs and "basic human nature"—men's and women's own intrinsic desires and aptitudes.

References

1. Weber, Max. "Science as a Vocation." In *The Methodology of the Social Sciences,* edited by E. A. Shils and H. A. Finch. Glencoe, Illinois: The Free Press, 1949.

2. Durkheim, Emile. *The Rules of the Sociological Method.* Glencoe, Illinois: The Free Press, 1938. Also *Suicide* (1951) and *The Division of Labor in Society* (1933). Glencoe, Illinois: The Free Press.

3. Etzioni, Amitai. "Basic Human Needs, Alienation and Inauthenticity." *American Sociological Review,* XXXIII, no. 6, December, 1968, 870–85.

4. Ruderman, Florence A. *Child Care and Working Mothers.* New York: Child Welfare League of America, 1968. A more general discussion of these and other materials will be contained in a forthcoming publication.

THE POSSIBLE BIOLOGICAL ORIGINS
OF SEXUAL DISCRIMINATION
by Lionel Tiger

Thus a picture emerges from generalizing about the terrestrial primates; it features the importance of bonds among males for the process of selection. An additional point of equal relevance is that the stability, order, and defense of the community depend on the male-bonded individuals: politics and reproduction are closely linked. *Hence the Darwinian processes of natural selection involve a combination of sexual competence with females and social competence with males.* This in turn appears to stabilize communities, provide models for the young males, and seems, indeed, to conduce to the "health" of females as well as dominant males.

(In one as yet unpublished study, it is noted that in a group of rhesus monkeys in which there was no male, the females were incapable of "governing" the group and social tension and disorganization were constant. The introduction of but one adult male into the group corrected the situation immediately, and a more normal political and social pattern quickly returned.)

What is relevant in all this to our concern here is that primate females seem biologically unprogrammed to dominate political systems, and the whole weight of the relevant primates' breeding history militates against female participation in what we can call "primate public life."

This is not only to say that female primates have no social bonds. Of course they do. First of all, they form intense bonds with their offspring and this bond is as crucial to group survival as the male-male bond seems to be.

Moreover, as we get more and better data about primate life it be-

From Lionel Tiger, "The Possible Biological Origins of Sexual Discrimination," in Impact of Science on Society, XX, no. 1 (1970): 29–44. Reprinted by permission of the author and Unesco.

comes clearer that there is something similar among some primates to "kinship systems" among humans.[1] Particular individuals born of certain females recognize certain intergenerational relationships between each other, and in terms of the group as a whole there is a tendency for the offspring of high-status females to become high-status themselves. Rudimentary but functioning "class structures" then appear to arise— not in connexion with any particular property or other resource but in terms of social relationships themselves.

That the young of dominant females should be more competent, more confident, and more capable of approaching the dominant males on whom "advancement" depends, should not surprise us altogether. But that this is also a function of rather elaborate group-kinship structures suggests that even such complex patterns as these may be broadly rooted in a biological foundation and that the contribution of females to these systems is meaningful not only for their offspring but for the entire group and—presumably for the species as a whole.

Further, that this female participation seems to tend toward the formation of stratified rather than egalitarian communities must be an item to consider among those schools of thought which are based on the broad belief that more primitive states of society—such as animals enjoy—are open and pleasant by comparison with human ones, and that the contribution of females to social procedures must be generally wholesome, egalitarian, and contrary—so runs the diagnosis—to the dismal and unhappy hierarchical structures which males create and endlessly refine.

The Genetic Foundation of Masculine Dominance

Let us return to the human case directly. In humans the bonding propensity of males—if it exists—would have been given an additional evolutionary emphasis by the function of hunting. It is important to remember that among nonhuman primates there is little if any differentiation between the sexes in the food-gathering activity. This is crucial, because if hunting in the human species was for males only, then a preexistent male bonding pattern which we might have inherited along with the primates may have been strongly and unambiguously accentuated by our special human innovation of cooperative hunting. In other words, while in other primates the sexual division of labor had

[1] Vernon Reynolds, "Kinship and the Family in Monkeys, Apes and Man," *Man*, III, no. 2 (June 1968).

chiefly to do with defence and politics, in the human case this was expanded to include economics too, and herein may lie some of the resistance which human communities appear to show still to even the most sophisticated and ardent efforts to achieve sexual equality.

Every human community displays some sexual division of labor. The allocation of tasks may vary enormously. In one society a particular job will be for men and in another the same job for females. Some jobs will be done by both. But the significant regularity is that there is always some distinction between male and female work for some jobs and on some grounds. Sometimes these are linked to obvious physical factors: they involve speed, danger, muscular strength, etc. Nonetheless, there is often no technological justification for the sexual distinction, and one is driven to the conclusion that the pattern of sexual division of labor may relate not only to real differences in skills, aptitudes and interests, but to a core pattern of the human primate: that in some circumstances, particularly those defined as dangerous, important for the community, or involving matters of high moment, males will exclude females from their groups and engage in male bonding undisturbed.

That this may be both a deliberate and an infrasocial, broadly unconscious pattern—in the same sense as the male-female bond, based on sexual attraction and reproduction, is both conscious and infrasocial—underlines the difficulty of doing something about this; it aggravates the difficulty of knowing precisely how to go about obtaining female equality in the labor, political, and associated spheres.

In other words, I am suggesting that a species-specific pattern of *Homo sapiens* is the creation of particular bonds between males, that these bonds are intrinsically related to political, economic, military, police, and other similarly power- and dominance-centered social subsystems, that equal female colleagues—even one—could interfere with these bonding processes, that one reflection of this principle is the constant division of labor by sex, and that while conscious social management of these processes may of course alter or reverse them, the propensity to behave in this way continue to manifest itself in each new generation until genetic change "breeds it out"—a process which even under current circumstances is very improbable in any foreseeable future.

Of course, all this is impossible to prove in the sense that an exact and reproducible cause gives rise to an exact and reproducible effect. However, biologically speaking, a species is an experiment without a control group—except insofar as it bears systematic and acceptable comparison with other species[2]—and in the human case we can use cross-cultural data to point toward items of behavior which are common to all cultures, thus species-specific, and those which are clearly culture-specific. Hence, I have argued that the ubiquity of the male dominance and female exclusion patterns which can be indentified is a serious indication of the possibility that these patterns may originate in our genetic codes, and in the interactions between genetic code and social group and particular circumstances in which individual codes work themselves out.

It should not surprise us that maleness and femaleness as biological categories have elaborate effects on even complex technologically based behavior. Both are clearly biological features of the core of individual beings, and while there are many similarities between males and females, it is scientifically parsimonious to attend to the possibility that behavioral differences in other spheres are as significant as those in the reproductive.

At the outset of this essay I suggested that social scientists have paid inadequate attention to biological science and noted that this was particularly marked in the matter of male-female differences. It may be of interest to try to overcome this inadequacy and try to follow out some of the consequences of a revised view of control-by-genetic-process of broad social patterns and particularly of the effect of genes on the situation of women as well as on our attitudes.

How Theoretical Equality Causes Factual Inequality

My basic proposition takes the form of a paradox: that the understandable and universally acceptable notion that males and females are equal and should have all equal rights of law, economy, politics, etc., has contributed to the practical inequality of females.

Theoretical sexual equality has forced rejection of any concern about sexual differences. The practical result of this has been the continued deprivation of females and the slowing-up of a process of opening opportunities to women in present structures, of changing the structures and of adding new ones to accommodate women. At the moment, it is women who must accommodate themselves, and they are being asked to compete with men in male-oriented institutions. The net result of this is their continued deprivation and a recently increased resentment and anxiety.

[2] Niko Tinbergen, "On Aims and Methods of Ethology," *Zeitschrift für Tierpsychologie*, XX, no. 4, (1963).

A number of obvious examples come quickly to mind. A variety of researches have confirmed what many other less-sophisticated communities have known all along—that the female menstrual cycle has some appreciable and predictable effects on female social, psychological, and even technical behavior. Crime rates, industrial accident rates, and incidence of illness, for example, have been correlated with the regular cycle.

A recent report by K. Dalton of the University College Hospital, London, reveals that young women writing examinations are affected by as much as 14 percent by the time of their cycle at which they undertake some tests. The implications of this simple finding are of course enormous. For example, persons wishing to enter graduate school in the United States of America must take special examinations on a national standard. Should a woman write these during her low-performance time, she begins with virtually a second-class result and the work of her previous years in the educational system and her own personal qualities and skills may be severely devalued. In good part this is because she participates in a system which does not formally recognize her femininity, admitting that it may be the cause of changes in behavior or performance of direct pertinence to the educational system which has so expensively provided her the opportunity for seeking graduate training.

The same effect will operate less dramatically but with persistent consequences throughout a young woman's educational career; it must also retain its impact during her functions in some job. This can become serious, not only for the individual woman's well-being and occupational success, but for the clients of her particular service or effort. The effect will be more clearly exposed as women increasingly perform tasks involving the exercise of technological judgement upon which depends the safety of other people. The relationship of the cycle to motor-car accidents has been pointed out; it seems inevitable that should women become airline pilots it will be necessary for their work schedules to conform to their biological rhythms—not because accidents are inevitable, but because they become somewhat more likely and hence a risk subject to control by conscientious managers.

Now, the writing of examinations and the flying of airlines are two rather extreme contrasts. But in both cases there is sufficient suggestion of the effects of the male-female difference on performance for sensitive communities to consider ways of mitigating the consequences of these for individual females and for the community at large. It seems likely that communities willing to take these factors into account will respond more suitably and immediately to situations involving real danger and the use of expensive artifacts such as aircraft and heavy industrial machinery.

The subtler and less tangible matter of scheduling educational, commerical, and other activities to take individual women's cycles into account seems much less likely to be implemented easily. Perhaps the two outstanding reasons for this are: (a) to do so would be to recognize formally and overtly real differences between males and females— something which communities have in a curiously successful and tenacious way managed to avoid doing, in the name of the ethic of equality, and (b) there appears to remain a widespread taboo of more or less severity against the formal statement by both men and women of the fact and occurrence of menstruation, though this depends on the attitude of the community involved, of course. It is not clear to what extent this is a function of females' desire to maintain some privacy in this respect, or of males' resentment and perhaps even fear of a process.

A study using the Human Relations Area Files by Young and Bacdayan describes an unusually bizarre correlation between political authoritarianism and the strength of taboos against various degrees of contact with menstruating females.[3] This suggests that there is considerable variation in this matter (as in any other) between communities and among individuals. It also portends that communities with relatively liberal political attitudes may be more likely to openly acknowledge the existence of the menstrual cycle and cope with its consequences. Yet, at the same time, in some such liberal communities —United Kingdom, the United States and Canada, for example— there is a particular reluctance to deal with such a female-specific matter as the cycle. Perhaps this is indeed for the first reason given above, namely that such an expression of difference might be construed as an expression of inferiority.

The particular reason for stressing the effect of menstrual cycling on work performance is that it is both relatively clear-cut and an excellent example of the general fact that the work patterns of industrial communities in particular are male-oriented. The 7-to-9-hour 5-to-6-day pattern of work of course represents the densest and apparently most efficient way of organizing the time of individual employees.

My point is very simple: were work adjusted to female propensities,

[3] F. W. Young and Albert A. Bacdayan, "Menstrual Taboo and Social Rigidity," *Ethnology*, IV, no. 2, (April 1965).

as it is now to those of males, a more humane and effective "fit" between system and individual could follow.

The same principle applies to the relationship of working mothers and children. It is customary that those employees with full privileges are full-time employees. Again, this is defined in male terms. However, there is no special reason, beyond habit, inertia, the reluctance to face complexity, etc., why mothers cannot be treated as full-time employees with full privileges—in proportion to their contribution—even if they work only a few hours a week, or one or two days, or three half-days, or according to any other arrangement which permits them to spend as much time with their young as they regard to be necessary, while participating in the wider tasks available in paid employment.

At the moment, in technologically elaborate communities it is chiefly the unpaid volunteer lady worker who is permitted a flexible participation in the socioeconomic network. If such arrangements can be made for volunteer employees, it is not inconceivable that they can be made, too, for paid employees. This is not to say that no part-time job possibilities are open to females, for of course there are. But such employment is always secondary in importance and individuals are discouraged from seeing their work as part of a continuing career; the very fact of their responsibility to their families permits them only a partial commitment to their employers.

The same comment applies to phasing of female work over years as well as days. The community spends great sums of money educating women to undertake jobs which the rigidity of its own structure makes it difficult for them to assume and maintain should they wish to bear children and spend considerable periods of time with them for several years or until they enter school. Similar problems of pension rights, seniority, retaining, and continuity arise for the mother whose working career is interrupted as for the part-time worker.

It is curious that at the same time as various organizations and governments claim difficulty in attracting and retraining committed and competent skilled employees, systematic and seemingly insurmountable barriers are placed in the way of the largest single pool of available personnel to fill these posts. And not only do the pertinent organizations themselves lose, but so does the community in general because of the resentment, confusion, and conflict of loyalties between past training and present situation which more and more females experience simply because more and more women are being elaborately and carefully educated.

DOWN WITH MYTH AMERICA

by Sandra Shevey

Movies have been a powerful influence in keeping woman in her place. In an industry run primarily by men—as studio heads, directors, writers, and producers—for the amusement of and in the interest of men, an independent woman has always been portrayed on screen as an unattractive crusader, the career girl left on the shelf. Even as early as 1912, in a film called "The Suffragette," women were being ridiculed as tough and overbearing.

The industry has passed down its prejudices in a sort of gentlemen's agreement" According to our moviemakers, women have but two identities—as a sex object or as a wife-mother figure. Any actress who wanted to work in motion pictures accepted these images, cashed her check, and kept her mouth shut. The American woman saw herself reflected on the screen either as a distilled goddess—Pola Negri, Hedy Lamarr, Elizabeth Taylor—or as marriage bait—Mary Pickford, Ginger Rogers, Doris Day. Unfortunately, cinematic fantasy became reality when little girls started modeling themselves after movie stars, aping the Clara Bow mouth, Joan Crawford shoulders, Rita Hayworth pizzazz, Marilyn Monroe inertia, and Debbie Reynolds vapid jubilation. Identity and integrity were of another era. The American woman was fast becoming a pop cartoon.

As incredible as it may seem, these stereotypes are still with us. And because of relaxed film restrictions on nudity, lust, and violence, the sex symbol stereotype is bigger and better than ever. At this year's Academy Awards, Raquel Welch looked like a mock Elizabeth Taylor —or her own put-on.

Woman as a sex object becomes almost a parody in *The Adventurers*. Author Harold Robbins and director Lewis Gilbert have assembled a melange of nubile females suggestive of a Busby Berkeley chorus

From Sandra Shevey, "Down with Myth America," in New York Times, *May 24, 1970, section 2, p. 13. Copyright © 1970 by The New York Times Company. Reprinted by permission.*

line. All the world is a hothouse, and every woman is a Venus's flytrap. Even Candice Bergen's climactic love scene, replete with blood, sweat, and tears, takes place in a conservatory.

When *MASH* opened in New York, it met with strong objections from feminist groups. I agree that it obscenely degrades women. A female army officer is the unit scapegoat because of her independent attitude toward sex. Director Robert Altman contends that because women now share man's sexual freedom, and perhaps his army, they are obliged to to shack up in his bunk. How can so competent a craftsman—one who is so hip to the hypocrisies of religion and war—know so little about sex? Unfortunately, this shortcoming has been true of almost all of the great American directors—D. W. Griffith, DeMille, Lubitsch, Wellman.

Beneath the chauvinistic attitudes of Donald Sutherland and Elliott Gould in *MASH*, there is an implied homosexuality. Similar relationships are shown in other recent films, including *Midnight Cowboy* and *Butch Cassidy and the Sundance Kid*. If one looks at film history, one sees that this pattern is typical not only of army pictures, but of cowboy films, gangster movies, and spy stories.

Female subjugation, male chauvinism, and homosexuality are a gay trio in Ken Russell's adaptation of the D. H. Lawrence novel *Women in Love*. Obsessed with Freudian dogma, Lawrence reinforced in modern literature the historical myths which existed about women in religion and folklore: that we are all evil temptresses who seek to destroy men, and that to survive they must subjugate us.

Freudian critics see both paranoid and homosexual feelings behind this arrogant attitude, and it is this veneer of male chauvinism that director Russell attempts to shatter. In a nude wrestling match cum love tryst between Alan Bates and Oliver Reed, Russell points up the fact that there's more to "jock" masculinity—or less—than a pair of gym trunks. Would that the director had challenged Lawrence's female stereotypes as well! Given the extraordinary creative instincts of Glenda Jackson and Jennie Linden, we might at last have seen something of a woman besides shackling wife or castrating bitch.

European filmmakers, such as Truffaut, Godard, Resnais, and Bergman, do not exploit women as brazenly as do the American directors. A sexual aura, however, still dominates women's personalities in their films while it merely complements men's. Michelangelo Antonioni is an exception. In *L'Avventura* this director is particularly sensitive to the need of women for self-expression and honesty in their relationships. Anna is destroyed by the "machismo" of her lover, Sandro, as subsequently Claudio is destroyed by his infidelity.

Antonioni's *Zabriskie Point* is boldly feminist, although the feminism is a part of the film's total nihilism toward traditional Western values. Curiously, what critics have found objectionable about the protagonist, Daria Halprin, is her unconventional female film image: she is aggressive, surly, and dominant. Reviewers cavil about the way she strides rather than walks, and about the inarticulate, natural quality of her speech. Her strident personality is a strong breakthrough for women's image in film.

With the disbanding of the big studios and the disappearance of the star system, with the possibility of young female writers, directors, and producers breaking down cinematic doors and actresses smashing old icons, we may at last see on the screen a representative image of ourselves—an image which until now has been a black comedy charade.

SEXUAL POLITICS

by Kate Millett

I

I would ask her to prepare the bath for me. She would pretend
to demur but she would do it just the same. One day, while I
was seated in the tub soaping myself, I noticed that she had forgotten the towels. "Ida," I called, "bring me some towels!" She
walked into the bathroom and handed me them. She had on a
silk bathrobe and a pair of silk hose. As she stooped over the tub
to put the towels on the rack her bathrobe slid open. I slid to my
knees and buried my head in her muff. It happened so quickly
that she didn't have time to rebel or even to pretend to rebel. In
a moment I had her in the tub, stockings and all. I slipped the
bathrobe off and threw it on the floor. I left the stockings on—it
made her more lascivious looking, more the Cranach type. I lay
back and pulled her on top of me. She was just like a bitch in
heat, biting me all over, panting, gasping, wriggling like a worm
on the hook. As we were drying ourselves she bent over and
began nibbling at my prick. I sat on the edge of the tub and she
kneeled at my feet gobbling it. After a while I made her stand
up, bend over; then I let her have it from the rear. She had a
small juicy cunt, which fitted me like a glove. I bit the nape of
her neck, the lobes of her ears, the sensitive spot on her shoulder,
and as I pulled away I left the mark of my teeth on her beautiful
white ass. Not a word spoken.

This colorful, descriptive prose is taken from Henry Miller's celebrated *Sexus*, first published in Paris in the forties but outlawed from
the sanitary shores of his native America until the recent Grove edition.
Miller, alias Val, is recounting his seduction of Ida Verlaine, the wife

of his friend Bill Woodruff. As an account of sexual passage, the excerpt has much in it of note beyond that merely biological activity which the narrator would call "fucking." Indeed, it is just this other content which gives the representation of the incident its value and character.

First one must consider the circumstances and the context of the scene. Val has just met Bill Woodruff outside a burlesque theater where Ida Verlaine is performing. In the rambling fashion of Miller's narrative, this meeting calls up the memory of the hero's sexual bouts with Ida ten years before, whereupon follow eleven pages of vivid re-enactment. First, there is Ida herself:

> She was just exactly the way her name sounded—pretty, vain, theatrical, faithless, spoiled, pampered, petted. Beautiful as a Dresden doll, only she had raven tresses and a Javanese slant to her soul. If she had a soul at all! Lived entirely in the body, in her senses, her desires—and she directed the show, the body show, with her tyrannical little will which poor Woodruff translated as some monumental force of character. . . . Ida swallowed everything like a pythoness. She was heartless and insatiable.

Woodruff himself is given out as a uxorious fool: "The more he did for her the less she cared for him. She was a monster from head to toe." The narrator claims to be utterly immune to Ida's power but is nonetheless subject to coldly speculative curiosity:

> I just didn't give a fuck for her, as a person, though I often wondered what she might be like as a piece of fuck, so to speak. I wondered about it in a detached way, but somehow it got across to her, got under her skin.

As a friend of the family, Val is entitled to spend the night at the Woodruff house, followed by breakfast in bed while husband Bill goes off to work. Val's initial tactic of extracting service from Ida is important to the events which follow:

> She hated the thought of waiting on me in bed. She didn't do it for her husband and she couldn't see why she should do it for me. To take breakfast in bed was something I never did except at Woodruff's place. I did it expressly to annoy and humiliate her.

In accord with one of the myths at the very heart of a Miller novel, the protagonist, who is always some version of the author himself, is sexually irresistible and potent to an almost mystic degree. It is therefore no very great surprise to the reader that Ida falls into his hands. To return to the picking, then, and the passage quoted at length above. The whole scene reads very much like a series of stratagems, aggressive on the part of the hero and acquiescent on the part of what custom forces us to designate as the heroine of the episode. His first maneuver, for example, is to coerce further service in the form of a demand for towels, which reduces Ida to the appropriate roles of a hostess and a domestic. That Ida dressed herself in a collapsible bathrobe and silk stockings is not only accommodating, but almost romance-like. The female reader may realize that one rarely wears stockings without the assistance of a girdle or garter belt, but classic masculine fantasy dictates that nudity's most appropriate exception is some gauze-like material, be it hosiery or underwear.

Val makes the first move: "I slid to my knees and buried my head in her muff." The locution "muff" is significant because it is a clue to the reader that the putative humility of the action and the stance of petition it implies are not to be taken at face value. "Muff" carries the tone, implicit in the whole passage, of one male relating an exploit to another male in the masculine vocabulary and with its point of view. What is considerably more revealing of the actual character of the action is the comment which follows: "It happened so quickly she didn't have time to rebel or even to pretend to rebel." Since the entire scene is a description not so much of sexual intercourse, but rather of intercourse in the service of power, "rebel" is a highly charged word. Val had already informed the reader that "she wanted to bring me under her spell, make me walk the tight-rope, as she had done with Woodruff and her other suitors." The issue, of course, is which of the two is to walk a tightrope, who shall be master?

Having immediately placed Ida under his domination, Val acts fast to forestall insubordination. This prompts the next remarkable event—Val brings her into his element, as it were, and places her in the distinctly ridiculous postion of being in a bathtub with her clothes on. Again the language indicates the underlying issue of power: "I had her in the bathtub." The reader is also advised that credit should be given to the narrator for his speed and agility; Ida is swooshed into the tub in a trice. Having assumed all initiative, Val then proceeds to divest his prey of her redundant bathrobe and throw it on the floor.

The display of stockings and nudity is brought forward for aesthetic delectation; it contributes to make Ida "more lascivious looking, more the Cranach type." The frail perfection of a Cranach nude had been

mentioned earlier as Ida's comparable body type. Juxtaposing the innocence and rarity of this image with the traditional "girlie" figure in
silk stockings is an eminent bit of strategy. The word "lascivious" implies a deliberate sensuality and is dependent upon a relish for the
prurient, and particularly for the degrading, in sexual activity, which,
in its turn, relies on the distinctly puritanical conviction that sexuality
is indeed dirty and faintly ridiculous. Webster defines "lascivious" as
"wanton; lewd; lustful" or a "tendency to produce lewd emotions." The
Cranach in question is most likely to be the delicate and rather morbid
Eve of the Genesis Panel, now depreciated to a calendar girl.

Val proceeds—his manner coolly self-assured and redolent of comfort: "I lay back and pulled her on top of me." What follows is purely
subjective description. Ceasing to admire himself, the hero is now lost
in wonder at his effects. For the fireworks which ensue are Ida's, though
produced by a Pavlovian mechanism. Like the famous programmed
dog, in fact "just like a bitch in heat," Ida responds to the protagonist's
skilled manipulation: ". . . biting me all over, panting, gasping, wriggling like a worm on the hook." No evidence is ever offered to the
reader of any such animal-like failure of self-restraint in the response
of our hero. It is he who is the hook, and she who is the worm: the
implication is clearly one of steely self-composure contrasted, to lower-
life servility and larval vulnerability. Ida has—in the double, but related, meaning of the phrase—been had.

In the conventional order of this genre of sexual narrative, one position of intercourse must rapidly be followed by another less orthodox
and therefore of greater interest. Miller obliges the reader with a quick
instance of dorsal intercourse, preceded by a flitting interlude of fel-
latio. But more pertinent to the larger issues under investigation is the
information that Ida is now so "hooked" that it is she who makes the
first move: ". . . she bent over and began nibbling at my prick." The
hero's "prick," now very centerstage, is still a hook and Ida metamor-
phosed into a very gullible fish. (Perhaps all of this aquatic imagery
was inspired by the bathtub.)

Furthermore, positions are significantly reversed: "I sat on the edge
of the tub and she kneeled at my feet gobbling it." The power nexus
is clearly outlined. It remains only for the hero to assert his victory by
the arrogance of his final gesture: "After a while I made her stand up,
bend over; then I let her have it from the rear."

What the reader is vicariously experiencing at this juncture is a nearly
supernatural sense of power—should the reader be a male. For the
passage is not only a vivacious and imaginative use of circumstance,
detail, and context to evoke the excitations of sexual intercourse, it is

also a male assertion of dominance over a weak, compliant, and rather unintelligent female. It is a case of sexual politics at the fundamental level of copulation. Several satisfactions for hero and reader alike undoubtedly accrue upon this triumph of the male ego, the most tangible one being communicated in the following: "She had a small juicy cunt which fitted me like a glove."

The hero then caters to the reader's appetite in telling how he fed upon his object, biting ". . . the nape of her neck, the lobes of her ears, the sensitive spot on her shoulder, and as I pulled away I left the mark of my teeth on her beautiful white ass." The last bite is almost a mark of patent to denote possession and use, but further still, to indicate attitude. Val had previously informed us that Bill Woodruff was so absurd and doting a groveler that he had demeaned himself to kiss this part of his wife's anatomy. Our hero adjusts the relation of the sexes by what he believes is a more correct gesture.

Without question the most telling statement in the narrative is its last sentence: "Not a word spoken." Like the folk hero who never condescended to take off his hat, Val has accomplished the entire campaign, including its *coup de grace*, without stooping to one word of human communication.

The recollection of the affair continues for several more pages of diversified stimulation by which the hero now moves to consolidate his position of power through a series of physical and emotional gestures of contempt. In answer to her question ". . . you don't really like me, do you?" he replies with studied insolence, " 'I like *this*, said I giving her a stiff jab." His penis is now an instrument of chastisement, whereas Ida's genitalia are but the means of her humiliation: "I like your cunt, Ida . . . it's the best thing about you."

All further representations conspire to convince the reader of Val's superior intelligence and control, while demonstrating the female's moronic complaisance and helpless carnality; each moment exalts him further and degrades her lower: a dazzling instance of the sexual double standard:

"You never wear any undies do you? You're a slut, do you know it?"

I pulled her dress up and made her sit that way while I finished my coffee.

"Play with it a bit while I finish this."

"You're filthy," she said, but she did as I told her.

"Take your two fingers and open it up. I like the color of it."

. . . With this I reached for a candle on the dresser at my
side and I handed it to her.
"Let's see if you can get it in all the way . . ."
"You can make me do anything, you dirty devil."
"You like it, don't you?"

Val's imperious aptitude sets the tone for the dramatic events which
follow, and the writing soars off into that species of fantasy which
Steven Marcus calls "pornotopic," a shower of orgasms:

I laid her on a small table and when she was on the verge of
exploding I picked her up and walked around the room with her;
then I took it out and made her walk on her hands holding her
by the thighs, letting it slip out now and then to excite her still
more.

In both the foregoing selections the most operative verbal phrases are:
"I laid her on a small table" (itself a pun), "made her walk on her
hands," "She did as I told her," and "I pulled her dress up and made
her sit that way." Ida is putty, even less substantial than common clay,
and like a bullied child is continually taking orders for activity which
in the hero's view degrades her while it aggrandizes him.

Meanwhile, the hero's potency is so superb and overwhelming that
he is lost in admiration: "It went on like this until I had such an erection that even after I shot a wad into her it stayed up like a hammer.
That excited her terribly." And emerging from his efforts covered with
so much credit and satisfaction, he takes account of his assets: "My
cock looked like a bruised rubber hose; it hung between my legs, extended an inch or two beyond its normal length and swollen beyond
recognition."

Ida, who has never demanded much of his attention, nor of ours,
is quickly forgotten as the hero goes off to feast in his inimitable adolescent fashion: "I went to the drug store and swallowed a couple of
malted milks." His final pronouncement on his adventure also redounds
to his credit: "A royal bit of fucking, thought I to myself, wondering
how I'd act when I met Woodruff again." Royal indeed.

During the course of the episode, Val obliges the reader with intelligence of the Woodruffs' marital incompatibility, a misalliance of a
curiously physical character. Mr. Woodruff possesses a genital organ
of extraordinary proportions, "a veritable horse cock." "I remember the
first time I saw it—I could scarcely believe my eyes" whereas Mrs.

Woodruff's dimensions have already been referred to under the rubric "small juicy cunt." But lest this irreconcilable misfortune in any way excuse her in seeking out other satisfaction, it is repeatedly underlined, throughout the section of the novel where she figures, that she is an uppity woman. Therefore the hero's exemplary behavior in reducing her to the status of a mere female. Moreover, we are given to understand that she is an insatiable nymphomaniac—thus his wit and prosperity in discovering and exploiting her.

The figure of Ida Verlaine appears to have haunted Miller's imagination. It is not enough that his hero should discover her "whorish" nature and bring her to paroxysms of sensual capitulation while congratulating himself on cuckolding her adulating husband. In an earlier work, *Black Spring,* she appears as a woman discovered at prostitution and properly chastised. Here Miller's didactic nature obtrudes itself and one is made to perceive the validity of his claim that his is a deeply moral imagination.

Bill Woodruff's brilliant reaction when the news is passed along to him by another buddy is narrated at length and with obvious relish. The narrator, again a version of Miller, regards the anecdote as "cute":

> This night, however, he waited up for her and when she came sailing in, chipper, perky, a little lit up and cold as usual he pulled her up short with a "where were you tonight?" She tried pulling her usual yarn, of course. "Cut that," he said. "I want you to get your things off and tumble into bed." That made her sore. She mentioned in her roundabout way that she didn't want any of that business. "You don't feel in the mood for it, I suppose," says he, and then he adds: "that's fine because now I'm going to warm you up a bit." With that he up and ties her to the bedstead, gags her, and then goes for the razor strop. On the way to the bathroom, he grabs a bottle of mustard from the kitchen. He comes back with the razor strop and he belts the piss out of her. And after that he rubs the mustard into the raw welts. "That ought to keep you warm for to-night," he says. And so saying he makes her bend over and spread her legs apart. "Now," he says, "I'm going to pay you as usual," and taking a bill out of his pocket he crumbles it and then shoves it up her quim.

Miller concludes the saga of Ida and Bill with a last joke at the cuckold's expense, for Bill is still a cuckold, and a maxim for the reader, in capital letters, is put forward as "the purpose of all this"—merely, "To prove what has not yet been demonstrated, namely that

THE GREAT ARTIST IS HE WHO CONQUERS
THE ROMANTIC IN HIMSELF."

Miller's educational intentions in the passage are abundantly clear. Females who are frigid, e.g. not sexually compliant, should be beaten. Females who break the laws of marital fidelity should also be beaten, for the barter system of marriage (sex in return for security) must not be violated by outside commerce. Rather more informative than this sober doctrine of the cave is the insight it provides into Miller's sexual/ literary motives and their undeniably sadistic overtones. They are closer to the vicarious politic of the cock-pit than of the boudoir, but the latter often casts considerable light on the former.

3

HOW ARE WOMEN EMPLOYED?

Women on the Home Front

Headlines do not often describe the activities of housewives, unless they deviate strongly from the traditional social roles—for example, when they murder or are murdered, are arrested for prostitution, or sue their husbands for wages. However, the overwhelming majority of women in this and other countries do become housewives, and most consider that the primary role in their lives. If domestic duties conflict with their wishes to engage in other role activities—play, work, self-development, most take for granted that those wishes must be discarded. Although most women in this country do enter the work force at some point in their lives, most do *not* view work or occupational achievement as the focus of their energies. They are not career-oriented, but home-oriented.

Paradoxically, women are not *prepared* for the task of homemaking. Not only do they often not possess the basic skills of cooking, housekeeping, budgeting, nursing, and so forth that are necessary, but they are not psychologically prepared for a central aspect of this role: Housewives are basically administrators, managers of human relations, engaged in running a complex enterprise.

It is also notable that young housewives (most women marry by age 21) show no great interest in preparing themselves for the role, even though they evidently feel some strain in discharging it. In this neglect, they are like most Americans, who seem to feel that, by some magical process, a woman who bears a child is automatically capable of rearing it wisely; that a woman who enters a kitchen is capable of quickly learning to cook and plan adequate diets; that the new couple is competent to work out any sexual or emotional problems they may face together. Ironically, Americans believe that education is a panacea for all problems, and a necessary step before tackling any job—except that of housewife.

As contrasted with outside occupations, the work of the housewife is not *evaluated*. People have definite opinions about how good or bad a performance the businessman, the baseball player, or the violinist turns in, but only the worst performance of a mother is recognized (for example, when her children are ill-fed to the point of malnutrition or when she beats them), and seldom is the excellent performance rewarded. Without evaluations and the possibility of satisfactions for good performance—or even the fear of disapproval for poor performance—the housewife does not have a solid sense of accomplishment.

The more affluent American corporation man's wife shares the same routines as her working-class sisters—cooking, housekeeping, overseeing of the children, and anticipating the needs of her husband. Her husband, like the working-class man, leads a life independent of his family for much of the day. The women in both contexts lead contingent lives—not determined by their own actions, but by their husband's choice of occupation.

In some ways, one might evaluate the American corporation wife's life as worse, since her activities are more closely scrutinized. Whyte's article provides clues to some of the patterns of family life that many young people are rebelling against today—the close interpenetration of family and corporation, the subordination of the wife's interests to those of her husband and thus of the corporation, the dedication of the husband to work and the corporation—all increasingly evaluated as sterile, unsatisfying, and constraining. Corporations find it harder and harder to locate young men who will become such husbands, and, in the future, neither the corporation nor the corporation man will find it easy to persuade women to accept the role of corporation wife, in the style that Whyte describes so vividly.

But even in the face of change away from the image painted by Whyte, many of the same patterns, and certainly the same priorities of attention, remain. Even the woman who would like to choose a different life style is limited by constraints created by her husband's choice of occupation and by the fact that society does not support independent options for her. Should she wish to work—at any level— it is still typically her mother to whom she must turn. Her husband cannot help; his job keeps him away from morning to night. Older children cannot help; they are at school. Nursemaids, scarce at best, are terribly expensive and there are few day-care centers to which anyone would care to send her children, to say nothing of centralized agencies to take care of home and clothing repair, food distribution, and so on. All the jobs now done by the housewife must be done by someone. Just how the family of the future might handle them—or who, besides the woman of the house, will do them—is certainly an important set of issues that will challenge our ingenuity in the period ahead.

Working Women

Women have always worked, but their *relation* to economically productive work and its meaning for them and their families has changed over the past century.

These are some of the issues:

> *Work and home are now separate*—geographically and socially—so that the housewife cannot fit her domestic tasks between her other tasks as she once could on the farm or in the small urban shop.
>
> *Child-rearing has come to be viewed as a twenty-four-hour a day responsibility,* unlike the past, so that the woman's commitment and attendance at a job is seen as a potential threat to her ability to be a good mother.
>
> *Women have the option of being housewives only* today because more families now enjoy comfortable incomes. This was not true of farm or urban families in past centuries.
>
> *Jobs are available to women independently* of husbands and other male kin, which reduces the power of the menfolk to control them. Women can make their own choices among a wider array of jobs than in the historical past.

Previously, they had to do whatever their husbands or fathers decided, whether it was weaving or feeding the cattle, making cheese or waiting on customers in the family restaurant. Women now have jobs as mail carriers and jockeys in the United States. They are transport conductors in England, doctors and ditchdiggers in the Soviet Union. As the articles in this chapter attest, however, exercising the options is not as easy as most people believe.

In the first selection, Nye and Hoffman present some basic descriptive data about the participation of mothers in the world of work. They note that, in recent decades, more middle-class mothers have entered the work force. Specifically, the authors point to three phases: In the first, the employed mother was likely to be the sole support of her family; then recruitment came from mothers who were drawn into employment in order to increase the total family income and raise living standards; in the third, which includes the present, more mothers are entering the labor force from families whose income is equal to the national average—that is, it is possible to infer that more mothers are participating because they *want* to enter the career world. These mothers also have more education than the average. Of course, this shift is gradual and, at any given time, the labor force of mothers includes all three categories.

Although women's participation in work seems to be generally increasing, Dean Knudson offers a sharply contrasting view. He uses census data to show that in many occupations their presentation has declined. Although the percentage of the total female labor force in the higher-level occupations *has* risen over the past three decades, he notes that the percentage of the total *male* labor force in those occupations has risen much more. That is, if you compare women's progress to men's, the women are falling behind. The expansion has occurred simply because of the upgrading of the labor force, as more jobs have been opened in areas such as teaching, accounting, librarianship, personnel, and technology. Women have not displaced or even seriously challenged male dominance.

Knudson's conclusions are similarly bleak with respect to income, a major reward for motivating women (or men) to devote their talents to work. Again, women have not been catching up at all over the past generation, but have instead lost ground. He suggests that most people hold contrary views because the spectacular cases of women who have been very successful are the only ones to be in the news. As to education, which in the United States is a major basis of rank or respect, women have again lost ground relative to men. More women receive higher education than before, but the increase for men has been greater still.

In the next article, Alice Rossi presents the complex set of factors that prevent women from being strongly represented in the sciences, where one might think that women would face fewer barriers. She notes the important social fact that, in the marriages coeds rank as successful (that is, with successful men), wives do not work, in spite of their college education. Since most young women want to marry in their "eligible years," they feel they must make the choice between popularity with the boys and the hard route of scholarship.

The choice to marry and have children is especially destructive to a career in science, especially if the talented young woman interrupts her research work to stay at home during the years before her children enter school. In many fields, it is the years immediately after graduate training when the scientist is most creative, and forms the associations that will help build her career. Research work demands long hours of concentration, independence, and solitude, but these are all antagonistic to the time demands she faces as a mother and housewife. Preference for these attributes also are not likely to be developed as psychological characteristics in females, who are taught as children to devote themselves to others' needs, to interrupt their own activities, and to value social interaction.

Men who train scientists confirm what Rossi asserts, that women with outstanding talent are more likely than men to decide not to go on with their education, to interrupt it for a period of time, to complete it but not to dedicate themselves to research, or to accept subordinate and auxiliary positions rather than to accept responsibility for doing work on their own. A consequence for society is the loss of a major source of creativity from the manpower pool, but surely of equal importance, is the deprivation experienced by tens of thousands of women who are not permitted to enjoy the development of their highest potential. Part of Rossi's report is focused on practical proposals for improving this situation.

One problem to which policy-makers in the United States have devoted almost no attention, in spite of the need for skilled manpower, is the establishment of child-care centers that would free women to work without anxieties about their children. The bureaucratization of work has exacerbated this problem over the decades, since both men and women are tied to rigid schedules. The professional outside a bureaucracy has much more control over his or her time allocation, but still faces a demanding set of challenges in the work itself. Since women recognize these difficulties, even those with great potential may feel the easier way is to avoid the sciences and professions, and take lesser jobs that they can also view as a smaller investment, entering them or leaving them as their domestic duties permit.

In the last selection in this chapter, Epstein describes both the contemporary participation of women in the professions and the causes for their failure to utilize the apparent opportunities. She then points out some of the changes in progress that may increase the percentage of women in the professions.

Her analysis also points to a fact noted elsewhere in this volume—the extent to which the more interesting and challenging jobs are allocated in all societies to men rather than to women. This is most striking when seen, over time, in the participation of men and women, as the jobs themselves change. Thus, as professional social work has yielded more rewards in prestige and money, more and more men have entered what was once considered a "female" profession. Men have almost completely taken over midwifery, as it has become incorporated into obstetrics. Once women were thought to be unfit for school teaching because it was intellectually too strenuous and because women were thought to command insufficient authority to control a class. Consequently, most teachers were men, at a time when that post commanded high prestige in the local village, if only a modest income.

The percentage of women college graduates who seek serious careers has certainly dropped since the period fifty years ago, when only dedicated women went to college and most of them married late, while many did not marry at all. Perhaps some of the modern stereotypes of the "professional woman" come from that era, when the barriers were so great that only women who could show aggressiveness in demanding their rights or exhibit a more than adequate desire to command others had any chance of entering the professions or succeeding once given the opportunity. Epstein argues, however, that the general pattern remains: Women still feel they must choose between marriage *or* career (and thus choose marriage), settle for lower level jobs, and not aspire to high achievement within the professions. Indeed, our society still gives some approval to talented women who "give it all up" for domesticity.

The articles in this chapter approach the topic of women's employment from various viewpoints and offer various proposals. They agree that although the United States has removed most of the formal and legal barriers that once kept women from taking part in careers, the social and institutional arrangements that would facilitate change have not been created; and the day-to-day social rewards—from childhood through adulthood—continually undermine the motivation of women. It seems likely, however, that an increasing number of people are now willing to create solutions for these problems.

THE WIFE PROBLEM

by William H. Whyte, Jr.

Over the last few decades American corporations have been evolving a pattern of social community able to provide their members with more and more of their basic social wants. Yet, the corporation now concedes, one of the principal members of its community remains officially almost unnoticed—to wit, the Wife. For the good of the corporation, many executives believe, it is time the matter was remedied. "We control a man's environment in business and we lose it entirely when he crosses the threshold of his home," one executive says mournfully. "Management, therefore, has a challenge and an obligation to deliberately plan and create a favorable, constructive attitude on the part of the wife that will liberate her husband's total energies for the job." Others, though they might not put it quite so baldly, agree that the step is logical.

Just how to do this is a problem that has many a management understandably baffled. On one very basic matter, however, management is not in the slightest baffled. It knows exactly what kind of wife it wants. With a remarkable uniformity of phrasing, corporation officials all over the country sketch the ideal. In her simplest terms she is a wife who (1) is highly adaptable, (2) is highly gregarious, (3) realizes her husband belongs to the corporation.

Are the corporation specifications presumptuous? It would appear not. The fact is that this kind of wife is precisely what our schools and colleges—and U.S. society in general—seem to be giving the corporation.

Let us define terms: we are discussing the wives of the coming generation of management, whose husbands are between 25 and 40, and in junior or middle echelons of management or with logical aspirations of getting there. There is, of course, no sharp dividing line between age groups, but among older executives there is a strong feeling that this

From William H. Whyte, Jr., "The Wife Problem," Life *(January 7, 1952): pp. 32–48. Reprinted by permission of the author.*

younger generation of wives is the most cooperative the corporation has ever enlisted. "Somehow," says one executive, "they seem to give us so much less trouble than the older ones." "Either the girls are better or the men are marrying better," says another. "But whatever it is with these people, *they get along.*"

The Negative Role

Perhaps it is merely that this generation of wives has not yet grown older and more cantankerous. Perhaps. But there is evidence that this group-mindedness is the result of a shift in values more profound than one might suppose. The change is by no means peculiar to the corporation wife but by the nature of her job she may be the outstanding manifestation of it. And a preview, perhaps, of what is to come.

First, how do the wives conceive their own role? Critical literature has been answering the question rather forcefully, with the result that many Americans (and practically all Europeans) assume that the wife of the American businessman not only is the power behind the scenes but wants to become more so. The picture needs considerable revision. For the striking thing that emerges from wives' comments is the negativeness of the role they sketch. As they explain it, the good wife is good by *not* doing things—by *not* complaining when her husband works late; by *not* fussing when a transfer is coming up; by *not* engaging in any controversial activity. Moreover, they agree heartily that a good wife can't help a husband as much as a bad wife can hurt one. And the bad wife, clearly, is one who obtrudes too much, whether as a "meddler," a "climber," a "fixer" or, simply, someone who "pushes" her man around.

Resolutely antifeminist, the executive wife conceives her role to be that of a "stabilizer"—the keeper of the retreat, the one who rests and rejuvenates the man for the next day's battle.

This stabilizing calls for more than good homemaking and training the kids not to bother daddy before dinner. Above all, wives emphasize, they have to be good listeners. They describe the job somewhat wryly. They must be "sounding boards," "refueling stations," "wailing walls." But they speak without resentment. Nurturing the male ego, they seem to feel, is not only a pretty good fulfillment of their own ego but a form of therapy made increasingly necessary by the corporation way of life. Management psychologists couldn't agree more. "Most top executives are very lonely people," as one puts it. "The greatest thing a man's wife can do is to let him unburden the worries he can't confess to in the office."

A Social Operator

In addition to listening she can do some judicious talking. If she is careful about it she can be a valuable publicity agent for the husband. "In a subtle way," says one executive, "they put in a plug for the husband. They tell things he wouldn't dare tell for fear of seeming immodest." In similar fashion they can humanize him if he's a boss. "About the time I get fed up with the bastard," says a junior executive, "here I am, going over to dinner at his house. And she's so nice. She jokes about him, kids him to his face. I figure he can't be so bad after all."

Low-key "stabilizing," then, the wife sees as her main task. There is another aspect to her role, however, and it is considerably less passive. For the good corporation wife must also be a social operator, and when husbands and wives sketch out the personal characteristics of the ideal wife it is the equipment for this role that comes first to their minds. What they ask for, more than any other quality, is gregariousness, or a reasonable facsimile. Here are some of the ways in which they spell it out.

> EXECUTIVE: "She should do enough reading to be a good conversationalist. . . . Even if she doesn't like opera she should know something about it so if the conversation goes that way she can hold her own. She has to be able to go with you if you're going to make a speech or get an award, and not be ill at ease."
>
> EXECUTIVE: "The hallmark of the good wife is the ability to put people at their ease."
>
> WIFE: "The most important thing for an executive's wife is to know everybody's name and something about their family so you can talk to them—also, you've got to be able to put people at their ease."
>
> EXECUTIVE: "Keeping herself so she is comfortable with people on the boss's level is important. I don't think reading and music and that kind of stuff are vital."
>
> EXECUTIVE: "The kind you want is the kind that can have people drop in any time and make a good show of it even if the baby's diapers are lying around."
>
> WIFE: "It's a very worthwhile bunch we have here. Edith Sampson down on Follansbee Road is sort of the intellectual type, but most of the gang are real people."

For the corporation wife, in short, being "sociable" is as important as stabilizing. Like the army wife, an analogy she detests, she must be a highly adaptable "mixer." In fact, she needs to be even more adaptable than the army wife, for the social conditions she meets are more varied. One year she may be a member of a company community, another year a branch manager's wife, expected to integrate with the local community—or, in some cases, to become a civic leader, and frequently, as the wife of the company respresentative, to provide a way station on the route of touring company brass.

"It Makes Me Laugh"

As a rule, she is inextricably bound up in the corporation "family," often so much so that her entire behavior—including what and where she drinks—is subtly conditioned by the corporation. "It makes me laugh," says one wife in an eastern city dominated by one corporation. "If we were the kind to follow the Pattern, I'll tell you just what we would do. First, in a couple of years, we'd move out of Ferncrest Village (it's really pretty tacky there, you know). We wouldn't go straight to Eastmere Hills—that would look pushy at this stage of the game; we'd go to the hilly section off Scrubbs Mill Pike. About that time, we'd change from Christ Church to St. Edwards, and we'd start going to the Fortnightlys— it would be a different group entirely. Then, about 10 years later, we'd finally build in Eastmere Hills." It makes her laugh, she says, because that would be the signal to everybody that she had become a wife of the top-brass bracket. Which she probably will.

Few wives are as articulate as that on the social role, but intuitively they are generally superb at it; their antennae are sensitive, and they know the rules of the game by heart. Second nature to the seasoned wife, for example, are the following:

> Don't talk shop gossip with the Girls, particularly those who have
>   husbands in the same department.
> Don't invite superiors in rank; let them make the first bid.
> Don't turn up at the office unless you absolutely have to.
> Don't get too chummy with the wives of associates your husband
>   might soon pass on the way up.
> Don't be disagreeable to any company people you meet. You
>   never know . . .
> Be attractive. There is a strong correlation between executive
>   success and the wife's appearance. Particularly so in the case
>   of the sales wife.

Be a phone pal of your husband's secretary.

Never—repeat, never—get tight at a company party (it may go
down in a dossier).

One rule transcends all others: *Don't be too good.* Keeping up
with the Joneses is still important. But where in pushier and more primitive times it implied going substantially ahead of the Joneses, today
keeping up means just that: keeping up. One can move ahead, yes—
but slightly, and the timing must be exquisite. Whatever the move, it
must never be openly invidious.

Perhaps it is for this reason that, when it comes to buying an auto,
the Buick is so much preferred: it envelops the whole executive spectrum and the jump from a Special to a Super, and from a Super to a
Roadmaster, can be handled with tact.[1] Not always, though. In one
eastern steel town, where cars have always been the accepted symbol
of rank, the chairman of the board has a Cadillac—certainly a high
enough ceiling. The president, however, has taken to buying Buick
Supers, with the result that people in the upper brackets are chafing
because it would be unseemly to go higher. Except for the chairman,
accordingly, only the local tradespeople drive Cadillacs and Road-
masters.

The good corporation wife, the rules continue, does not make friends
uncomfortable by clothes too blatantly chic, by references to illustrious
forebears or by excessive good breeding. And she avoids intellectual
pretensions like the plague.

Are these rules of the game merely the old fact of conformity? In
part, yes. But something new has been added. What was once a fact
has now become a philosophy. Today's young couples not only concede
their group-mindedness; they are outspokenly in favor of it. They blend
with the group not because they fear to do otherwise but because they
approve of it.

While few young wives are aware of the sacrifice involved, the role
of the boss's wife is one that they very much covet. In talking about the
qualities of the ideal wife—a subject they evidently had thought over
long and often—they were at no loss. In one third of the cases the
American woman's favorite cliché "gracious" came instantly to them,
and in nearly all the others the descriptions spelled out the same thing.
Theirs is a sort of First Lady ideal, a woman who takes things as they

---

[1] The present equivalents of yesteryear's ranks shows a reach for the exotic.
Special has become Le Sabre; Super is now Electra; and Roadmaster is Electra
225—*Eds.*

come with grace and poise, and a measure of *noblesse oblige;* in short, the perfect boss's wife. But how near do they come to the ideal?

What A Wife Faces

What, for example, of the listening job that wives take such pride in? How well can they listen? Consensus of a cross section of U.S. executives: not very well. ("And for God's sake, don't quote me.") There are excuses aplenty. "If he has had a rough day," says one wife, "I don't want to hear about it. He'd only get mad and say things the children shouldn't hear." The husband, however, may be the one chiefly to blame. He asks for active, intelligent listening, yet seldom wants advice ("Women just don't understand").

And how well does she handle the special social problem? In advancing the husband in the office, the corporation is quite likely to advance him socially as well. There is no easy out for the couple in such cases, and for the wife the inward tug of war between the social *status quo* and the prospect of advancement can be extremely poignant. "I must have made some terrible mistakes," laments one wife now in midpassage. "I love people and I've made many intimate friends in the company, but since Charlie got his new job it's just been hell on us. He has so much control over their lives, and it's all gotten so complicated." . . .

A common feminine observation is that a man's major satisfactions come from the home. If he's happy there, he can be happy in his work, and vice versa. The belief is probably necessary. Is it correct as well?

Item: As management psychologists note, the average executive shows a remarkable ability to repress his home worries while on the job; rarely, however, can he shut out office worries at home.

Item: The reaction to this Hobson's-choice question: "If you had to make the choice, which would you take: an increasingly satisfying work life and a proportionately souring home life—or the opposite?" The answers would surprise wives. "The business of doing it all for the family," as one husband confesses, "it's just a rationalization. If I got a windfall today I'd still knock myself out."

"Man's love is of man's life a thing apart," Byron once observed. " 'Tis woman's whole existence." So, for all the group integration and communication skills she can muster, it will probably remain.

The schism between Home and Office has been even more accentuated recently. Thanks, in part, to the way the tax structure has accumulated, the corporation now provides the man with a higher standard of living in his work than in his home—and, it might be added, a higher one than his wife enjoys. From 9 to 5 he may be a minor satrap, guiding the destiny of thousands, waited on by secretaries and subordinates; back in his servantless home he washes the dishes. Nor is it merely the fact of his satrapy; the corporation virtually rigs it so that he can have more fun away from home. . . .

What kind of background for the woman, then, is the optimum? A serious career can be dismissed easily; there is almost universal agreement among wives, husbands, and corporations on this score. Work before marriage, however, is generally approved. "I feel the fact that I worked before marriage," says one wife, "is a help. I know what goes on in an office and can understand what Charles is up against."

College? Here is the *summum bonum*. There are some obvious reasons; because virtually all executives now go to college, the couple in such cases starts off with shared values. But corporation people mention a reverse factor almost as much. It is not so important for the wife, they say, to have gone to college, but it is very important not to have *not* gone to college. If she hasn't, corporation people warn, she is prey to an inferiority complex that makes it difficult for her to achieve real poise. Some corporations, accordingly, make it their business to find out whether or not the wife has a degree.

More and more corporations these days are interviewing the wife before hiring an executive, and some are not uninterested in fiancées. There are many holdouts ("This railroad picks its executives and lets its executives pick their wives and so far it's been okay"), but roughly half of the companies on which *Fortune* has data have made wife-screening a regular practice and many of the others seem about ready to do so. And the look-see is not academic. About 20 percent of its otherwise acceptable trainee applicants, one company estimates, are turned down because of their wives.

Ordinarily, the screening is accomplished via "informal" social visits. Many executives, for example, make it a point to call on the wife in her own home. Louis Ruthenburg, board chairman of Servel (which never hires an executive without a look at the wife), likes to recall how one college president used to insist on eating breakfast with a candidate's family; the wife who didn't fix her husband a good breakfast, he used to say, wasn't a good risk. To help them spot such key indicators many executives rely heavily on their own wives. "My wife is very, very keen on this," says one president. "She can spot things I might miss. And if the gal isn't up to par with her, it's no go." . . .

What are the wife's basic unadjusted feelings about all this? The answer is clear: she likes the way of life. To picture her as a helpless sort of being pushed around by the corporation would be to attribute to her a sense of plight she does not feel; she must be considered not only an object of the integration but a force for it in her own right. She has become such an ally of the corporation, in fact, that on several matters it would almost appear that she and the corporation are ganging up on the husband.

Whatever else she may think of the corporation, on three main points she and her sisters agree:

The corporation means opportunity. The big company, wives explain, plays fair. "We went over all the pros and cons of bigness before Jim joined Du Pont," say one wife, "and we've never regretted joining. The bigness holds out a challenge for you."

The corporation means benefits. "Eastman Kodak has wonderful good-will policies," a wife explains. "I used to have to attend to all the home details like insurance and bills. Now the company has someone who does those things for you—they even plan vacations for you."

The corporation means security. "Some companies may pay more at the start, but employment is not so secure. Here they never fire anybody, they just transfer you to another department."

Few wives go on to articulate their image of "the Company." But there is an image, nonetheless, that of a beneficent "system," at once impersonal and warm—in a nice kind of way, Big Brother.

There is, of course, another side to the picture. Many companies that have extensive wife programs do not attempt social integration, and some not only look on the wife—to borrow one executive's explanation—as none of their damn business, but take active steps to see that she *doesn't* get close to them. A sampling of executive views— oil company: "We are just as happy if we never see her at all." Tool company: "If wives get too close to management they always get too status-minded. That means trouble." Motor company: "Wives' activities are their own business. What do some of these companies want for their $10,000? Slavery too?"

THE SOCIO-CULTURAL SETTING

by F. Ivan Nye
and Lois Wladis Hoffman

The Changing Face of the Employed Mother:
Extent and Trends of Employment

Census data show a steadily increasing proportion of women in paid employment over a sixty-year period, but, unfortunately, early reports do not distinguish between women who were mothers and those who were not. Estimates are available from the 1940 census, and after 1948 adequate data indicate the presence and age of children in the family.

There has been a "moderate" increase in the proportion of all women gainfully employed—from 25.7 percent in 1940 to 34.8 percent in 1960. By contrast, the proportion of employed married women living with their husbands increased from 14.7 to 30.5 percent in the same twenty-year period, and the proportion of mothers with children under eighteen increased even more dramatically (Table 1).

Women with children of school age have entered the labor force in greater numbers than mothers of preschool children, but the *rate* of increase of both groups is about equal. The *increase* from 1948 to 1960 is 116 percent for the mothers of the school-age children and 108 percent for the mothers of preschool children.

Almost one third of all employed women in 1960 were mothers with children under eighteen. While the latter grew over 400 percent in absolute numbers in a twenty-year period, single employed women declined in actual numbers, and the widowed, divorced, and separated groups showed only small increases. Within this period, the employed mother changed from a negligible social and economic phenomenon

From F. Ivan Nye and Lois Wladis Hoffman, The Employed Mother in America *(Chicago: Rand McNally and Company, 1963), pp. 7–17. Copyright © 1963 by Rand McNally and Company and reprinted by their permission. References in parentheses direct the reader to the list of references at the end of the article.*

TABLE 1. WOMEN IN THE LABOR FORCE, 1940–1960

Marital Status	Employed Women						
	1940	1944	1948	1952	1955	1958	1960
	Number (Millions)						
Single	6.7	7.5	5.9	5.5	5.1	5.4	5.4
Married, living with husband	4.2*	6.2	7.6	9.2	10.4	11.8	12.3
No children under 18	2.7		4.4	5.0	5.2	5.7	5.7
Children 6–17 only ⎫	1.5*	†	1.9	2.5	3.2	3.7	4.1
Children 0–5 ⎭		†	1.2	1.7	2.0	2.4	2.5
Widowed, divorced, living apart	2.9	4.7	3.7	4.1	4.6	4.8	4.9
All women	13.9	18.5	17.2	18.8	20.1	22.0	22.6
	Percent						
Single	48.1	58.6	51.1	50.0	46.6	45.4	44.1
Married, living with husband	14.7	21.7	22.0	25.3	27.7	30.2	30.5
No children under 18			28.4	30.9	32.7	38.8	34.7
Children 6–17 only ⎫	8.6*	†	26.0	31.1	34.7	37.6	39.0
Children 0–5 ⎭			10.7	13.9	16.0	18.2	18.6
Widowed, divorced, living apart	35.4	42.0	38.3	38.8	38.5	40.8	40.0
All women	25.7	35.0	31.0	32.7	33.4	35.0	34.8

Sources: *Current Population Reports, Labor Force* (4) and *Special Labor Force Report No. 13* (14).
* Estimated. Source: *Women as Workers* (15).
† No information available.

to one that affects almost two in five households in which there are children under eighteen.

In total numbers there were 22 million women aged fourteen or over in the labor force (employed or seeking employment) in 1958, which was 35 percent of the total female population aged fourteen or older. Of these, slightly more than half were married and living with their husbands, one quarter were single, and one quarter had been married but were now widowed, divorced, or separated (Table 1). The highest proportion employed is among the single women (45.4 percent) and, second, those previously but not now married (40.8 percent); however, women with children aged six to seventeen and living with husbands are not far behind (37.6 percent). It should be considered that practically all women with dependent children are within the age range in which women are defined as employable, whereas many single and previously married women are not.

The Changing Face of the Employed Mother

Less obvious changes have occurred in the type of work performed by an employed mother, the type of woman employed, and the type of family from which she comes. The 1940 estimate gave 1.5 million mothers living with husbands as being employed full- or part-time. At a time when unemployment was near 10 million, these women were probably in most cases the only or principal means of support of their families. This assumption is further buttressed by the strong social pressure that existed from business and labor to "spread the jobs" by having no more than one wage-earner in each family. The employed mother typically was forced into employment regardless of the size of her family, specialized education, talents, or personal wishes. Since unemployed men were (and still are) recruited in largest numbers from those with the least education and skills, the mothers involved were likely also to come from the bottom socioeconomic strata and were unlikely to have advanced educational or vocational training. Mothers in such educational and soioeconomic strata are also more likely to have large families.

In general, the employed mother prior to World War II (as nearly as it can be reconstructed) had several children and was forced into an unskilled, physically tiring, low-paying job by direct economic necessity. Although there undoubtedly were exceptions, this image is in harmony with the available facts (7, chap. 11).

The stereotype has persisted, but the reality has changed in the postwar era, particularly as American society enters the 1960s. Now married women living with husbands are not usually forced into employment because of a need for their income as the principal support for their families. The large majority live with husbands who are employed, and this factor allows them to enter employment selectively. Thus working mothers living with their husbands may fall into two possibly overlapping categories—(a) those to whom employment gives an opportunity to use their individual talents and vocational training, and (b) those women who are least likely to experience major conflicts in their responsibilities toward their children or to receive negative reactions from their husbands.

This, together with the rapid upgrading of the occupations of both sexes, has radically changed the kinds of jobs held by employed mothers (Table 2). The demand for unskilled and slightly skilled labor has declined sharply. The proportion of women employed as household workers and farm laborers has shown a particularly large decline. In contrast, clerical and kindred workers have shown a tremendous increase, with large gains also in sales workers and managers, officials, and proprietors. However, though professional, technical, and kindred workers increased, steadily until 1930, this category has shown a slight decline since then.[1] Paid employment for the most part has become less physically tiring, has more status, yields more income, and is accompanied by better working conditions. In the current situation, mothers are *choosing* employment; they are not being forced into it in any absolute sense.

TABLE 2. OCCUPATIONS OF THE EMPLOYED FEMALE POPULATION FOR THE UNITED STATES, 1900–1960

Occupation	Percent of Women Working						
	1900	*1910*	*1920*	*1930*	*1940*	*1950*	*1960*
Professional, technical, and kindred workers	8.1	9.7	11.6	13.4	12.7	12.2	13.3
Farmers and farm managers	5.8	3.7	3.2	2.4	1.2	.7	.4
Managers, officials and proprietors, exc. farm	1.4	2.0	2.2	2.7	3.2	4.3	4.6
Clerical and kindred workers	4.0	9.2	18.6	20.8	21.4	27.4	30.0
Sales workers	4.3	5.1	6.2	6.8	7.3	8.6	7.2
Craftsmen, foremen, and kindred workers	1.4	1.4	1.2	1.0	1.1	1.5	.9
Operatives and kindred workers	23.8	22.9	20.2	17.4	19.5	19.9	16.1
Private household workers	28.7	24.0	15.7	17.8	18.1	8.8	9.8
Service workers, exc. private household	6.7	8.4	8.1	9.7	11.3	12.6	15.4
Farm laborers and foremen	13.1	12.0	10.3	5.9	2.7	2.9	2.0
Laborers, exc. farm and mine	2.6	1.4	2.3	1.5	1.1	.8	.3
Total	99.9	99.9	100.0	100.0	100.0	99.9	100.0

Source: *Occupational Trends in the United States, 1900 to 1950* (13), and *Special Labor Report No. 13* (14).

[1] This point is discussed further by Theodore Caplow, *The Sociology of Work* (Minneapolis: University of Minnesota Press, 1955), p. 230.

TABLE 3. EDUCATION LEVEL AND EMPLOYMENT STATUS
OF 1,972 WASHINGTON MOTHERS

Education	Not Employed	Part-Time Employed	Full-Time Employed	Total	Total
	Percent				Number
1–6 years	2.0	1.4	.3	1.6	32
7–9 years	15.1	13.0	8.6	13.7	270
10–12 years	60.9	59.6	64.9	61.4	1211
13–16 years	20.0	24.2	20.1	20.6	407
17 or more	1.9	1.8	6.0	2.6	52
Total	99.9	100.0	99.9	99.9	1,972

Better educated mothers are moving into the labor force. Although adequate data prior to World War II are unavailable, present data indicate the employed mothers to be better educated, generally, than those not employed (Table 3). For many jobs, for both men and women, high school graduation is a prerequisite. Increasingly, it is the educated women who have the opportunity for employment.

These opportunities for more highly skilled and educated women cause working women to come from different types of families. Dornbusch and Heer have analyzed 1940 and 1950 census data and have shown that although there was an inverse correlation between the rate of female employment and median male income in 1940, there was a reversal for Causasian women in 1950. That is, the 1950 data show a higher rate of employment for women in *the more prosperous* communities (5). More recent census releases have also shown a trend toward the increased involvement of the middle-class family. Data prior to 1950 generally show that the lower the income of the husband, the more likely was the employment of the mother. A 1957 census release indicates that this is no longer true. If there were no children under eighteen, the women whose husbands made an average wage—$4,000 to $5,000 yearly—were most likely to be employed. If minor children of school age were present, the husband earning $2,000 to $3,000 was most likely to have an employed wife; next came husbands earning $3,000 to $4,000, only slightly below the median male income in that year (Table 4).

This trend of maternal employment upward into the middle-class family is further substantiated by its increasing presence in families

TABLE 4. LABOR FORCE STATUS OF WIFE BY PRESENCE OF
CHILDREN AND INCOME OF HUSBAND, 1957

Income of Husband	All Women 14 Years of Age and Over	Percent of Wives Working 20 to 44 Years of Age			
		Total	No Children under 18	Children 6 to 17 Only	Children under 6
Total	30.2	31.9	60.4	39.9	18.2
Under $1,000	31.3	42.3	....	45.9	28.2
$1,000 to 1,999	28.7	40.0	59.8	47.3	28.3
2,000 to 2,999	34.3	39.3	59.1	57.3	22.9
3,000 to 3,999	36.0	37.7	63.9	49.4	22.4
4,000 to 4,999	34.2	34.2	64.1	42.8	21.1
5,000 to 5,999	27.9	27.2	59.7	34.7	15.0
6,000 to 6,999	27.8	26.4	57.5	36.7	13.4
7,000 to 9,999	20.5	18.3	53.5	26.9	6.2
10.000 and over	14.6	14.8	....	16.2	9.3

Source: *Current Population Reports, Labor Force,* No. 87 (4).

in which the husband is engaged in a middle-class occupation (Table 6). For example, the highest proportions of married women gainfully employed are found among non-farm proprietors; those following have husbands who are clerical and kindred workers, service workers, operatives, sales workers, laborers (except farm), craftsmen, professionals, farmers and farm managers, non-farm managers and officials, and farm laborers and foremen.

In brief, in two decades the employed mother has passed through two states and into a third. In the first state, she provided sole support for herself and her family; in the second, her husband was employed or partially employed in the lowest income bracket; and at present, her husband is employed with an income only slightly lower than the median for the entire society. During the same period a transition was made from a situation in which women were *forced* into employment with their labor the primary source of family income, to one in which women are *drawn* into employment to raise family living standards or for other reasons. A rapid upgrading of occupations has raised the pay and status of the employed mother. This has required more vocational training, which has involved more and more middle-class families.

Social Differences between Employed and not Employed

All studies have shown family size to differentiate among women entering employment. In the Washington sample (Table 5), the number of children averaged one more per family among the nonemployed women; moreover, the proportion of families with four or more children is much larger for this group. The difference is even greater with respect to the presence of preschool children in the home—65 percent for the nonemployed compared to 23 percent for those employed full-time.

The relationship of socioeconomic status to employment of mothers is not entirely clear from the census data. Employment of the wives of profesional men is low, but it is high for the wives of business owners and proprietors. It is high for wives of men in clerical work but low for wives of agricultural laborers (Table 6). These differences appear to stem partly from the availability of suitable work in family-operated businesses and the absence of suitable employment for wives of agricultural laborers; however, they also result from limitations in the census classification. In the Washington study, the Empey scale for measuring occupational prestige was employed. Unlike the census category, it differentiates between businesses of various sizes, assigning lower prestige to those employing primarily family labor (8). This criterion does discriminate between families in which the mother is or is not employed. A smaller percentage of employed mothers come

TABLE 5. NUMBER OF CHILDREN AND EMPLOYMENT STATUS OF 1,976 WASHINGTON MOTHERS

Number of Children Born or Adopted	Not Employed	Part-Time Employed	Full-Time Employed	Total	Total
		Percent			*Number*
1	3.8	4.3	12.7	5.4	*107*
2	23.1	28.0	34.7	25.7	*509*
3	27.3	27.6	25.2	26.9	*532*
4	24.0	21.9	15.9	22.3	*440*
5	10.3	11.5	4.6	9.5	*188*
6 or more	11.6	6.9	6.9	10.1	*200*
Total	100.1	100.2	100.0	99.9	*1,976*

from families in which the husband is the owner or manager of a large business. That there is some relationship to social class is also indicated in the slightly lower incomes of husbands of employed women (Table 4). The Washington data also show that *within* an occupational category the wives of husbands earning less are more likely to be employed. It appears evident, therefore, that although more and more employed mothers are coming from middle and upper socioeconomic levels, they are still overrepresented in the lower and lower-middle classes.

Employed mothers as a category have somewhat more education than mothers not in the labor force. In the sample of Washington mothers, the differences are greatest between the proportion of employed and not employed who have junior high or less education (Table 1.3). In the same sample, more employed mothers also had some college education, but the differences are less.[2]

If broken homes are considered as a single category, they are more prevalent among employed mothers. However, when they are divided into those in which the mother has and those in which she has not

TABLE 6. LABOR FORCE STATUS OF WIVES BY OCCUPATION OF HUSBAND

Occupation of Husband	Wives in Labor Force
	Percent
All categories	30.9
Farm laborers and foremen	22.4
Non-farm managers and officials	25.4
Farmers and farm managers	26.2
Professional, technical, and kindred workers	27.2
Craftsmen, foremen, and kindred workers	28.9
Laborers, except farm and mine	32.8
Sales workers	33.4
Operatives and kindred workers	34.0
Service workers (inc. private household)	35.7
Clerical and kindred workers	36.6
Non-farm proprietors	36.8

Source: *Current Population Reports, Labor Force* (1).

[2] Since "absolute need" is presumably greater for mothers who have no more than a junior high school education, this provides more evidence that more women are choosing than are being forced into employment.

TABLE 7. MARITAL STATUS AND EMPLOYMENT STATUS
OF 1,975 WASHINGTON MOTHERS

Marital Status	Not Employed	Part-Time Employed	Full-Time Employed	Total	Total
		Percent			*Number*
Original marriage	86.3	87.0	74.1	83.8	*1665*
Solo mother	1.8	2.5	13.0	3.8	*76*
Remarriage	11.9	10.5	13.0	11.8	*234*
Total	100.0	100.0	100.1	99.4	*1,975*

remarried, the relationship is quite different for the two. In the Washington study, 13 percent of the families of the employed mothers and 1 percent of those of nonemployed mothers included no male adult (Table 7). Stated another way, over 80 percent of the female heads of households were employed compared to less than 40 percent of women who were not heads of households.

Remarriages (in which there is a male head of household) present a very different picture. Almost identical proportions of remarriages were found in the three employment categories (Table 7).

Census data (1959) show a higher proportion of nonwhite women in the labor force; 46.2 percent of nonwhite and 34.8 percent of white women work. This can be refined slightly by taking the age group from thirty-four to forty-four—in which individuals are likely to be married and have dependent children of school age. In this age range, 60.8 percent of the nonwhite females were employed compared to 41.1 percent of the white females (1).

The proportion of women employed reaches its peak in the age range from thirty-five to forty-four, but there is no sharp peak. Rather, a plateau of high employment extends from age twenty through fifty-five. Between the forty-five to fifty-four and fifty-five to sixty-four categories, a substantial decline occurs—from 54.3 to 40.9 percent employed. For the purposes of the present inquiries, it is of interest that the years of peak employment for women are twenty-five to fifty-four, the same years in which their household and family responsibilities are heaviest. Finally, after sixty-five only 16.5 percent are employed (1).

Summary

The American mother moved into paid employment in significant numbers during World War II. Contrary to the expectation of American society in general and social scientists in particular, her numbers continued to increase rapidly during the postwar era. By 1960, almost 40 percent of mothers of children six to seventeen years of age were in the labor force, and almost 20 percent of those with preschool children were employed.

This massive movement was made possible by: (a) new labor-saving machinery in the home and new inventions and distributive techniques in industry and trade which permitted the mother's economic tasks to be performed more efficiently outside the home; (b) smaller families; and (c) the spread of equalitarian family ideology. The continued dominance of the value of an increased standard of living, broadly defined, provided strong positive motivations.

The rapid upgrading of occupations following World War II created a demand for well-educated women. This increasingly involved not only more middle-class women but, as a consequence, middle-class husbands and children. The employed wife presently is likely to have more education than her nonemployed counterpart, but her husband is likely to have a slightly lower occupational level and lower income than the husband of a woman not employed.

By 1955 the continued surge of mothers into paid employment had been noticed by social scientists and laymen alike. The more vocal laymen, in most instances, denounced the trend and even intimated that action should be taken to reverse it. Social scientists were divided and without adequate research from which to generalize.

References

1. "Annual Report of the Labor Force, 1958," *Current Population Reports, Labor Force.* United States Department of Commerce, Bureau of the Census. Washington, D.C.: Government Printing Office, 1959.
2. Bossard, James H. S. *The Sociology of Child Development.* New York: Harper, 1954, pp. 282–86.
3. Caplow, Theodore. *The Sociology of Work.* Minneapolis: University of Minnesota Press, 1954.
4. *Current Population Reports, Labor Force.* United States Department of Commerce, Bureau of the Census, Series P-50, Nos. 22, 62, 73, 76, 81, and 87. Washington, D.C.: Government Printing Office.
5. Dornbusch, Sanford M., and Heer, David M. "The Evaluation of Work by Females, 1940–1950," *American Journal of Sociology,* LXIII (July, 1957), 27–30.
6. Durand, John D. "Married Women in the Labor Force." *American Journal of Sociology,* LII (November, 1946), 217–24.
7. Elliott, Mabel A., and Merrill, Francis E. *Social Disorganization.* New York: Harper, 1950.

8. Empey, LaMar T. "Social Class and Occupational Aspiration: A Comparison of Absolute and Relative Measurement." *American Sociological Review,* XXI (December, 1956), 703–9.
9. Kirkpatrick, Clifford. "Inconsistency in Marriage Roles and Marriage Conflict." In *Readings in Marriage and the Family,* edited by Judson and Mary Landis. Englewood Cliffs, N.J.: Prentice-Hall, 1952, pp. 386–92.
10. Komarovsky, Mirra. *Women in the Modern World.* Boston: Little, Brown, 1953.
11. Landis, Paul H. *Making the Most of Marriage.* New York: Appleton-Century-Crofts, 1955.
12. Lundberg, Ferdinand, and Farnham, Marynia F. *Modern Women, The Lost Sex.* New York: Harper, 1947.
13. *Occupational Trends in the United States, 1900 to 1950.* United States Department of Commerce, Bureau of the Census, Working Paper No. 5. Washington, D.C.: Government Printing Office, 1958.
14. *Special Labor Force Report No. 13.* United States Department of Labor. Washington, D.C.: Government Printing Office, 1961.
15. *Women as Workers.* United States Department of Labor, Women's Bureau, D.-65. Washington, D.C.: Government Printing Office.

THE DECLINING STATUS OF WOMEN: POPULAR MYTHS AND THE FAILURE OF FUNCTIONALIST THOUGHT

by Dean D. Knudsen

A common theme of much literature in the social sciences has developed the idea of a gradual but persistent equalization of statuses of men and women. It often has been assumed that the battle for women's rights is won, and whatever inequity still persists derives entirely from a failure of women to exercise their legal, educational, occupational, and social prerogatives.

. . . Further, the institutionalization of this inequality will be used to illustrate the conservative nature of much modern social science research.

The Modern Context of Sex-Defined Statuses

While the modern industrial society has effectively destroyed the narrow definition of appropriate female roles that persisted throughout most of the early Hebrew-Christian era and into Colonial America, the idea of complete legal and social equality did not finally emerge as a viable ideal for the majority of the population until the early twentieth century. However, even during this recent period such equality has not been accepted without contest, despite legal sanctions. Enactment of *Title VII* of the Civil Rights Act of 1964 resulted in 2,031 complaints of discrimination against women, about one-third of the total number

From Dean D. Knudsen, "The Declining Status of Women: Popular Myths and the Failure of Functionalist Thought," Social Forces, 48 (December, 1969): pp. 183–93. Reprinted by permission of the University of North Carolina Press. References will be found at the end of the article.

presented to the Equal Employment Opportunity Commission during its first year of operation (Interdepartmental Committee, 1966: 43). Such numerous complaints offer significant evidence of a continuing antifemale discrimination in employment.

However, both professional and popular publications have frequently assumed that discrimination has ceased, and that the trend is toward equality of opportunity and equality of fact. Thus it is stated that "The status discrepancy has narrowed considerably in recent years yet men remain dominant in many spheres. Initiative in dating and proposing marriage, the double sex standard, and a broader field of occupational choice for males are illustrative" (Babchuck and Bates, 1963, p. 377).

Similar optimistic interpretations emerge from an investigation of publications of U.S. Government agencies, as is evident from the following statements:

> Women's Gains, 1950–60. During the 1950s, the professions in which women made their most significant employment *gains*— either in terms of percentage increases or number of workers— were those relating to service and social needs of society. . . . Challenging careers for qualified college women have never before existed in such variety—*nor offered so many rewards* (U.S. Department of Labor, 1964, p. 71, italics added).

Comparisons of historical data between the sexes are thus crucial to an understanding of the status of women. Only by examining the position of women relative to men in 1940, 1950, and 1960 can an adequate assessment begin. In an effort to make statuses comparable, male and female achievements will be examined in the three most commonly operationalized measures of social class and status: occupation, income, and education.

Occupation As A Measure of Status

Probably no aspect of feminine behavior has received the attention that has been focused since World War II upon the employment of women, especially mothers of young children. Though there has been a substantial amount of research, there is no agreement about empirical findings concerning the supposed negative effects that out-of-home work by married women has upon family life in any aspect—themselves, their marital relationships, or their children (e.g., Nye and Hoffman, 1963). Increases in the percentage of the labor force that is female suggests an increased interest in work-for-pay outside of the home, what-

TABLE 1. PERCENT OF EMPLOYED WOMEN AND MEN IN EACH OCCUPATIONAL CATEGORY FOR 1940, 1950, 1960, AND 1966

Occupational Categories*	Female				Male			
	1940†	1950†	1960†	1966‡	1940†	1950†	1960†	1966‡
Professional, technical and kindred	13.4	12.4	13.0	14.0	6.1	7.3	10.3	12.6
Managers, officials and proprietors	3.5	4.3	3.7	4.4	9.6	10.7	10.7	13.6
Clerical and kindred	21.1	27.3	29.7	32.5	6.0	6.5	6.9	7.2
Sales workers	7.3	8.5	7.8	7.0	6.7	6.3	6.9	6.0
Craftsmen, foremen and kindred	1.2	1.5	1.2	0.9	14.9	18.6	19.5	19.3
Operatives and kindred	18.1	19.2	15.4	15.8	17.9	20.1	19.9	21.1
Laborers, except farm and mine	1.0	0.7	0.5	0.4	9.0	8.1	6.9	7.0
Private household workers	17.7	8.5	7.9	7.5	0.3	0.2	0.1	0.0
Service workers	11.0	12.2	13.4	15.6	5.8	5.8	6.0	7.0
Farmers and farm managers	1.4	0.7	0.6	0.5	14.7	10.4	5.5	4.3
Farm laborers	2.9	2.9	1.1	1.4	8.3	4.9	2.8	2.0
Not reported	1.0	0.7	0.5	....	0.7	1.1	4.6	....
Total	100.0	100.0	100.0	100.0	100.0	100.0	100.0	100.0
Number employed (thousands)	11,178	15,772	21,172	25,236	33,892	40,662	43,467	45,847

* Slightly different totals and percentage figures are obtained for 1940 and 1950 if "Experienced Labor Force" or "Economically Active" are used as the basis of computation. However only for the "operatives" category in 1940 is the difference greater than 1 percent (−1.4) and greater than 0.5 percent for "professional, technical, and kindred" in 1940 (−0.6 percent) and for "operatives" in 1950 (−.8 percent). If data in the 1967 Statistical Abstract are used to compute 1960 figures there are four changes: professional, technical and kindred, −0.08 percent; managers, officials and proprietors, +1.3 percent; private household workers, +1.9 percent; service workers, +0.7 percent. These differences may be due to definitions and also to date of data collections.

† Source: U.S. Bureau of Census *U.S. Census of Population:* 1960: Vol. 1 (Washington, D.C.: Government Printing Office, 1964), Table 89, pp. 1–219.

‡ Source: U.S. Bureau of Census, *Statistical Abstract of the United States, 1967* (Washington, D.C., Government Printing Office, 1967), computed.

ever the motivation, though the majority of positions filled by women can hardly be classified as creative and intellectually demanding.

Table 1 shows the within-sex occupational distribution of both female and male workers, 1940–66, a period during which the relative size of the clerical and kindred category for women increased by over 50 percent, drawn largely from private household workers and operatives. It should be noted that during the 25-year period there has been only a slight change in the relative sizes of the two highest-status categories, the professional and managerial positions for women, though considerable increases for men.

Additional information is provided by an examination of the percentage in each occupational category that was female during the same period, in Table 2. Several complementary patterns emerge from a consideration of trends. There has been a slight but persistent decline in the proportions of professional, technical and kindred workers that were female, while either a definite increase or a leveling occurred for every other category. For clerical and kindred workers, sales, service

TABLE 2. EMPLOYED PERSONS: PERCENT FEMALE FOR OCCUPA-
TIONAL CATEGORIES FOR 1940, 1950, 1960, AND 1966

Occupational Categories*	1940†	1950†	1960†	1966§
Professional, technical and kindred	41.6	39.5	38.1	37.9
Managers, officials and proprietors	11.2	13.5	14.4	15.3
Clerical and kindred	53.9	62.3	67.6	71.3
Sales workers	26.1	33.9	35.8	39.5
Craftsmen, foremen and kindred	1.9	3.0	2.9	2.5
Operatives and kindred	25.3	27.1	27.4	29.1
Laborers, except farm and mine	3.3	3.7	5.4	3.0
Private household workers	94.4	94.8	96.5	98.0
Service workers	38.4	44.6	52.3	55.0
Farmers and farm managers	3.0	2.7	4.7	6.0
Farm laborers	10.3	18.7	16.8	28.8

* Some slight differences are obtained if "Experienced Labor Force" or "Economically Active" are used as the basis of computation.

† Source: U.S. Bureau of Census, *Census of Population: 1950:* Vol. 2 (Washington, D.C.: Government Printing Office, 1953), computed from Table 124, pp. 1–261 to 1–266.

‡ Source: U.S. Bureau of Census. *U.S. Census of Population: 1960:* Vol. 1 (Washington, D.C.: Government Printing Office, 1964), computed from Table 202, pp. 1–528 to 1–533.

§ Source: U.S. Bureau of Census, *Statistical Abstract of the United States: 1967* (Washington, D.C.: Government Printing Office, 1967), No. 327, p. 230 (computed).

and farm workers, the increase was substantial—a shift of over 10 percent from male to female workers in every instance. Thus, while there are now more women professionals than in earlier years, their proportion of the total number of professionals has declined, from about two-fifths to slightly over one-third during the past 25 years.

Further consideration of professional workers shows only slight gains for women, as illustrated by the data in Table 3. All specific professional categories involving 5,000 or more women in 1960 are included. It is significant that the Women's Bureau publication (U.S. Department of Labor, 1964) used these categories to provide evidence of employment gains by females during the 1950 decade. However, an assessment of the changes suggests no great increase in professional occupations by women when compared to men, but rather a modest decline. In twelve of the twenty-one categories listed, the percentage increase for males exceeded that of females, and the overall increase for males was greater, despite a much larger base of population in 1950. Further, in only two of the nine cases where the female percentage increase was greater did the number of women exceed that of men, those of musicians and therapists and healers. In six of the twelve cases where the male increase was greater, however, the number of men was at least twice that of women.

Such data suggest several conclusions regarding female participation in professional employment during the past quarter century. First, while there has been an increase in the number of women employed in professions, the percentage increase is considerably less than that of men, and the female has neither displaced nor seriously challenged the American male's dominance in professional positions. Second, greatest relative female increases occurred primarily in those specific categories which already had an overwhelming majority of men—auditors and accountants, personnel and labor-relations workers, sports instructors and officials, physicians and surgeons, lawyers and judges, and public-relations workers and publicity writers. Third, in the remaining categories of relatively greater female increase are those occupations uniquely compatible with homemaking responsibilities, and thus lend themselves to part-time or irregular patterns of work involvement, especially in the case of musicians and music teachers. Finally, the frequently mentioned claim of increased varieties of work and rewards can be validated only if placed in the context of historical comparisons rather than in relation to male opportunities, since the growth in numbers of women employed has occurred predominantly in the lower-status occupations.

**TABLE 3. NUMBER OF EMPLOYED PERSONS IN 1960 AND
PERCENTAGE CHANGE 1950–60 IN SPECIFIC
PROFESSIONAL CATEGORIES BY SEX**

Occupational Category	Female*		Male†	
	Number 1960	*Percent Change: 1950–60*	*Number 1960*	*Percent Change: 1950–60*
Total employed	2,753,052	+41	4,479,358	+51
Teachers‡	1,196,526	+43	475,388	+66
Nurses, professional	567,884	+45	14,495	+51
Musicians, music teachers	109,638	+40	82,246	+8
Accountants, auditors	79,045	+41	392,257	+22
Librarians	71,836	+46	12,045	+90
Social welfare, recreation workers	60,667	+15	36,029	+54
College presidents, professors, instructors	38,850	+30	138,889	+45
Editors, reporters	37,438	+40	63,279	+43
Religious workers	35,099	+21	21,239	+66
Personnel, labor relations workers	30,215	+100	67,957	+81
Sports instructors, officials	24,931	+123	51,957	+53
Dietitians, nutritionists	24,237	+15	1,882	+40
Therapists, healers	19,752	+62	16,902	+18
Physicians, surgeons	15,513	+32	213,413	+18
Recreation, group workers	15,497	+129	20,858	+121
Natural scientists	14,738	+10	134,592	+30
Social scientists	14,177	+24	42,403	+77
Lawyers, judges	7,434	+19	204,974	+13
Engineers, technical	7,211	+11	853,738	+62
Pharmacists	7,129	−2	85,026	+5
Public relations workers, publicity workers	7,005	+258	23,358	+41

* Source: U.S. Department of Labor, Woman's Bureau, *Job Horizons for College Women in the 1960s* (Washington, D.C.: Government Printing Office, 1964), Table 2, p. 67.

† Source: U.S. Bureau of Census, *U.S. Census of Population:* Vol. 1 (Washington, D.C.: Government Printing Office, 1960). Table 202, pp. 1–528 to 1–533 (computed).

‡ Category does not include art, music, dancing, or physical education teachers who are classified elsewhere.

Income As A Measure of Status

Income provides another basis for relative evaluation of the recipient's status, by focusing upon the economic rewards offered and
may be especially meaningful in terms of filling the more repetitive and

less creative positions that have often been assigned to women. In terms of historical data, incremental rewards for women relative to men may be interpreted as evidence of an increasing status, while increased inequality of reward suggests a relative loss if occupational levels are similar in status ranking.

TABLE 4. MEDIAN WAGE OR SALARY INCOME IN DOLLARS OF YEAR-ROUND FULL-TIME FEMALE WORKERS, AND PERCENT OF MALE INCOME EARNED BY FEMALES IN SPECIFIC YEARS BY OCCUPATIONAL CATEGORY

Occupational Category	1939†		1949‡		1959§		1966†	
	Median Income	Per- cent	Median Income	Per- cent	Median Income	Per- cent	Median Income	Per- cent
Professional, technical and kindred	$1277	60.8	$2615	60.6	$4385	64.2	$5826	65.1
Managers, officials and proprietors	$1218	54.0	$2382	57.3	$3934	56.9	$4919	54.0
Clerical and kindred	$1072	78.5	$2255	70.2	$3493	68.1	$4316	66.5
Sales workers	$745	51.3	$1658	49.3	$2340	42.2	$3103	41.0
Craftsmen, foremen and kindred	$995	63.7	$2280	67.2	*	*	$4345	60.4
Operatives and kindred	$742	58.5	$1926	64.9	$2916	63.3	$3416	55.9
Laborers except farm and mine	$738	74.5	$1912	79.9	*	*	*	*
Private household workers	$339	61.7	$799	53.1	$1146	*	$1297	*
Service workers	$607	59.6	$1455	58.2	$2241	56.0	$2815	55.4
Farmers and farm managers	$403	93.7	$854	51.6	*	*	*	*
Farm laborers	$245	67.1	$474	42.0	*	*	*	*

† Source: U.S. Department of Commerce, *Current Population Reports: Consumer Income*, Series P-60, No. 53 (Washington, D.C.: Government Printing Office, December 28, 1967), Table 34, p. 51 (computed).

‡ Source: David L. Kaplan and M. Claire Casey, *Occupational Trends in the U.S., 1900 to 1960*, U.S. Department of Commerce, *Current Population Reports: Consumer Income*, Series P-60, No. 35 (Washington, D.C.: Government Printing Office, January 5, 1961), Table 38, p. 52 (computed).

§ Source: U.S. Department of Commerce, *Current Population Reports: Consumer Income*, Series P-60, No. 35 (Washington, D.C.: Government Printing Office, January 5, 1961), Table 38, p. 52 (computed).

* Data for comparisons not available for year-round full-time workers due to insufficient numbers of women or men in the category.

In Table 4, the median salaries for only those women who were full-time year-round workers within various occupational classifications during the past quarter century are presented. The 1939 data are for the prewar end-of-depression period and in comparison to that income level, the 1966 incomes indicate an increase of at least 400 percent in nearly every case. Of greater significance, however, is the proportion of male income that was received by females within the various categories. In only one instance was the proportion greater in 1966 than in 1939, that of professional, technical, and kindred workers, but even this difference was less than 5 percent.

When occupation and income are considered simultaneously, however, even this apparent gain is minimized. Since the professional, technical, and kindred category contained relatively fewer women in 1965 than in 1940, the apparent gain was achieved by relatively fewer women. Further, clerical and kindred workers, that category with the greatest relative numerical increase in employment, was subject to the largest relative loss in income, a decrease of 12 percent.

For women, the relationship between levels of income and numbers employed in any occupational category is clearly a negative one: as the proportion of workers being female in any occupational category increased, the relative income of women has declined over the past quarter century. It is a strong, if not perfect, negative correlation with the greatest gains in one measure offset by the greatest losses in the other.

To account for such losses of relative income, it could be argued that women have gradually shifted from a broadly dispersed distribution throughout each occupational category toward a concentration at the lower income levels of each classification. Data in Table 3 offer no support for such an interpretation, at least among professional workers. Even this suggestion, however, assumes that women either have demonstrated a gradual but persistent loss of motivation for competitive positions or have been systematically discriminated against by employers. Either of these choices tacitly recognizes the pattern of incremental inequality in relative income at given occupational levels.

Perhaps it should be noted that the well-publicized but only occasionally successful professional woman often is idealized much as the self-made man was through the "American dream" of earlier years. The myth of female equality rests in some measure upon the glamorization of these exceptional cases, making it appear that individual effort is the lacking ingredient in success, rather than a lack of equal opportunity.

Education As A Measure of Status

Education is the third generally used measure of social status. Because education is highly correlated with both occupation and income, it was expected that data regarding educational achievement would also indicate a relatively disadvantaged situation for women. In addition, since education is the primary means by which women can effectively enter the competitive market, it may reflect most clearly the normative expectations of females and their parents in occupational achievements.

In Table 5 median educational achievements are presented for males and females at various ages under age 40, when most formal education has ceased. Females at all ages in 1940 had higher grade levels of completion than males, with most differences involving a half grade or more. In 1950, these differences had declined in size, and had practically been eliminated by 1960. For college age persons, 19–24, median male achievement was practically identical to that of females in 1960,

TABLE 5. MEDIAN EDUCATIONAL ACHIEVEMENTS FOR MALES AND FEMALES BY AGE FOR 1940, 1950, AND 1960, AND PERCENT INCREASE BY SEX

Age	1940†		1950‡		1960‡		Percent Increase 1940–60	
	Male	Female	Male	Female	Male	Female	Male	Female
17	10.2	10.7	10.4	10.8	10.8	11.1	6	4
18	10.7	11.3	11.2	11.7	11.6	11.9	8	5
19	11.0	11.8	11.9	12.2	12.2	12.3	11	4
20	11.0	11.7	12.1	12.2	12.3	12.4	12	6
21	11.0	11.8	12.0	12.2	12.3	12.4	12	5
22	10.9	11.6	11.9	12.2	12.3	12.4	13	7
23	10.8	11.3	11.8	12.1	12.3	12.3	14	9
24	10.7	11.1	11.8	12.1	12.3	12.3	15	11
25–29	....	....	12.0	12.1	12.3	12.3	2*	2*
30–34	....	....	11.4	11.8	12.1	12.2	6*	3*
35–39	....	....	10.3	10.7	12.1	12.2	17*	14*

† Source: U.S. Bureau of the Census. *U.S. Census of Population: 1950:* Volume 2 (Washington, D.C.: Government Printing Office, 1953), Table 114, pp. 1–223 to 235 and Table 115, pp. 1–236 to 243.

‡ Source: U.S. Bureau of the Census. *U.S. Census of Population: 1960:* Volume 1 (Washington, D.C.: U.S. Government Printing Office, 1964), Table 173, pp. 1–404 to 410.

* 1950–60 comparisons.

TABLE 6. COMPARISONS OF EDUCATIONAL PARTICIPATION FOR 1940, 1950, 1960 AND 1964, AND PERCENT CHANGE BY SEX

Educational Participation	1940	1950	1960	1964	Percent Change 1940–64
Instructional staffs†					
Percent female	77.8	78.7	71.0	68.9	−14.9
Mean salary (1964 dollars)	3182	3922	5434	6240	+96.1
Enrolled in school, aged 20–24‡					
Percent female	7.5	4.6	7.4	12.4*	+65.3*
Percent male	9.3	14.2	19.9	29.2*	+214.0*
Students enrolled for degree credit§					
Percent female	40.2	30.3	35.3	38.0	−5.5
Faculties in institutions of higher education§					
Percent female	27.6	24.5	22.0	22.1	−19.9

† Source: U.S. Bureau of Census, *Statistical Abstract of the United States, 1967* (Washington, D.C.: Government Printing Office, 1967), No. 166, p. 120 (computed).
‡ *Ibid.*, No. 151, p. 112 (computed).
§ *Ibid.*, No. 189, p. 133 (computed).
* Data used are for 1966.

in spite of military service, work responsibilities, and other demands which interrupt educational efforts for males. This fact is particularly important in terms of competing in the modern work force, since inadequate education leads to employment with less rewards, both in economic and in prestige terms.

The columns at the right in Table 5 further illustrate the recent trends in education. In every instance, median education of males increased more rapidly than that of females, and twice as rapidly at several age levels. The same trend exists for those ages with equal educational achievement in 1960, suggesting that males will receive more education than females in the coming years.

Additional data in Table 6, concerning various aspects of educational participation offer further evidence of greater male achievements. As the average salaries for elementary and secondary teachers have increased, the proportions of teachers that are female have declined. Despite a sizeable increase in school enrollment for females aged 20–24, the percentage increase for men for the 1940–66 period is over three times that for women. From 1940 to 1950, the data indicate that there was a sizeable relative and absolute loss for women in terms of enrollment, probably due to the postwar demands for education on the part of male veterans and the limited facilities available. However, the special deference to males during that period—to the later detriment of females—reflected a general perspective about women as being less worthy or beneficial to society than men if resources permit only one to be educated. Thus, only after a partial solution of the postwar space limitations did enrollment by women increase, though the percentage increase figures from 1950–66 mask a persistent pattern of greater relative and absolute enrollment by males.

Consistent with these interpretations, the data show a slight loss in the percentage of degree students who are females from 1940 to the present, though a gradual increase since 1950 has occurred. Finally, in terms of the faculties of institutions of higher education, females comprised a somewhat smaller proportion in 1964 than in 1940, despite the demand for teachers.

The data on education support and illustrate the earlier findings regarding the status of women. There appears to be considerable evidence that not only have women failed to achieve equality in terms of occupation and income, but in education—the one area of historic superiority—women are relatively less well off now than 25 years ago. Regardless of the type of data examined, it appears that the effects of lower educational participation, especially during the late 1940s and 1950s, are currently reflected in occupational and income data. The emphasis on education for men, however, has had the effect of creating a higher level of education precisely in those areas related to greatest rewards in occupational status and income—graduate training toward professional employment.

Thus, while women presently comprise an increased proportion of college enrollments, it appears that men are becoming better educated, especially beyond the baccalaureate, making the educational data more significant for future activities. The ultimate effect is the perpetuation of the system of employment which places women in low-level occupational positions. Their earlier educational superiority eliminated, women will increasingly be forced to create alternative channels to effect meaningful competition in the occupational sphere, or to accept the relative deprivation deriving from inferior education if out-of-home employment is desired. This situation exists despite some current evidence which suggests that already women are better educated, more experienced, and better qualified than men of equal levels (Harrison, 1964. See Simon *et al.*, 1967 for an alternative view).

References

Babchuck, Nicholas, and Alan P. Bates, "The Primary Relations of Middle-Class Couples: A Study in Male Dominance," *American Sociological Review*, 28 (June, 1963): 377–384.

U.S. Department of Labor, Woman's Bureau, 1964. *Job Horizons for College Women in the 1960s*, Bulletin 288.

Nye, F. Ivan, and Lois W. Hoffman, *Employed Women in America*. Chicago: Rand McNally, 1963.

Harrison, Evelyn, "The Working Woman: Barriers in Employment," *Public Administration Review*, 24 (June, 1964): 78–85.

Simon, Rita J., *et al.*, "The Woman Ph.D.: A Recent Profile," *Social Problems*, 15 (Fall, 1961): 221–36.

WOMEN IN SCIENCE: WHY SO FEW?

by Alice S. Rossi

. . . Why are there so few women in science? Why are they less apt to get advanced degrees than men? Why are they less apt to marry? Why do they withdraw from their fields?

The Priority of Marriage

What a man "does" defines his status, but whom she marries defines a woman's. In meeting strangers, one can "place" a man socially by asking what he does, a woman by asking what her husband does. This is particularly true for the top professional and technical strata of American society. Only small proportions of the wives of doctors, scientists, engineers, and lawyers are employed, ranging (in 1960) from a low of 16 percent of doctors' wives to a high of 25 percent of scientists' wives (7, Table 12). In contrast, 44 to 47 percent of the wives of librarians, social workers, and school teachers are employed.

This has decided implications for the paths young women see as open to them for success in American life. A man must express his intelligence and ambition in the occupational sphere. A woman's ambition can find an outlet in marriage or in work, seldom in both. If a woman has a successful husband, there are no cultural pressures upon her to use her intelligence or training in the work of the world. In fact her husband may resist a desire on her part for such a separate career, for a wife with leisure is one symbol of his success, and a wife's career might require him to carry some of the parental responsibilities his wife has carried for him.

I think it is the awareness that marriage and careers are not now compatible for women in the upper-middle class (despite protestations to the contrary in recent years) that lies behind the often pathetic vacillations of high school and college girls between the pursuit of

From Alice S. Rossi, "Women in Science: Why So Few?" Science, 148, no. 3674 (May 28, 1965), 1196–1202. Reprinted by permission of the author. Copyright 1965 by the American Association for the Advancement of Science. References will be found at the end of the article.

social popularity (a route to successful marriage) and excellence in scholarship (a route to successful careers). Surely it plays a role in the different concerns parents have for their adolescent boys and girls—the educational goals of their sons and the dating patterns of their daughters.

A sample of women college graduates 3 years beyond graduation were asked the following question (11): "An American woman can be very successful in a variety of ways. Which of the following would you most like to be yourself?" The most frequent answers were: to be the mother of several accomplished children and to be the wife of a prominent man. Yet some echoes of earlier aspirations and the imprint of their college education are found in their responses to the further question, "Which of the following do you personally admire very much?" Four out of five chose winners of scientific, scholarly, or artistic awards. They admire the minority within their sex who have careers, but choose themselves to live in the shadows of their husbands' and children's accomplishments.

Unless there are changes in the organization of professional and technical work or in the attitudes of men toward women's roles, it seems likely that fewer rather than more college-trained women will pursue serious careers in the future, for there has been a steady increase in the proportion of the male labor force found in the top occupations. This is not to say that wives of such men will not work. They will, particularly early in the marriage when their earnings supplement university stipends to support the graduate training of their husbands. And we shall hear from these women again when they reach their forties. As long as their husbands are not "too" successful, they may become social workers, teachers, computer programmers, professional or technical aides in laboratories or offices. Only rarely will they become doctors, lawyers, scientists, or engineers. Harriet Martineau's observation in 1834 that the "prosperity of America is a circumstance unfavorable to its women," meaning women are not "put to the proof as to what they are capable of thinking and doing" (12), is as true for the upper-middle class in 1964 as it was when she compared America with England on her first visit to the young nation.

It is ironic that with a life span now long enough to experience many and varied adventures of the mind, the spirit, and the senses, the major life experiences of marriage and parenthood and the intellectual excitement of advanced study are compressed into the same narrow few years of early adulthood. Instead of savoring each to the full and in their turn, we feast upon all three simultaneously as on a triple-decker sandwich. This quickened pace of life and the earlier age at which marriage, parenthood, and occupational success take place play an important role in lowering the career aspirations of women and in deflecting them from the pursuit of such goals as they have. There is not enough time in late adolescence for young women to evolve a value system of their own and a sense of direction toward an individual goal, for they are committing themselves prematurely to marriage and adapting to the goals of their husbands at the expense of their own emotional and intellectual growth.

Men are more conservative than women concerning the role of careers in the lives of women. Much larger proportions of college-trained men than women in the NORC career development study (11) believed women should not choose a career difficult to combine with child-rearing, and disapproved of women's working when they have preschool children. The same men were between two and three times more likely than the women to say there was "no need at all" for the major recommendations made by the President's Commission on the Status of Women—increased child-care facilities, equal opportunity in hiring and promotion, and encouraging more women to enter the professions and national political office.

Women see the sharp differences between their own views and those of "most men." Women in the NORC sample were given a brief account of a hypothetical family conflict and asked how they themselves would resolve it and how they thought "most wives" and "most husbands" would resolve it. In the story, a woman graduated from college with honors in biology, married, and held a teaching job while her husband completed law school. Now he has a degree and a good job. Both wish to have children, but she would like to take an advanced degree in biology and eventually pursue a career in biological research. The respondents were asked what decision the couple should make: to start a family and have the wife get the degree later; to start a family and give up the wife's career goal; to postpone child-bearing and let the wife get the degree now; or carry out both wishes simultaneously. Only one-fourth of the women thought the couple should start the family now, with the wife either giving up or postponing her training and career plans; but half of them believed these two decisions would be favored by "most wives," and three-fourths that it would be favored by "most husbands."

In actual fact, most women do as they say most husbands would prefer: they are less apt to complete any advanced training, highly likely to work after marriage and then withdraw for the child-bearing and -rearing years. The typical pattern of work for American women shows two peaks of employment, the first in their early twenties, the

TABLE 1. VOLUNTARY WITHDRAWAL FROM LABOR FORCE* IN
SELECTED PROFESSIONS, BY AGE AND SEX (7);
EXPRESSED IN PERCENTAGES.

Profession and Sex	Age		
	25 to 44	*45 to 64*	*65 or older*
Natural scientists			
Women	51	13	61
Men	2	1	57
Engineers			
Women	31	13	42
Men	1	4	58
Secondary school teachers			
Women	34	13	65
Men	2	2	54
Physicians-surgeons			
Women	19	10	31
Men	2	2	25

* The labor force is defined as all persons, whether currently employed or not,
who have worked in the stated capacity during the last 10 years. The figures are as
of 1960.

second in the 40 to 55 age group. As seen in Table 1, this withdrawal
in the 24 to 44 age group is particularly high for women in the sciences.
Thus in their expressed attitudes, women are less conservative than
men, but their actual behavior reflects an adaptation to the views of
men.

Effect of Interruption of Career

During the last five years there has been a mushrooming of
centers for counseling and retraining older women who wish to return
to professional employment. I think there is a danger that by thus
institutionalizing the withdrawal-and-return pattern of college-educated
women, we may reduce even further the likelihood that women will
enter the top professions. Older women who have not worked for
many years may be retrained and contribute significantly to personnel
shortages at the lower professional levels as laboratory assistants,
technical writers, nurses, and school teachers, but only rarely as doctors,
full-fledged scientists, and engineers. Not only is training for such
fields a long and difficult process, but the pace of technological and
scientific knowledge has been so rapid that even those who remain in

these fields have difficulty keeping up, let alone those who return to advanced training after a ten-year break.

Even more fundamental, however, is the effect on potential creativity of withdrawal precisely during early adulthood. Lehman's researches into the relation between age and achievement (13) have shown that the quality of intellectual output is strongly related to age, and that in the sciences the peak of creative work is reached in the late twenties and early thirties. The small number of women included in his samples showed their most creative years to be no different from those of the men. They were making their major contributions during the very years when most American women withdraw and devote a decade or more to home and family.

If more women are to choose science and remain active in science, it must be possible for them to do so without lengthy interruption of their careers during their potentially most creative years. There has to be a better balance between marital, parental, and career obligations and pleasures for both sexes: work must be *less* dominant than it is in the lives of men in order for it to be *more* dominant in the lives of women.

New View of the Maternal Role

Women will not be strongly motivated to remain active professionally during the early years of child-rearing simply out of concern for the effect of withdrawal upon their intellectual creativity. The development of their children is a concern equal to if not greater than their own work. Until very recently, there was a widely held belief that any separation of the mother and the child would have dire consequences for the emotional development of the child, and many women who worked throughout their children's early years did so with considerable anxiety about the effect of their daily absence upon their children. It is only very recently that this myth has been laid to rest. A current volume of some twenty-two empirical studies on the employed mother (14) has shown that maternal employment has no unfavorable effects upon children. Of much greater importance than employment per se are the mother's reasons for working, the quality of the care the child receives in her absence, and the attitudes of her husband. In the last few years, social scientists have begun to stress the desirable rather than the unfavorable consequences of maternal employment (15, p. 615).

There is a second body of research on child development that reflects a further shift in the concept of the maternal role. For years psychologists focused rather exclusively on the mother's feelings toward and physical care and training of the child. Now there is increasing emphasis on the role of mothers in their children's cognitive development. It has been found that how well the child takes to his early school experiences is strongly related to whether he has had stimulating experience with language and ideas during his preschool years. The better educated the mother, the greater will this stimulation of the child tend to be. There is research currently under way testing the hypothesis that it is the lack of cognitive stimulation that contributes most heavily to poor school performance among lower-working-class children (16).

The implications for social action in behalf of children in culturally deprived homes are clear: enrich the environment of the very young child by means of child-care facilities designed to provide such cognitive stimulation (17). The implications as regards children of college-educated parents are less clear-cut. Some child specialists may say that the mother is more necessary at home than ever, not only to love and care for the child but to stimulate the growing mind of the child. This is to stress the role of the mother as a *teacher*. She may be even more effective, however, as an *example* to the child. If she is utilizing her education in a professional job which keeps her alert and involved with things of the mind, she may transmit far more zest for learning than the educated mother who shelves her books along with her diploma. With the view that maternal employment will harm the child now shown to be unfounded, younger women are potentially free of one source of anxiety if they choose to pursue a profession.

Women and Science: Incompatible?

What is there about women on the one hand, and science on the other, that leads to such a very low affinity between them in American society? What are the major characteristics of the scientist, and why are women in our society less apt to have these characteristics than men?

The following thumbnail sketch of the scientist is based largely on the intensive research of Roe (18) on eminent physicists and biologists. Two caveats must be noted. First, there have been no detailed psychological studies of women scientists in any way comparable to those of men scientists. Some studies suggest that differences in students' interests and values are more closely related to their fields of study than to sex differences, but in drawing a portrait of the characteristics of the scientist it is an assumption rather than an empirically established fact that women scientists do not differ from men scientists in the major characteristics relevant to their occupational role. Secondly, Roe's studies of scientists were conducted in the 1940s with men largely in their fifties at that time. Whether younger men entering the considerably changed world of science in the 1960s and 1970s will differ we do not know, though a comparison of physics students with the physics faculty at a major university in the 1950s shows such striking similarity in personality and social traits as to suggest little change from generation to generation (19).

The four characteristics Roe found most typical of outstanding natural scientists are the following:

1. *High intellectual ability*, particularly spatial and mathematical.

2. *Persistence in work*; intense channeling of energy in work such that the greatest personal satisfaction was experienced when working.

3. *Extreme independence*, showing itself in childhood as a preference for a few close friends rather than extensive or organized social groups, and preference for working alone; in adulthood as a marked independence of intense relations with others and a preference for being free of all supervision.

4. *Apartness from others*; low interest in social activities, with neither preference for an active social life nor guilt concerning such tendencies toward social withdrawal.

All four characteristics manifest themselves early in life; hence a predisposition toward science as a career goal is established long before the college student makes a formal commitment to a "major." Furthermore, these are all characteristics girls in American society are considerably less apt to have than boys. Both at home and at school, girls are socialized in directions least likely to predispose them toward science as a career. What are these sex differences during the formative years?

Intellectual Ability

For many years it was assumed that there were practically no sex differences in intelligence, for studies relying on the Stanford-Binet intelligence test showed almost no differences between boys and girls. It had somehow been forgotten that, in standardizing this test, items which revealed consistent sex differences were discarded so that the scores of boys and girls could be evaluated against the same norms.

During more recent years, as specific tests were constructed to measure different dimensions of intellectual and creative ability, consistent sex differences began to emerge.

These differences may be summarized as follows (20): Girls talk at younger ages, put words together into sentences somewhat sooner, and learn to read more easily than boys. After the fifth or sixth grade, however, boys do as well as girls in reading comprehension, though girls show somewhat greater verbal fluency. In mathematical skills there are no sex differences during the early school years, but during high school boys begin to excel, and by the time they take the Scholastic Aptitude Tests the boys score an average of fifty points higher on the mathematical portion, while girls score only eight or ten points higher on the verbal portion. Throughout school boys do better on spatial tests (for example, detecting a simple figure embedded in a more complex one), which suggests that "boys perceive more analytically, while the girls are more global, more influenced by all the elements of the field together" (20, p. 29).

Thus girls develop cognitive abilities along somewhat different lines than boys, and enter adolescence with a style of thinking less appropriate to scientific work. Any final interpretation of this sex difference awaits further research, but what is known to date is that one key lies in the kind and degree of training in independence the child receives. Bing (21) found that high verbal ability is fostered by a close relationship with a demanding and somewhat intrusive mother, while high mathematical abilities were enhanced by allowing a child a considerable degree of freedom to experiment on his own. Children whose scores on standard intelligence tests rise between their sixth and tenth years are highly likely to have been six-year-olds who were "competitive, self-assertive, independent and dominant in interaction with other children," while those who showed declining scores were "passive, shy and dependent" youngsters at six (20, p. 33).

Early Family Influences

If we look more closely at the family environment of the young child, we can guess at some of the sources of this difference in cognitive style between boys and girls. The scientist's characteristics of independence, persistence in work, and social isolation are mirrored in significant differences between the father and the mother as seen through the eyes of the child. No matter what the father works at, the child sees him leave the family to pursue it; it is a normal part of every day's expectation that father will not be present. Mother, in contrast, is usually at home and instantly available, someone who takes care of the thousand details of home and family life, none of them so important that she cannot be easily interrupted. Even when he is at home, father may be far less "available" than mother.

It is easy for the child to conclude from daily observation that men work for long stretches of time at something important, and that men are less involved with people than women are. There is a consistency between these observations of the parents and the characteristics of young children. Very young girls have a greater interest in other people than boys have and are influenced to a greater extent by what other people think of them. Coleman (22) has found that in adolescence, girls are far more often involved in same-sex cliques than boys, who are more often independent loners. Girls comply with the demands of social situations more than boys do, whether at home in doing what parents ask of them or at school in doing what teachers ask. In short, by the example of their parents boys receive encouragement to stand on their own, to be alone, to aim high, and girls are encouraged to be cooperative and responsive to people and to minister to their needs.

The result of these early influences is a marked contrast between men and women in the values that underlie their career choices. Rosenberg (23) and more recently Davis (24) have indicated that the occupational value which most sharply differentiates the career choices of women from those of men has to do with the orientation toward people. Women strongly prefer fields in which they work with people rather than things, and hence we find college-trained women most heavily represented in the humanities, the applied aspects of the social sciences, education, and the health professions. Some of these differences persist even among men and women who have chosen the same occupational field. Women are more often found teaching science than doing science. Women college teachers mention as most satisfying about their campus jobs "good students" and "desirable colleagues," whereas men teachers stress "opportunity to do research" and "freedom and independence" (25).

For most American women, growing up has meant shifting from being taken care of in a well-peopled social environment to taking care of others. If we want more women to enter science, not only as teachers of science but as scientists, some quite basic changes must take place in the ways girls are reared. If girls are to develop the analytic and mathematical abilities science requires, parents and teachers must encourage them in independence and self-reliance instead of pleasing feminine submission; stimulate and reward girls' efforts to satisfy their curiosity about the world as they do those of boys; encourage in girls not unthinking conformity but alert intelligence that asks why and rejects the easy answers. A childhood model of the quiet, good, sweet girl will not produce many women scientists or scholars, doctors, or engineers. It will produce the competent, loyal laboratory assistant "who will not operate so readily on her own," as Pollard wrote recently in describing his preference for a female rather than a male laboratory assistant (26).

Summary and Conclusions

American society has prided itself on its concern for the fullest development of each individual's creative potential. As a nation, we have become sensitive to the social handicaps of race and class but have remained quite insensitive to those imposed because of sex. Those women who have entered the top professional fields have had to have extraordinary motivation, thick skins, exceptional ability, and some unusual pattern of socialization in order to reach their occupational destinations. In their backgrounds one is likely to find a professional mother, an unusually supportive father, or dedicated and stimulating teachers.

If we want more women scientists, there are several big tasks ahead:

1. We must educate boys and girls for all their major adult roles—as parents, spouses, workers, and creatures of leisure. This means giving more stress in education, at home and at school, to the future family roles of boys and the future occupational roles of girls. Women will not stop viewing work as a stopgap until meaningful work is taken for granted in the lives of women as it is in the lives of men.

2. We must stop restricting and lowering the occupational goals of girls on the pretext of counseling them to be "realistic." If women have difficulty handling the triple roles of member of a profession, wife, and mother, their difficulties should be recognized as a social problem to be dealt with by social engineering rather than be left to each individual woman to solve as best she can. Conflicts and difficulties are not necessarily a social evil to be avoided; they can be a spur to creative social change.

3. We must apply our technological skill to a rationalization of home maintenance (15). The domestic responsibilities of employed women and their husbands would be considerably lightened if there were house-care service firms, for example, with teams of trained male and female workers making the rounds of client households, accomplishing in a few hours per home and

with more thoroughness what the single domestic servant does poorly in two days of work at a barely living wage.

4. We must encourage men to be more articulate about themselves as males and about women. Three out of five married women doctors and engineers have husbands in their own or related fields. The views of young and able women concerning marriage and careers could be changed far more effectively by the men who have found marriage to professional women a satisfying experience than by exhortations of professional women, or of manpower specialists and family-living instructors whose own wives are homemakers.

The physiological differences between male and female are sufficiently clear and so fundamental to self-definition that no change in the direction of greater similarity between male and female social roles is going to disturb the sex identity of children or adults. No one would be confused if men were more tender and expressive and women more aggressive and intellectual. If anything, greater similarity in family and occupational roles would add zest and vitality to the relations between men and women and minimize the social segregation of the sexes. An increase in the number of women scientists would be only one of many desirable outcomes to the social changes that I have here urged.

References and Notes

1. *American Women: Report of the President's Commission on the Status of Women, 1963* (Government Printing Office, Washington, D.C., 1963).

2. *Report of the Committee on Federal Employment to the President's Commission on the Status of Women* (Government Printing Office, Washington, D.C., 1963), pp. 104–105.

3. *1960 Census of Population* (Government Printing Office, Washington, D.C.), vol. 1, pt. 1, Table 202.

4. Scientific personnel in government employment do not show so high a proportion of women in the biological sciences: the proportion female by major scientific field among those federally employed is 8 percent for physical sciences, 4 percent for biological sciences, 1 percent for engineering (2, Appendix D).

5. D. Hiestand, *Economic Growth and Employment Opportunities for Minorities* (Columbia Univ. Press, New York, 1964).

6. 1962 National Register data, reported in *Physics: Education, Employment, Financial Support, A Statistical Handbook* (American Institute of Physics, New York, 1964).

7. *1960 Census of Population: Characteristics of Professional Workers* (Government Printing Office, Washington, D.C.).

8. Ibid., rates calculated from data in Tables 3 and 6.

9. J. Davis, *Great Aspirations: The Graduate School Plans of America's College Seniors* (Chicago; Aldine, 1964), pp. 154–155.

10. N. Miller, "One year after commencement," *National Opinion Research Center, Chicago, Report No. 92* (1963), pp. 125–126.

11. Preliminary results of a recent questionnaire sent to the same sample as in Davis (9).

12. H. Martineau, *Society in America*, S. M. Lipset, Ed. (New York: Doubleday, abridged ed., 1962), p. 295.

13. H. Lehman, *Age and Achievement* (Princeton, N.J., Princeton Univ. Press, 1953).

14. A. Rossi, *Daedalus* 93 (1964), 615.

15. F. I. Nye and L. W. Hoffman, *The Employed Mother in America* (Chicago: Rand McNally, 1963).

16. R. Hess, J. *Marriage and the Family* 26 (1964), 422.

17. One experimental day-care center in Syracuse, New York, will test the effect of an optimal environment for 6-month-to-3-year-old children on learning readiness at school age. B. M. Caldwell and J. B. Richmond, ibid., p. 481.

18. A. Roe, "A psychological study of eminent biologists," *Psychol. Monograph No. 65* (1951), p. 331; "A psychological study of physical scientists," *Genet. Psychol. Monograph No. 43* (1951); "Psychological study of research scientists," *Psychol. Monograph No. 67* (1953), p. 2; "Crucial life experiences in the development of scientists," in *Talent and Education*, E. Torrance, ed. (Minneapolis: Univ. of Minnesota Press, 1960); *The Making of a Scientist* (New York: Dodd, Mead, 1963).

19. G. Stern, M. Stein, B. Bloom, *Methods in Personality Assessment* (Glencoe; Free Press, Ill., 1956).

20. E. Maccoby, "Woman's intellect," in *The Potential of Women*, S. Farber and R. Wilson, eds. (New York: McGraw-Hill, 1963), gives a more detailed summary of sex differences in intellectual ability.

21. E. Bing, *Child Development* 34 (1963), 631.

22. J. Coleman, *The Adolescent Society* (Glencoe, Ill.: Free Press, 1961).

23. M. Rosenberg, *Occupations and Values* (Glencoe, Ill.: Free Press, 1957).

24. J. Davis, Undergraduate Career Decisions, in press.

25. R. Eckert and J. Stecklein, "Job motivations and satisfactions of college teachers," *U.S. Office of Education Coop. Res. Monograph No. 7* (1961).

26. E. Pollard, *Science* 145 (1964), 1018.

WOMEN AND THE PROFESSIONS

by Cynthia Fuchs Epstein

In spite of astounding changes in the status of women throughout the world, American women's participation in the professions has remained constant during the past seventy years. Women in professional life are as unusual in the 1960s as they were in the 1890s, though they may be somewhat less of an oddity.

Most legal obstacles which once barred them from many occupations have now been eliminated, but women who do work have settled for a fraction of the job opportunities offered by the economy and there has been a striking lack of advance in the rate of increase of women in the prestigious and traditional professions of law, medicine, teaching in higher education, the natural sciences, and engineering (leaving aside those most enduring male preserves, the ministry and the military).

On the one hand we still have the debate over whether women should work outside the home *at all*, a rather recent issue (the home being defined as the "natural abode of women"), and on the other hand the question of which occupations are most "suitable" or "natural" for women.

Several elements are crucial to an understanding of the context within which these contradictory questions are raised. The most important of these elements—themselves often contradictory—are the following:

1. The radical legal changes in the direction of equality for women. These reforms are now worldwide and are to be found in the most traditional societies. In our country even the secondary legal inequalities have been reduced, some as recently as this decade. Under the Civil Rights Act of 1964 employers are no longer permitted to refuse to hire or promote women on the ground that their fellow workers or customers would not accept them; to classify certain jobs

From Cynthia Epstein, "Women and the Professions," New Generation (Fall, 1969): pp. 16–22. New Generation *is a quarterly journal of the National Committee on Employment of Youth. Reprinted by permission of* New Generation.

exclusively for males or females unless sex is a *bona fide* qualification; to establish separate seniority lists based on sex; to label jobs "light" or "heavy" if it is merely a subterfuge for the terms male or female; to forbid the hiring of married women if the ruling is not also applied to married men; to place newspaper help-wanted advertisements excluding applicants of one sex and limiting the job to applicants of the other sex.

2. The legal reforms are themselves an indicator of the sweep throughout the world of the *ideology* of equality for all. The inclusion of women in the national economic life has not only been a necessity in many technologically advancing countries, but an expression of their emancipation from second-class citizenship.

3. Industrialization has resulted in the creation of new occupational roles and has created demands for skilled personnel, both of which require additional manpower that often must be recruited from the female population. Some of these new industrial roles have not been institutionalized to the extent of becoming stringently sex-defined.

4. Women's participation in the labor force has been at issue only during the past century, and only in industrial societies where work is separated from the home. Even so, in much of the Western world, including the United States, women constitute between a third and half of the labor force.

5. Women have equal access to higher education and professional training in many countries. Although discrimination still exists at this level, the opportunities for initial entry to professional training often are underutilized by women.

6. In the advanced Western societies, and particularly in the United States, the participation of women in upper-level positions and professions does not show clear gains as it does in the modernizing societies.

Considering the broad participation of women in the world of work, it is noteworthy that women are underrepresented in responsible positions and in jobs where individual creativity and talent are combined. Why do women continually settle for the lower-ranking, low-paying, and often personally unchallenging work of the society? What are the factors which influence their decision to work, their choices of occupation, and their levels of occupational aspiration? And, most provocative for the purpose of this investigation, why have women in the United States, where the drive for equality and legal reform was first initiated and realized, lagged in advancement into economically and intellectually rewarding positions in industry and the professions?

Some striking—and informative—statistics come to light when we compare relative progress of boys and girls in the world of education. There is a greater number of girls than boys in high school graduation classes, but this radically declines in the college years, a pattern that has not changed since the start of the century. One of the principal successes of American education has been the increased *number* of young people, both men and women, who are receiving higher education. Yet there appears to be no relative improvement in women's share in higher education, and one might argue that they have failed to maintain the place they had reached earlier, since the *proportion* of women attending colleges and universities has decreased.

It has also been suggested that girls pursue less demanding programs than boys and are more carefully selected to begin with. Moreover, studies show that fewer of the gifted women than men even enter college; more of the gifted women than men drop out; more women who take physical science and professional programs quit than do men; and as one climbs the ladder of higher education the proportion of all women steadily declines, even in the "female" fields. The percentage of women applying to medical school is lower than it was ten to fifteen years ago. Similarly, in the 1930s two out of five BA's and MA's were women and one out of seven PhD's. In 1962 women received one out of three of the BA's and MA's and only one in eleven of the PhD's.

Most importantly, of those women who do complete higher education and professional training, less than half use their training, and even fewer become part of the professional elite or rise to positions of eminence, even in the so-called feminine occupations. And this is true as well for women in other societies, although the proportion of women who do work and do succeed varies from country to country. While the proportion remains small in most countries, women's representation in *professional* occupations in Sweden, Great Britain, France, the Soviet Union, and Israel has doubled or more in the past twenty years.

The existence of a large stratum of educated, trained, and professionally active women makes it unnecessary to argue the question of women's innate intellectual capacity or their ability to do sustained high-concentration work. The question of whether women are as intelligent as men, of whether or not they can handle abstract ideas and solve problems, has been eliminated by their achievement in mathematics, chemistry, physics, and the social sciences. Although the extent of women's capacities is still argued at dinner tables, in newspaper columns and by educators, the truth is that women *do,* therefore they *can.* What is interesting is the question of why so many of those who can, *do not.*

We all know that not all smart men do well in their occupations and that men with demonstrated abilities in science and engineering may run into a career dead-end. But, unlike women, smart men generally *expect* to do well occupationally. They expect financial rewards and job satisfaction as well as approval and encouragement by their families and associates. But smart women must decide if they will even enter the occupational world, and once having entered must decide if they will stay. They also must decide if they will try for the rewards men expect as a matter of course: money, prestige, power, and job satisfaction. Although men may often compromise in one or two of these areas, it is more likely for women to feel they must compromise far earlier and for far less.

It would be inaccurate, however, to focus only on career choice as an individual decision. Which women will enter the economic sphere and which realm within it they will populate is also an indicator of larger cultural attitudes and of social dynamics, including pressures and demands from every institution in society. Thus, while a growing economy may need additional workers and seek out women, religious leaders may counter the demand by urging women to stay home, care for families, and go to church.

Changes in marriage patterns, too, have altered the structure within which work choices are made. In the past generation women often chose between marriage and a career, and "career women" were most often spinsters, divorcees, or widows. Many studies indicate that among those who rose to the top of their profession, the incidence of unmarried women was also greater. Probably it is true that single women who chose careers generally did better than their married colleagues because they had more continuous work experience or because many women who combined marriage with work did not take their jobs seriously or were in other ways diverted from work-achievement goals.

Since the spinster has become almost as much a relic in fact as in name, women have chosen marriage, with or without a career. The decision has been made more binding because of the lowered age at which couples now marry (we have the lowest average in the Western world), and that means early motherhood and less time and resources to devote to advanced training, a pattern that has had deleterious effects on women's participation in the professions. Thus, though more married women work (one-third of them are mothers with children under eighteen), they are most often found in the lower ranks of the occupational hierarchy, and far fewer single women are available to fill the reservoir of potential career women that existed in the past.

The presence of large numbers of married women in the work force has led to institutional and cultural disharmony despite unchanging social attitudes toward career women. Today women who choose both marriage and a career face a nearly normless situation in that there is no formal structure to aid them in apportioning time and resources between their two major responsibilities. The ability to deal with the complex roles of wife, mother, and working woman, especially at the professional level, is still largely a matter of individual adaptation, compromise, and personal arrangement, and is often characterized by strain.

The married middle-class woman who works knows she can choose to stop working at any time and that, on balance, the decision to give up working probably would meet with more social support and approval than any arrangement she might be able to work out for combining her work and home life.

Consider the relevance of "image" on the working patterns of women. The American image of working women is limited and negative. In contrast, the popular impression of Soviet society is that women *do* work. Indeed, it is expected that Russian women will work outside the home at a wide range of jobs, including those normally considered men's work in the United States (mining, bus driving, etc.), and they are being channeled into such "masculine" professions as medicine, engineering, and law.

Social definitions are part of an individual's self-concepts, and further determine hierarchies of choice, definitions of rewards, and pressures creating guilts. These have direct consequences for the sex-division of labor. If women are to work only if they *have* to, then they will not have the foresight to train, prepare, and orient their lives in the direction of work. They will drift to the easily accessible and unskilled jobs. In addition, the fact that many occupations are considered "male" and others "female" has considerable effect on the early socialization process of the individual and in later recruitment and performance.

The history of the sex-typing of certain occupations and professions would be an interesting study in itself. In the early days of the United States much of the work of the agrarian economy was shared by men and women. Of course, many tasks were sex-defined; men did the heavy physical labor while women did much of the household work, although men performed work in the home (especially during the winters), and women were involved in a range of farm activities. With the Industrial Revolution, men lost many of the household and homeshop tasks which they formerly had performed and women lost the work of the farm but retained the work of the household. Thus, housework was designated as an exclusively feminine domain with some occupational work assigned to women as an extension of the female role, and other occupational work relegated to the male.

But the course of occupational sex-typing has not been logically consistent—occupations have shifted in definition from male to female and vice versa. For instance, midwifery traditionally was a female job and the assistance of men at childbirth was considered a serious breach of modesty. Not until recent times, and mainly in the West, has delivery of the newborn become the work of the (mostly) male medical practitioner.

Although the prejudices against men assisting at childbirth are now thought to be primitive superstitions or Victorian notions, other rationales which support sex-typing in the professions generally have not been questioned. By and large these rationales are used to exclude women from the prestigious male occupations, though they act as well to limit men's entry into female professions such as nursing and social work.

Sex-typing links occupational roles with sex roles and makes "female occupations" of those which involve nurturing, helping, and empathizing (e.g., teaching, nursing, and social work), and are seen as extensions of the female role. Occupations which are seen as requiring such characteristics as coolness, detachment, object-orientation, and outspokenness (e.g., law, medicine, science) are not considered appropriate for women.

However, there is much social and historical evidence to indicate that there is far more flexibility to sex-role and occupational-role typing than is apparent from observing the proportion of each sex in most of our occupations today.

Several illustrations: In colonial and pioneer days, primary-school teaching was a male occupation ostensibly because women did not have the necessary stamina of mind to educate the young. Only with the shortage of men during the Civil War and the growing press of mass education did the demand for teachers require the recruitment of women. Women eventually became predominant in the teaching profession, with a concomitant change in public attitudes toward the suitability of education as an essentially female prerogative.

A similar pattern occurred in the secretarial field. Though at one time male secretaries and typists were common, today they are an anomaly. Only in such conservative, all-male work cultures as are found in certain Wall Street law firms are male secretaries still to be found. Part of the answer may be the proliferation of jobs in the white-collar sector of the economy, where women provided a source of cheap, transferable, nondemanding labor. Yet it is still unclear why males have become excluded from many lower-level white-collar jobs when there is no defined masculine or feminine characteristic in the nature of the work. Women may simply make better subordinates because they accept their position and do not aim higher.

Some spheres of work remain unaffected by sex-typing. Jobs as bank tellers, for instance, seem to be open to both men and women, and it will be interesting to see whether new jobs which have come about through scientific innovation (e.g., computer technology) will provide opportunities without sex definition. One may expect that they too will become polarized.

There are also large differences in sex-typing of jobs from country to country. One rarely hears of an American woman dentist, although 75 percent of the dentists in Denmark are women and dentistry is considered a female profession in some South American countries. Women account for 1 percent of the profession in this country.

Although there is no hard evidence of the fuller acceptance and utilization of women in the professions, many observers have pointed to changing trends which should lead to democratization of career opportunities. The changes within the professions are an outgrowth of wide social change in American society. The civil rights movement and the accompanying pressures for elimination of all barriers to free recruitment in the job market are but one example of the interplay between changes in ideology and social structure.

Indications of change in the society leading to changes in the professions may be found in the following:

1. Young men are becoming more at ease with educated women as elite education, once strictly separate, has become coeducational. One might expect that these young men, as adults, will be less resistant to working side by side with women.

2. The traditional professional training centers are being restructured. As in pioneer days, there are said to be more opportunties in the West, and in fact there are fewer traditions and a greater need for trained people there, which gives entree to those whom the traditional centers have deemed undesirable.

3. The expansion of population everywhere and the need and rising expectations for specialized personnel create pressures on the professions to recruit from a broader base than they might prefer.
4. Ideological changes have upset traditional modes of education and work. The "establishment" now has vociferous and gifted challengers.

Although women's special problems have not yet been enunciated to the same extent as those of the other disadvantaged, women may benefit from the steamroller effect of rapid social change. But whether the trends toward equality will be stronger than the forces which inhibit women's choice and ability to work is still unknown.

4

THE CHANGING POSITION OF WOMEN
IN CHANGING SOCIETIES

The revolutionary programs of all nations in which fundamental transformations of the society are imposed have aimed at improving the condition of women and the family. These nations vary greatly in their traditional social structures, their economic bases, and their political foundations, but, in all of them, the leaders are aware that there could be no revolution that did not employ women and that did not give them freedom.

This chapter looks at women in two revolutions: Cuba and Soviet Russia. To some extent, we are hampered in measuring the amount of real change that has taken place in these societies because of the lack of good studies in the past. There is little material on Cuba and almost no adequate historical research on the family has been done in the Soviet Union. Scholars have had to rely on analyses of changes in the law, on literary sources, on the reports of former citizens or travelers, and on the official statistics concerning marriage and divorce.

Some of the changes attributed to a revolution were initiated before it took place. Olesen notes, for example, that, prior to the Cuban revolution, many educated Cuban women had substantial achievements to their credit, had participated in politics, and even had assumed high positions in the occupational sphere.

No lasting changes can be made by a revolution that is not based on groundwork laid much earlier. Certain structures in societies—the family is one—are very resistant to change. In addition, because revolutions advocate change in many spheres, new governments must decide what their priorities will be.

Contrary to Marxian predictions, the modern revolutions have occurred mainly in the technologically less advanced nations. In such societies, freedom and opportunity for women were possible for only the few members of the upper social stratum who had received a Western education. Oddly enough, these women often did better than American women in obtaining important posts or achieving professional success. Olesen notes, for example, that although few women were doctors or lawyers in Cuba, they formed a higher percentage of these fields than did women in the United States (13 and 7 percent respectively). (The phenomenon of educated women having access to top-level jobs in countries considered "backward," while they fail to do so in most Western countries, is an interesting problem for social scientists to solve.) But in general, family systems in the revolutionary societies were patriarchal. Women were expected to stay at home and men were expected to be the natural rulers.

Cuba has provided an interesting modern revolution in which to study the problems of women, because it has been typified as a "male vanity culture." In addition, it is the only Latin American nation to undergo a genuine revolution—one that has sought to transform the entire social structure.

Even in revolutionary societies not characterized by a male vanity culture, where women have been given new economic opportunities and freed from male domination, and where the official propaganda encouraged their emancipation, men continue to resist the new social arrangements. Cuban men still want their old rights and feel threatened by women who seek equality. Olesen notes the many tensions generated by the discrepancy between attitudes formed in another era and the *new* doctrines and opportunities. This has certainly been the experience in the Soviet Union as well.

Yet the *direction* of change seems apparent. Although some societies begin with a program of emancipation that is swift and extensive and find they have to retrench (Premier Castro, for example, has deferred a full-scale assault on Cuban attitudes about sexual behavior), there is no doubt that women in all cases are better off than they were prior to revolution.

Men may wish that women be kept at home and sheltered from other predatory males while they themselves are free, but once women have tasted freedom, it is impossible to convince them to give it up. In addition, the labor needs call for a greater utilization of women's talents. By now, Cuban women do not as yet number as much as one-seventh of the nonagricultural working population, but half of all the students in medical training are women. Women have even entered occupations once considered too "heavy," such as driving tractors.

Geiger's analysis of the Soviet situation places emphasis upon the wide *differences* in the position of women in different social statuses. Many Russian peasant men and women still accept traditional views of marriage (the husband is the absolute patriarch), but such attitudes are much rarer in urban Russian life. Even in rural regions, however, traditions are crumbling. Divorce was once viewed as nearly impossible, wife-beating was expected, love was unimportant, and the public display of affection was looked upon as taboo. All this is changing.

The Russian situation is instructive because it is the oldest contemporary revolution available. The revolutions in Vietnam, Cuba, China, and Algeria are recent. In the Soviet situation, we can best study how ancient family traditions can be altered by a modern political apparatus that is determined to change the old patterns and attitudes.

Geiger discusses some of the changes during the half-century of modern Soviet rule and some of the tensions that still exist between the official doctrines specifying equality of women and the traditional sex-division of labor. Although Russian women may come closer than any others to the ideal of being given access to all spheres of work, at each higher level of professional or administrative achievement, an increasingly smaller percentage of Russian women is found. Women are also clustered in the traditional spheres of women's work (teaching and nursing) as they are in the United States. And, once the work day is over, Russian women seem no more emancipated than women anywhere else. They must then turn to the cooking and housework—typically not shared by their husbands; equalitarianism has not pervaded the home to any substantial degree.

These cases examine a wide variety of experiences that women are undergoing in revolutions thousands of miles apart. Both the difficulties and resistances, and the successes, suggest where traditional social structures can be altered and what the costs and benefits are of doing so.

LEADS ON OLD QUESTIONS FROM A NEW REVOLUTION: NOTES ON CUBAN WOMEN, 1969

by Virginia Olesen

> *That is a problem now, too, getting married. I like to dominate my wife and that is not so easy any more.*
>
> *I know I am married to an exaggerated case, but his point of view is very Cuban. The position of Cuban women is terrible.*
>
> *. . . God knows there is something she can do. . . . In case you have not noticed it, there has been a revolution here and women do not have to put up with that kind of treatment.*

Cuba is a society where change has been rapid and dramatic, where elements indicating emergent or reduced strains between the sexes are highly discernible, and where composition of the society allows meaningful analysis of wide sectors of that society. . . .

Sociohistoric Situations of Cuban Women

In the years immediately preceding 1959 Cuba enjoyed a healthy economic profile, an attribute unique among Third World nations and among those nations, characteristic only of Japan. Within both underdeveloped and developed nations in its own size, under 6.5 million, Cuba's GNP in those years was less than that of such countries as Finland, Switzerland, Denmark, New Zealand, Norway, Venezuela, where the GNP was over $600 million. It stood on a par, in terms of a GNP between $300 and $600 with such countries as Ireland, Israel,

From Virginia Olesen, "Leads on Old Questions from a New Revolution: Notes on Cuban Women, 1969." Reprinted by permission of the author.

Costa Rica, Lebanon, Panama, and Uruguay and definitely outranked poorer nations whose GNP was less than $300, such as Albania, Saudi Arabia, Dominican Republic, Ecuador, El Salvador, Guatemala, Honduras, Iraq, Nicaragua, Haiti, Paraguay or Bolivia. It was not therefore an "underdeveloped" country in the usual sense, though one must recognize that apparent wealth was badly and unevenly distributed in the population. What concerns us here is the part that women played in the labor forces of that time: What was the opportunity structure for women? How many women were in the labor force? What were their prospects as women workers?

In the Cuban labor force of the mid and late 1950s there were few women, the number being around 17 percent of the economically active population over 14 years of age. This small percentage points to the prevailing Latin norms which severely restrict and govern activities of females outside the domestic arena. Only since 1936 had Cuban women been able to vote and only since 1940 had they been assured the legal privilege of owning property. Moreover, this small number suggests that women's occupational choices were limited even for those bold enough to wish or to have to step outside the bounds of the culture's restrictions on women's work.

The types of occupational choices available to Cuban women varied in those years, however, and in ways which suggest that both the economic structure of the country and the maldistribution of wealth influenced the kinds of choices women could make in this sphere of their lives. Examination of a list of occupations shows that of all occupations domestic service numbered more women workers (89 percent were women) than any other. The occupational category with the next greatest number of women workers was that of teacher, where 82 percent were women, a situation not unlike other Latin nations, for example, Brazil. Clearly, the two occupations which drew most women represented radically different paths and choices available to women whose background provided or denied them access to an education for the opportunities at hand. This duality is apparent in the rest of the occupational list: whereas almost half (45 percent) of social workers were women, as were a substantial number of pharmacists (34 percent), a significant number of women were also employed in such critical industries as food and tobacco (24 percent) and the clothing industry (45 percent).

Judging from this analysis it would seem that for those women whose life chances had included the possibility of education, a theme of some importance in Cuba since the nineteenth-century pronouncements of such feminists as Maria Luisa Dolz y Arnago, the opportunity structure provided some chance for professional employment, albeit a limited one judging from the sparse numbers of women in medicine (13 percent) or law (a meager 7 percent). For those whose station was much humbler, domestic service or industrial work was their lot. For those whose situation fell between these extremes, the occupational structure held open the possibilities of work in clerical areas and to these large numbers of Cuban women were drawn, for example, typists (53 percent were women), or telephone operators (23 percent), women who, in the vivid description found in a novel on Cuban life of the period, "waged a battle between penury and decorum, struggling to get a hold on the fringes of the middle class; too smart to stop at high school, too poor to go to college or train for a career; too proud to end her anguished pretense by either marrying into the declared blue collar class or becoming the mistress of a minor merchant or political upstart."

To this picture of the variable opportunities afforded by the occupational structure of pre-Castro Cuba it must be added that agricultural work drew very few women (less than 2 percent), for it was regarded as being too heavy. Women who worked in pre-Castro Cuba therefore were largely the urbanized women of the cities, particularly those whose social station permitted them access to an education which would for some lead to such professions as teaching, social work, and pharmacy. Such was the picture from the viewpoint of women's choices. To turn the picture around, it may be noted that even though women were only 17 percent of the labor force in the mid 1950s, their substantial numbers in such professions as teaching, in such significant support activities as clerical work, in such basic industries as tobacco work which had utilized women since the 1850s, were clear contributions to the economy of the 1950s.

These figures also point to the public sector of life for Cuban women in those days and suggest that as participants in that public sector, irrespective of Latin norms, they had already begun to emerge from the convent-like dwelling of the home before the Castro phase of Cuba's long revolutionary history. Indeed, pre-Castro Cuba and Cuba of earlier times had been peopled with women, particularly certain members of the upper and middle classes whose activities at very high political and professional levels gave them and females like them what has felicitously been termed "a strong public character." Women such as Dona Socorro Mancebo whose correspondence with Simon Bolivar advocated Cuban independence in the 1820s, Dona Maria Luisa Dolz y Arnago, nineteenth-century educator and feminist; Terresa

Casuso, student activist of the 1930s and later Cuban ambassador to the United Nations for a time, come to mind in this connection.

At the same time, however, that Cuban women had begun to enter public life in small numbers and along with the symbolic facts of these women of "strong public character," the mode of Latin culture as found in Cuba surrounded these and other women of all classes with norms and sanctions which both pampered and restricted their lives, which emphasized sexuality whilst condemning women for extramarital infidelities, which in all social levels made women subordinate to the Cuban male in matters of intellect, family life, and, of course, sexual response. A few examples . . . will illustrate: Common-law marriages, frequent in pre-Castro Cuba, particularly in rural areas, were more binding on women than on men; social visiting in city cafes was appropriate for men but not for women; even after marriage women remained symbolically part of their father's family; adulterous behavior on the husband's part was not grounds for divorce unless it had created public scandal; marital infidelities on the male's part were expected and indeed encouraged, but similar wifely behavior was regarded as flightiness; in rural Cuba women frequently did not sit at the same meal with their menfolk, but ate with the children.

These behaviors were supported by much more than the influence of the Roman Catholic church, which in pre-Castro Cuba was significantly weakened and had had limited appeal, that largely to urban women of the upper-middle classes. Such behaviors were thoroughly grounded in and nourished by the cultural themes of *hildalgoism* and *macho. Hildalgoism,* the courtly sense of nobility, was balanced by the theme of *macho,* the demand to display manliness in matters sexual, physical, and intellectual by defying convention but with the type of style and flair which would earn admiration not only of womenfolk, but of other men. The enactment of *macho* in the Cuban setting was, and indeed, still is, heavily implicated with notions of honor and shame which link the psychological aspects of Cuban sexual identity with the social and behavioral norms noted above.

Rather importantly from the standpoint of social pressure on Cuban women, these experiences of honor and shame derived not only from the proper male enactment of *macho* and *hildalgoism,* but on the continued proper conduct of women in any male's life. Ideal women, chaste and hopefully, indeed preferably sexually innocent, contributed to their own honor and the honor of their men through their decorous behavior. In such a society it is not surprising that marital infidelity for males was condoned, even encouraged, that there were well-established institutions for prostitution. Clearly, the cultural pressures on women and their choices redounded on Cuban men, too, and may very well have been part of the reason for the jump in the divorce rate (from .83 to 1.17) between 1962 and 1965 when divorce laws were liberalized.

Quite aside from these observations concerning sexual behavior and its prescribed limits, the Cuban family in the pre-Castro years was thought to be a significant social unit for the rearing of children and the provision of a stable society. Family size in 1953 averaged 4.86 persons with 4.35 being the norm in the urban settings and 5.75 the rural average, reflecting the very large families of peasants, families often headed by a woman. Family planning and the choices which it represented were not a factor in the lives of Cuban women, by virtue of on the one hand the influence of the Church, however weak, and on the other, the impress of the cultural themes just discussed.

To summarize briefly the situation of Cuban women before the Castro years, it may be noted that their partial entry into the labor market represented for different classes differential access to the education necessary to pursue occupations other than those of service or very low skills. In spite of the contributions, both symbolic and otherwise, of women with "strong public character," the Cuban woman was strongly influenced by strong cultural themes which in demanding manly sexual aggressiveness from males in the society muted and diminished female attempts at sexual forwardness in choices other than those rigidly circumscribed by these cultural themes. The realization of personal honor and the penance of public shame were closely related for both men and women to proper enactment of these cultural themes.

The Current Situation

With respect to the occupational structure and opportunities now open to women for education and occupational placement, contemporary Cuba is characterized by a much wider range of these than was the case formerly. Women, as well as men, have been the beneficiaries of the extensive literacy campaign of 1961, which, for many of humble station or what would have been thought of as humble station in an earlier time, has meant greater access to clerical work, from which they would have been barred in an earlier era by virtue of limited education. Nor is it the case that education for clerical work is the major outlet for many women who wish to or have been encouraged to work outside the home. The nationalization of some 55,363 small private businesses in 1968 necessitated the creation of a managerial class, largely recruited from the ranks of housewives whose background or skills were suitable for this purpose. Nearly half of all medical school classes are now women, and their numbers have begun to appear in such diverse pursuits as barbering, driving tractors, and agricultural work of the sort deemed too heavy in former days.

Not only are more opportunities for work open to women, but many more women are at work. By Cuban estimate, the number of women in nonagricultural pursuits jumped from 90,000 to 370,000 between 1965 and 1968, an increase which they hope to continue with addition of 100,000 more women in agricultural and industrial work in 1969 and which will eventually culminate, they hope, with one million women engaged in nonagricultural pursuits by 1975. Assuming that the Cuban population remains somewhat stable or increases only slightly (it was 7,833,000 in 1966), this means that by 1975 one out of every seven Cubans would be a working woman. From the official standpoint these efforts to bring women into the labor force are determined and dictated by the economic necessity to increase the labor pool as an economic resource. Such efforts are, moreover, attempts to involve Cuban women in the moral aspects of the revolution, to make them a part of creating the new revolutionary man and to urge them to take part in bettering the nation.

Although it may be reasonably assumed that many Cuban women earnestly have taken up work as their own commitment to the revolutionary ideals, it may also be noted that economic pressures on the individual which involve rising costs and stable salaries have also prompted the move of many women to the labor force. In the advent then of increased numbers of working women we see the tensions between issues of *conciencia,* the amalgam of conscience, conscientiousness, and commitment to revolutionary ideals and *egoismo,* the concerns for material matters or rewards. For some these tensions play their part with respect to the types of choices women can and do make with respect to the types of family lives they and their husbands work out, as, for example, the comments of a regional secretary of the Cuban Federation of Women who noted that:

> I have been married two years. My husband was at Guantánomo during the alert and since I had been in Santiago at school just before that, we did not see each other for four months. Now he is at Banes and we see each other once a week. It has to be, it is no sacrifice. My ambition is to see our work succeed. . . .

Along with broadening the opportunity structure for women, necessitated in part by the economic and moral demands of the new situation, there has been an effort to institute the types of social services which women need if they are to enter the labor force, particularly women with families. Chief among these has been the establishment of nursery schools which enable women to take full-time work or to undertake studies which will later lead to work.

The wider participation of women in work, several-fold beyond the modest 17 percent of the mid 1950s, has also been accompanied by the further emergence of the Cuban woman with "strong public character." To the familiar names of Mariana Grajelas, renowned as the mother of an early hero (Antonio Maceo), and Ana de Moro Betancourt, another nineteenth-century feminist, have been added the names of women whose participation in various phases of Castro's ascent to power nominates them for martyrdom or heroic stature. For example, Olga Guevara, formerly a guerrilla fighter who is now a trouble-shooter in mountain settlements; Celia Sanchez, Castro's personal secretary; Haydee Santamaria, heroine of the attack on the Monchada barracks, now head of the cultural services, La Casa de Las Americas, who has been celebrated in song and in poem. The emergence of these women as potent symbolic figures of strong female public character has paralleled the increasing prominence of the Federation of Cuban Women, an organization headed by Castro's sister-in-law, Vilma Espin, and an organization devoted to the eradication of the inferior status of Cuban women as well as their induction and integration into the new situation.

Whilst these themes have strongly emerged in contemporary Cuba, much of the cultural arrangement from earlier times appears to have survived with respect to certain emphases on women's roles. For one matter the family unit continues to be regarded as critical in Cuban life. The positive view with which the society as a whole looks upon the family and especially upon the role of mothers is clearly reflected in the large sections of the Communist paper *Granma* devoted to Mother's Day and in one foreign observer's notes on Mother's Day wherein he had observed that Cuban bakers devoted their entire capacity and perhaps even the entire daily ration of flour to the production of special Mother's Day cakes.

This observation leads to the question of pressures on sex role behavior and the matter of women's choices. In this connection it is to be noted that the cultural themes discussed in the earlier section of the paper, e.g. *macho* and *hildalgoism*, are still very much an influence on sexual behaviors and judgments, as witness the report about a former Monchada fighter, now a disburser of scholarships at the university, who is reputedly notorious among students for refusing to allocate scholarships to young women who are supposed to have slept with their boyfriends, no doubt basing his judgments on the old standards of chastity and innocence. Other informal reports of negative responses from Cuban husbands to such fashions as mini-skirts suggests that the former ideals of honor and shame are still realized to a significant extent through the wife's behavior.

With respect to choices in the matter of child-bearing, since Cuba does not utilize the pill, the older methods of contraception, where accessible, must be relied upon. Abortions, while available, are not encouraged since the question of population increase to restore numbers lost through immigation and in order to assure a sufficient labor pool is clearly one of importance to the regime. Studied efforts, however, to enforce productivity and to realize a higher birth-rate have not been undertaken by the Castro government, even though there has been an increase in the birth-rate. For this reason the analysis of women's choices in this area remains one in which the cultural, economic, and social proscriptions around sex role and family, not the dictates of the regime, are the salient considerations. Interestingly, as recounted in the statements of some young Cubans, an almost Puritanical attitude toward sexual relationships exists among some of the young, although by no means among everyone, certainly not among the *campesinos,* whose large families on the one hand give assurances of future workers, but who on the other hand pose critical problems for food supplies in an economy of scarcity where crop lands once devoted to food become increasingly taken over by sugar cane.

The eradication of prostitution, an official attempt on the part of the regime to do away with this institution to which many women of poorer classes had been drawn in pre-Castro Cuba, has been accompanied by official recognition that not all of the former traditions, most especially the *posadas,* inns where lovers could dally at leisure and in private, could be dispersed with and that certain traditions around sexual behaviors would have to grow out of the mix of the old and the new. Castro himself has indicated that:

> Traditions and customs can clash somewhat with new social realities and the problem of sexual relations in youth will acquire scientific attention. . . . All of this (discussion on prostitution) raises the future necessity, too, of approaching the problem of sexual relations in a different way. But we believe that these are problems of the future that cannot be determined by decree—not at all.

Women's own responses to the revolution and to the meaning of these changes for them as women seem somewhat mixed. Inferentially, based on findings which show that women workers had a more conservative response to the revolution than did their fellow male workers, the question has to be raised as to whether women were prepared or even willing to realign their roles in accordance with the new times. Moreover in an earlier part of the Castro decade, mixed comments from women about the role of a queen in a Havana carnival suggested that women themselves had radically differing ideas about their place as women, either as symbols of female roles or as participants in the revolution.

To summarize, a series of tensions seems apparent in the observations just noted: For one matter, the effort to bring women into the labor market, both as an economic necessity for the country and for individual gain cross-cuts the continued emphasis on the importance of the Cuban family. The sacrifices to enact *conciencia* and to create the new Cuba and the new Cuban man may well articulate choices for family rearing and planning that far transcend the conventional choices and modes of control known elsewhere. Much of the resolution of this tension would appear to depend on the success of the child-care centers. For another matter, the same effort to bring women into the public arena in the labor market serves to draw attention to the fact that although they had earlier begun to be active in that public area, they nevertheless are newcomers with as yet no well-developed norms or themes with which to work out the tensions generated from this arrival and its impact on the cultural themes of *macho* and *hildalgoism* or the effect of these themes on their arrival in the work force. Clearly, what is implied in this particular tension is not only an emergent set of ideals or values to cover this particular situation, but an emergent set of ideals which would be shared by males as well as females.

ELEMENTS AND TYPES IN SOVIET MARRIAGE

by Kent Geiger

"There is no love so ardent that it will not be cooled by marriage," says a traditional proverb. Some idea of the distance Soviet men and women have been invited to travel since the Revolution can be obtained by contrasting the sense of the proverb with the marxist notion that no marriage is valid *unless* it is bonded by love. As we know, the Soviet regime under Stalin felt obliged to compromise with the marxist ideal and urged husbands and wives to seek, at least in the transition period, other sources of bondedness in addition to that individual sex love so praised by Engels. Nonetheless, the record suggests that many in the population have found the ideal marriage pattern not only desirable but attainable. These two positions can be regarded as the extremes of the Soviet continuum of marriage types. . . .

In the peasant marriage sexuality is seen as a need and prerogative of the man, and sexual relations are usually suffered more than enjoyed by the wife. Marital fidelity on the part of the husband is not considered important—"men are like that"—but both virginity before marriage and fidelity after marriage are expected of the wife. Not only in sexual behavior, but also in other realms of impulse release, the double standard is very strong. Drinking, smoking, fighting, swearing are all prerogatives and symbols of masculinity and are denied to the proper peasant wife. She is expected to obey and to please her husband as best she can, and if he fails to reciprocate with wisdom and kindness, that, too, even though it is resented, is to be expected from men. The chief solace to the wife in an unhappy marriage is the church and her children.

In sexual relations the peasant woman is expected to be innocent, passive, and relatively uninterested. The man takes full initiative, looking upon sexual intimacy as a right which a wife can under no circumstances deny him. To a considerable extent his positive feeling for his

Excerpted from Kent Geiger, The Family in Soviet Russia *(Cambridge, Mass.: Harvard University Press, 1968), pp. 217–39. Copyright 1968 by the President and Fellows of Harvard College. Reprinted by permission of the author and Harvard University Press.*

wife is linked directly to her sexual desirability; as a consequence, the Soviet peasant husband sees the first period in his marriage as most enjoyable by far—the high point in his relation with his wife. After the initial excitement furnished by novelty, the relations with his wife settle down to a routine form both sexually and in more general terms. A young peasant girl says: "Of course your first year is the best. Your husband treats you better the first year. After that the children—after three or four years."

In the past such a marriage was embedded in a larger, usually patrilocal, extended family, and the tie between the young spouses was only one of the factors to be considered. Central, for instance, was her capacity to adapt to the already established routines of her husband's family of orientation. The submissiveness of the wife was supported by the residence custom, in which she was literally given away by her parents to become a member of another family and thus became economically dependent upon her new family. The real ruler of the family in those days was the old man, the husband's father. The wielding of power was determined primarily by age and sex, the order of precedence being from husband's father to husband's mother to husband. For the newly married husband and wife this worked well in the beginning of their marriage, giving them a chance to get used to each other without the immediate responsibility of exercising power, though by tradition the young wife was "always a stranger in the household of her husband."

These patterns have gradually crumbled, because the economic and legal basis for the aged father's authority has ended. On the kolkhoz, for example, work and payment are assigned and made to the individual, not by the head of household, and the new opportunities and outer status of women make the role of dependent daughter-in-law quite unattractive. Today, when a new wife feels uncomfortable with her parents-in-law she and her husband quickly decide to live by themselves. As noted in the previous chapter, there are definite advantages to living separately, but the responsibility for maintaining the marriage is thrown directly upon the participants' shoulders. Unfortunately, in the countryside, love—in the sense of that institutionalized expectation of permanent romantic attachment which elsewhere is important as a binding factor—is usually present, if at all, only in the early stages. Thus, it offers little support.

Village custom, religious opposition to divorce, dependency of wife and children on continuation of the marriage, and official divorce policy have all continued to exert some pressure. Sometimes when a peasant wife feels ill-treated and threatens to leave her husband, he uses naked threat of bodily harm, and she stays because she is afraid of what he will do to her. To some degree the traditionally low expectation of what peasant marriage provides helps to maintain it. If "a wife is only dear twice—when brought into the house and when carried out in her coffin," then the peasant husband is not too disappointed about it. Nevertheless, in a time of rapid economic and social changes all these forces have lost some of their sustaining capacity, and Soviet peasant marriage has become more and more unstable with the passing of time.

Equal Rights with Love

This pattern corresponds to the relations deemed proper by modern urban populations around the world. Both spouses share power by conscious agreement and deliberate effort. Sharing does not mean an absence of friction over the question, but when power is abused by one or the other of the sides, usually the husband, it is the wife's right to demand her say. Nor are the spouses required to perform in other respects in any set manner.

In many of the marriages observed the question seems to have been solved without great difficulty. The social unrest and uncertainties in the larger society seem to have combined with the challenging tasks offered by Soviet daily routine to make many Soviet husbands and wives only too glad to share rather than monopolize responsibility and power. The pattern seems often to involve a very rational alternation between two spouses, with an attitude of easy permissiveness for the most qualified to exercise influence, as in a Stalingrad working-class marriage. "In their partnership he predominated at times, and sometimes she did. He then gladly acceded to her guidance."

Often the husband, especially if he is at all "coopted" by his occupation, is content if the wife takes full charge of running the family household. This is a common factor to the equal-rights pattern. The wife of the busy Moscow factory director, for instance, did not work on the outside, but did take full charge of the furnishing of their luxurious five-room modern apartment near the Kremlin and of planning how to spend the couple's free time. Such spouses often seem quite highly specialized in their marital roles. In the relationship of a research chemist and his wife, also a trained chemist and serving as his assistant at work, the specialization by sex is muted but still noticeable. Their personalities and relationship are described this way: "He was quiet, controlled, serious, and reserved; she was the same. He was very active in his work, but as a person more passive. With her it was somewhat the other way around. While at work she was under him; at home she was really somewhat more the leader. Added together, this led to complete equality of rights between them. All problems were dealt with in common with complete calm." Other equal-rights marriages seem more tense, and apparently much effort has to go into the preservation of the equal status of the spouses. It seems that underlying, less conscious needs press the husband and occasionally the wife in a direction that diverges markedly from their conscious ideal of equality. This situation is especially common in younger families, where idealism is stronger, when husband and wife are still adjusting to each other, and where the limits of each other's desires and capabilities are not clearly understood.

Sometimes, perhaps as frequently as the wife, it is the husband who most seeks this kind of relationship. A young man from Viriatino, a recent version of the "progressive Komsomol youth of the 1920s with its uncompromising view of religion as a class-alien ideology, and with its urge to break with the routine of family life," married a young peasant girl with whom he wanted to establish an equal-rights relation. He became quite a proselytizer, taking his wife to the cinema and Komsomol meetings, reading to her aloud, and "insisting on a baby sitter on evenings when meetings or some other activities were going on in the village club." Another example is a young marriage between a twenty-six-year-old military officer and the daughter of a university professor: "Relations between them were very affectionate, and they did a lot of things together, though she did not share his occupational life. Surprisingly, he was more for equal rights in the marriage than she, who preferred to be somewhat subordinate and made no use of the liberties he was ready to extend to her." The affective bond in this kind of marriage is a deep sense of intimacy and sharing of all aspects of the self. The partners see each other as unique and look upon their relationship as irreplaceable. There is considerable self-control exercised, with the mood swings so typical among the peasantry occurring only rarely. Love is expected and spoken about, the partners are self- and relationship-conscious.

To be sure, mutual understanding and aid are also stressed, as is respect. When referring to the spouse in talk with an outsider (such as an interviewer), a respondent is apt to refer to his spouse as a "friend," or "life comrade" as well as a wife or husband. In general, such spouses seem decidedly more conscious of each other as separate personalities than is the case in the preceding pattern, and also more consciously dependent upon each other. Research into the personalities of Great Russians has repeatedly furnished evidence that dependency and affiliative needs are strong. Marriage is an obvious form for their satisfaction and seems to be the more strengthened by the presence of these needs, provided that they can be integrated with a pattern of distributing power that makes it possible to express them.

As a matter of fact, successful marriages that follow the equal-rights-with-love formula impress one with not only the conscious recognition but the considerable degree of enjoyment afforded by satisfying dependency and affiliative needs. A white-collar worker, age sixty-five, says: "It is easier to meet all life's problems when one has a close friend, when one can be of assistance to one another. In that sense I consider my wife as a source of life-giving energy, which enables me to have the strength to meet the struggle for life." In the case of the factory director and his wife, "If he came home from work exhausted, she cheered him up, so that he became visibly transformed—more cheerful and relaxed. . . . The link between them as two human beings was extremely deep." If peasant-style marriage ranges from relatively unfeeling familiarity at best to savage oppression at worst, those at the opposite extreme range in terms of the typical emotional experience from reasonably sympathetic at worst to impressively rich at best. The capacity to enter into a full, intimate relation seems great; perhaps there is an unusual reservoir of stored emotion in the Russian psyche. A Stalingrad couple has an almost idyllic relationship: "They cared for each other not only in the usual sense of marriage, but took an interest in each other's work. Thus she visited him on her free days at his construction site. They also shared the same values and opinions . . . when they had nothing to do, they sat together in front of the door of the house, the wife played the balalaika and the family sang, or the husband and wife played chess." . . .

The Trend of Change

Even in rural areas the old days, when the reins were firmly in the hands of the oldest male, have gone. A saying that until recently the men liked to repeat—"woman has long hair and a short wit"—has ceased to be true or amusing, and the unequal terms of address—by which the patriarchal male was likely to address his wife with the familiar *ty*, while she in speaking to her husband was well advised to use his name, patronym, and the formal *vy*—have been long since replaced by the familiar form. The patriarchal pattern, both as an ideal form for peasant family life as a whole and as an implicit ordering principle for absolute male dominion in marriage, has undergone a gradual and uneven weakening. The process has been under way for some time. Urbanization, education, the emancipation of women—

these worldwide trends have had their effect in Russia as elsewhere, and the Revolution has greatly accelerated them.

All sources agree that Soviet marital life is tending toward more equality between husband and wife. The changing pattern of relative age of the two spouses is one particularly significant symptom of the degree to which this is so. Table 1 is based on a sampling of three thousand marriage registration records for the three years, 1920, 1940, and 1960, for two urban districts and one rural district in the Leningrad region. If the decline in age disparity indicated by these data is typical for the whole country, the change is a striking one indeed.

Male dominance is still frequent in the peasant marriage, especially in the older generations. Yet even those who still subscribe to the pattern in their own lives express a presentiment of change. A peasant woman says of the new pattern she observes around her: "I am your wife. You say, 'You will not go there. I don't want you to go there.' But I say, 'You have no right. I'll go where I please. The husband does not have the right to tell his wife what to do.' There is a law . . . they call it equality of rights. The wife may want to go into the Komsomol or do something, and she does what she wants, not what her husband wants." In many worker and peasant marriages the confrontation of the old pattern by the new equality brings considerable malaise. As in the above case, there is a tendency for some lower-class women to

**TABLE 1. RELATIVE AGE AT MARRIAGE OF SPOUSES,
LENINGRAD REGION, 1920, 1940, 1960**

Location of registry office and year	Relative Age of Spouses			
	Same or groom younger (percent)	Groom 1–6 years older (percent)	Groom 7 or more years older (percent)	Total (percent)
Urban				
1920	19.0	49.5	31.5	ı100.0
1940	32.5	51.0	16.5	100.0
1960	40.0	46.5	13.5	100.0
Rural				
1920	17.5	46.0	36.5	100.0
1940	26.5	50.5	23.0	100.0
1960	41.0	48.0	11.0	100.0

Source: Adapted from Kharchev, *Brak i semia*, p. 190. The rural sample numbered 1,500 and was taken from Mginski district, Leningrad region. The urban sample also consisted of 1,500 cases, taken from Kirov and Kuibyshev districts, Leningrad city.

see the legal equality of woman as extending to family relations as well as economic and political life. Another wife, from a working-class marriage, says, "In the Soviet Union the husband had no say about his wife's working or about his adult children."

Most peasant men have been unwilling to grant such a radical shift in power so quickly, and most of their wives, I believe, have not wanted it either. The transition from the old order has been slow and often painful. Even where the man has remained dominant, however, the nature of his relationship with his wife has been different. Consultation and mutual agreement about important decisions have become prescriptive. A young collective farm wife is asked who makes the decisions in her family. She says, "My husband, of course. Of course he talks it over with me, asks whether I agree. But he is the husband, he decides mostly. Because he understands more." While the old order involved absolute and irrational hegemony, the new male supremacy is more temperate. Frequently, as in the case above, it is rationalized as "he understands more." Another peasant, who became a tractor driver, presents a different rationalization: "Of course a man should be head of the family. Because I can earn more than my wife. If I get anything my wife has it too."

Actually, in many peasant families today there is a characteristic arrangement, by which the husband is the ruler "in principle," while it is the wife who often makes important decisions and wields considerable influence in other ways. The distinction between public appearance and private reality is more apparent, I suspect, to the wives than to the husbands. An old collective farm woman says: "The husband is the boss, but it's I who tell him 'Father, we need such and such a thing.' I know the needs of everyone in the family better than he does. I wash their clothing and can see better than he who needs something."

The contradiction between the still lively cultural norm of masculine dominance and the observed behavior of such partners leads to a kind of ritual patriarchalism which can easily be misinterpreted by the casual observer who sees only the outer form and concludes that masculine dominance is more thoroughgoing than is actually the case. A Soviet ethnographer described (perhaps with some exaggeration) the new situation in the families on a *Kazakh* kolkhoz: "In the overwhelming majority of families in the absence of outsiders the wife has an equal position with the husband, and at times in some families even is the ruler. But in the presence of outsiders, by tradition she must exhibit her supposed submissive position . . . [for example,] when visiting she does not sit in the place of honor [*tör*]."

This is probably close to the situation today in the typical Soviet marriage (taking typical to mean modal with respect to the entire population). Masculine dominance, while still present, has become more moderate, and humane, tending gradually toward acceptance of full equality for the wife, though there is still a long way to go among the peasantry. A study of three hundred Leningrad working-class families conducted in 1961 offers some good evidence in support. Two types of marital relationships are distinguished, both of which involve masculine predominance—"by tradition the overwhelming majority of women name the husband head of the family." In the first the personal power of the husband is conserved, but it is said to be based not upon constraint but upon "the moral authority of the husband with more or less voluntary submission on the part of the rest of the members of the family to this authority." In the second type the predominance of the husband is merely formal and masks a *de facto* equality of rights in deciding basic intrafamilial questions. Of course, it may be significant, as the researcher claims (but does not support with evidence), that these are all families in which the wife is employed. In any case, the second type, in which the masculine dominance is merely a formal one, is the majority pattern, found in 60 percent of the sample.

Marital patterns change much more slowly than behavior in public contexts. To the Russian man surrender of power over his wife—a right extended by God, customary law, tradition, and superiority of physical strength—however justifiable in a rational sense and on a conscious level, nonetheless gnaws at his self-esteem. For this reason the outer form so often remains patriarchal even while things are more equal in private and even if feelings of affection and love may have become strongly influential. Thus the typical marriage today combines, in friendly coexistence, male dominance and tender affection, attitudes which do not merge well when they are found in extreme forms. A good example is given by the marriage of a thirty-five-year-old construction foreman from Kiev. His wife is twenty-eight, and they are described as in love: "They met before the war during their student days at a dance, and were married at the time he was drafted. . . . Both expected a mildly patriarchal marriage, and conducted their marriage accordingly. He led the way, but in a gentle and less absolute way than had been the case in the marriage of her parents, his father-in-law. . . . The main influence on both their attitudes was that of their parents' home, mellowed by the advances made by the society which surrounded them."

In addition to ritual patriarchalism with love, there are other signs of what is happening in Soviet marriage. Patterns of the future as well as the past are found in the changing nature of the association between social relations and ceremony. It is usual in Viriatino to go through two wedding ceremonies, one in the Civil Registry or ZAGS office and a second, traditional, service in the home of the husband's parents. Significantly, it is reported that sexual relations often are initiated after the first of the two, though the girl continues to live with her own parents until the second ceremony has been completed.

It seems that the link between the girl's continued residence in her parents' home and the traditional wedding ceremony in her husband's parents' home is furnished by the larger circle of persons, mainly kinsmen, who are in some way involved with the young couple. Moving out only after the traditional wedding symbolizes their continuing willingness to see their marriage as contingent upon the larger community, specifically the two parental families, and, perhaps, their desire to express respect for the traditions of their peasant heritage.

The association between the official Soviet agency and their sexual intimacy is also important, the connecting link here being the marriage itself. The initiation of sexual relations before the girl moves out of her parents' home, but only after a trip to the ZAGS office, suggests that the couple sees the Soviet order as supportive of their right to live a separate and independent life as a married couple, and in particular to behave in a fashion independent of and different from that of their parents. However, they assert this right unobtrusively, in terms of the most private aspect of their life together, sexual relations, so as not to offend too greatly against their relatives' or their own sense of respect for tradition.

Such behavior patterns reveal social change in process and the extent to which cultural malintegration is creatively adjusted to by the partners of individual marriages. It is also not without significance that sexual intimacy, perhaps love too, between spouses seems to find its defender in the new Soviet order, whereas the traditional way of life appears to uphold the more repressive, less spontanous aspect of marriage, namely, the power of the community to influence the young couple's life together.

Of course, this trend toward more individualism in marriage is by no means novel. The shift of solidarity priority from the larger kin group to the marital pair is shown by changes in other patterns of peasant life. In the old days the relationship of man and wife was influenced by the general assumption of male superiority, in connection with which the women were subjected to discrimination and segregation in various guises. The older folks in Viriatino still remember when the mealtime seating order at table in the peasant cottage required the men to sit on one side and the women on the other. But, they report, married couples had begun to sit together before the turn of the twentieth century.

To conclude this portion of the discussion, it is worthwhile to stress several facts about the most typical of Soviet marriages, that which is in transition between the peasant pattern and the pattern of equal-rights-with-love. . . . In this marriage not only are power and affection governed by contradictory forces, but often so are other aspects of married life, such as the spouses' religious and political views. Consequently, the continuity from one generation to another is not great, there is a certain fitful unrest to the marriage, as if elemental spontaneity and conscious self-control are vying for supremacy, and very often the spouses work out their uncertainties on their children. In a highly sublimated form of this unrest, husband and wife divert attention from themselves and their own relationship and focus their conscious thoughts and goals upon their children. Such seems to have happened in the case of the happily married Stalingrad couple already referred to: "The children were the purpose of the family. They were to get a better education. He carefully supervised their school work. And when they won prizes for good work he was very proud of them. Their social intercourse was also controlled: the children were not allowed to play with the children of Volga River workers. . . . The family was passively religious, and the children were so reared and they crossed themselves." . . .

Up to this point we have inspected the two extremes of Soviet marriage that correspond with the two ideal patterns, peasant and equal-rights-with-love, [and] have discussed the transitional form that falls between those extremes. . . . In social-class terms the most noticeable distinction is between peasant and urban marriages. Most of the former seem to fall into the transitional category, leaning toward the more purely peasant pattern. Probably most urban marriages also are transitional—masculine dominance going together with love—but tending more in the other direction, that of equal rights. Once outside the influence of peasant traditionalism, marriage patterns seem to fan out, presenting a varied assortment to the choice of the individual, but are not correlated in any discernible way with urban social classes.

The breadth of the variation is in itself important, for it contributes, along with the two competing cultural patterns, to what sociologists call anomie, a situation in which important actions have to be taken without a normative standard to provide guidance. From one point of view this generates confusion and uncertainty. From another it suggests greater freedom for the individual couple to attend to its own preferences without too much concern for what others will think.

It is my strong impression that in matters of love and authority in Soviet marriage today there is an extraordinary tolerance and permissiveness among the people, if not in the regime. Not only do individual needs and personality differences play a great role, but many Soviet citizens feel that it is quite proper that they should. For instance, in regard to the proper locus of authority, many would oppose any standardized pattern and would feel, as one respondent suggested to me, that "authority should be enjoyed by the spouse who is better able to organize a family life." Indeed, it is possible to see a parallel between the role of "personal gifts" in determining eligibility for re-election to political posts at the top level in the Soviet Union and the role of the same factor at the bottom level in determining eligibility to wield power in marriage.

5

FEMINIST MOVEMENTS IN THE UNITED STATES: BEFORE AND AFTER

On August 26, 1970, tens of thousands of women marched down Fifth Avenue in New York City to commemorate the occasion of a similar march exactly fifty years before. Suffragettes then marched to celebrate passage of the Nineteenth Amendment, giving women the vote. In 1970, their daughters and granddaughters declared August 26 a day to strike out against oppression and to declare their intention to work towards the achievement of equality for women, which the suffrage movement had failed to accomplish. Accompanied by a sizable contingent of male supporters, old and young women from various groups and associations of all political persuasions, rallied to ask for equal opportunities in employment and education, abortion on demand, and twenty-four-hour a day child-care centers. The women's rights movement that was dormant for a half-century showed its emerging strength.

Today, few people realize that there were many voices calling for radical reorganization of the family, as well as for the vote, in the early part of the nineteenth century. Many of the important issues of those early days became subverted or reduced in scope as the achievement of the vote became central. William O'Neill describes the social forces and the individuals who set the women's movement into motion in that early period.

Although the times were not receptive for change then, or women and their supporters were not politically astute enough to carry their plans forward, many of the issues brought forth then seem to have a better chance of being realized now. Helen Dudar (writing in the popular press) charts the course of the modern women's movement.

Why did the women's rebellion start so late in the Western world? O'Neill's work suggests some reasons. The Victorian household was a great burden on the woman. In it she was viewed as a wan, ethereal, frail person who, nevertheless, was expected to perform substantial tasks. Personal stress may well have been increased in many cases by the rhetoric of antislavery arguments that were—and are now—applied to the plight of women. Women played a large role in the abolition movement and became infused with the need for freedom.

The Civil War also drew women from the home as they chose the opportunities to participate in national life as nurses and relief workers, as spies and ideologists. Wars typically have an emancipating effect because, as women's services are called for to free men to become soldiers, they also exhibit their capacity to do men's work.

But the suffragists had to wait until after World War I to attain the vote; riding the coattails of abolition did not achieve their ends. And perhaps their ability to direct their attention to the more basic issues of women's inequality was one cause for the undermining of the movement. Those who raised the question about restructuring the family were viewed askance. The cause was also hurt by advocates of widespread social change who tended to be colorful, if not bizarre characters, who became involved in complex personal scandals. To make matters worse, several experimental utopian communities in the nineteeth century made the threat of "free love" real enough that an attack on the foundations of "the family" was viewed as an attack on morality, purity, and the whole fabric of society. All these factors obscured the issue of women's rights.

It is somewhat ironic that many supporters and opponents of the extension of suffrage to women believed that *it* (much less any other specific set of actions directed at improvement of women's condition) would have such important consequences, whether for good or evil. Now, fifty years later, it would be difficult to prove that *anything* important resulted from granting the vote to women.

Although now the events that surround that activity evoke images of high drama and conflict, doubtless most ordinary citizens of the time devoted little attention to the issues before World War I. Even people who read of such happenings would have considered the heroes and heroines of this movement odd and curious, not at all as the heralds of the future. The champions of women's freedom were often viewed as ridiculous, much like today. Then, as now, most women were opposed to the feminist movement.

There is a wide range of political and social arguments that focuses on women's liberation today. The National Organization for Women (NOW) founded by Betty Friedan in 1966, was the first, and now is only one of the rapidly growing groups that have mobilized their energies in this battle. Some groups call for a complete restructuring of the society, alleging that women can never achieve equality until marriage and all the supporting property and legal foundations of sexual exploitation are abolished. Others are pressing for more moderate demands, such as the lifting of quotas in professional schools and the abolition of derogatory and demeaning images of women in the popular media.

But the composite Women's Liberation Movement, as it is called, has created widespread reactions and ramifications. Here are some of the important ones:

The response of men. Although some men are concerned that women will compete with them for jobs in a truly open market, many are expressing even more concern about how women will interact with them in love, in marriage, and in daily social relations. They sense correctly that if women achieve equality, men will no longer be able to take their own dominance for granted. The place of men is likely to change as women's place in society is altered. Although many of the consequences of reducing rigid definition of tasks along sex lines would free men as well as women from the old constraints, fear of the unknown is always generated and men cannot yet assess the relative merits and costs for them of women's equality.

The reactions of women—both inside and outside the movement. Not only is the social structure being altered; alterations are taking place within *women themselves* today. Women are becoming more assured of their own worth and integrity. They demand serious treatment and full respect. Those who once would have dropped out of a graduate training program or from competition for a higher level job, now stay and fight, prove their dedication and competence, and reject the disparaging ways that they are treated. Formerly alone, many now have the support of their "sisters" and a collective sense of obligation to assert their rights.

The reaction of the "liberal" public. Similar to the attitudes of many in the revolution of the Blacks in the 1960s, it is apparent that many "liberals" are really very conservative. They favor higher education for women, but feel that it ought to be used in the home. They think women should work, but that jobs should come second to home duties. They admit that women have talents, but believe that all-out exploitation of talent is more suitable in building a man's career than in molding a woman's life. They belived that victims of rape ought to be permitted abortions, but that all women ought not have the right of abortion on demand as an expression of the individual's right over her own body. Many liberals, however, have developed a less antagonistic view of women's liberation when presented with its full range of arguments, and, increasingly, are entertaining the possibility that it generally holds the promise of a better society.

THE ORIGINS OF AMERICAN FEMINISM

by William O'Neill

. . . Having already taken the economic context of American life as essentially given, feminists went on to do the same thing for the marital and domestic system, accepting, for the most part, Victorian marriage as a desirable necessity. In so doing they assured the success of woman suffrage while guaranteeing that when women did get the vote and enter the labor market in large numbers, the results would be bitterly disappointing.

Neither the Woodhull debacle nor the general climate of Victorian opinion fully explain the feminist position on sex in the late nineteeth century. Also important was the social purity crusade which played a prominent role in the woman movement. Of course, campaigns against prostitution in a century as sexually obsessed as the nineteenth were inevitable, but social purity meant much more than the suppression of vice. Its origins lay in the mothers' associations which began as early as 1815 and, especially during the 1830s and 1840s, developed a considerable interest in suppressing vice and "uplifting" fallen women. Thereafter, maternal societies seem to have lost interest in these matters. It was not until the 1870s that social purity became a coherent and persistent movement, in reaction to the growth of regulated prostitution in both England and the United States. In the 1860s the British Army tried to license prostitution in the continental manner, inspiring a counterattack which spilled over into the United States once regulation had been turned back in England.

The scattered efforts of American vice reformers were crystalized in 1877 when a delegation of English antiregulationists visited this country. Vigilance committees were formed in New York and elsewhere, and the movement swelled until it reached a peak in 1895 with the formation of the American Purity Alliance. Like all such reforms, social

From William O'Neill, Everyone Was Brave: The Rise and Fall of Feminism in America (*New York: Quadrangle Books, 1968*), *pp. 30–37. Copyright* © *1969 by William L. O'Neill. Reprinted by permission of Quadrangle Books, Inc.*

purity progressed erratically. In the early 1880s it languished, but was revived in 1885 by W. T. Stead's exposures of the vice industry, which occasioned almost as great a scandal here as in Britain. Mothers' meetings were held around the country, the WCTU's Social Purity Department was energized, and another department for the suppression of obscene literature added. By the 1890s social purists had not done much to eliminate prostitution, but they had destroyed any chance of regulating it. The physicians, military men, and public health officers who supported regulation had either been persuaded or intimidated, and with this threat removed social purity lost its separate identity.[1]

Social purity was by no means an entirely feminine affair, but its ranks were largely filled with women, and it represented in an especially intense and emotional way the woman movement's characteristic attitudes on sexual questions. It stood for the abolition by law of impure practices, and the censorship for moral reasons of all forms of expression. Famous censors like Anthony Comstock and Josiah W. Leeds of Philadelphia were highly regarded by moral reformers. Female moralists were, however, by no means unsympathetic to the prostitute herself, whom they tended to see as an innocent victim of economic want and masculine lust—as against the still popular view of the inherently depraved harlot.

Less durable than these convictions, which continued to be widely held in the twentieth century, was the Victorian feminists' opposition to birth control. Because the public fight for birth control was won in the United States by a coalition which included emancipated women, it is sometimes assured that feminists always favored contraception. In the Victorian age, however, organized women invariably opposed it. English feminists consistently preferred continence to contraception and saw birth control as merely another way of encouraging masculine lust. Hence the militants' slogan in 1913, "Votes for Women and Purity for Men." American social purity forces took much the same line, not only out of their fear and hatred of sexual intercourse but because they believed in the conservation of energy. Since they visualized the body as an energy system that was running down, they were eager to avoid the physically depleting effects of coitus.

Social purity, with the Victorian woman's antieroticism, completed the work of reorienting feminism away from a serious consideration of sexual issues. Especially after the Woodhull affair it was almost impossible for suffragists to see sexual irregularities as anything but

[1] See the unpublished doctoral dissertation by David Jay Pivar, "The New Abolitionism: The Quest for Social Purity, 1876–1900" (University of Pennsylvania, 1965), p. 304.

immoral, and immorality as something that could not be suppressed by votes for women. As one suffragist put it while discussing Stead's exposures of the London vice scene, "One thing is evident, without the votes of women no vice that appeals peculiarly to the appetites of man can ever be suppressed or the laws enacted for the suppression of such vice be properly enforced." [2] While there were feminists, particularly after the turn of the century, who did not share these prejudices, the leadership of the woman movement united under the banner of absolute purity. Two important consequences flowed from this. By closing their eyes to the sexual elements regulating the life of women, feminists prevented themselves from developing a satisfactory analysis of the female dilemma. And, as we shall see, when the great changes in female sexual behavior became visible in the 1920s, feminists were unable to react to it in such a way as to command the respect of emancipated young women. It was their sexual views more than anything else that dated the older feminists after World War I, and made it difficult for them either to understand or to speak to a generation moved by quite different ambitions.

This blind spot was true even of a woman like Charlotte Perkins Gilman, almost the only major second-generation feminist to continue attacking the cult of domesticity.[3] The original suffragists were fully aware that "concentrating all woman's thoughts and interests on home life intensifies her selfishness and narrows her ideas in every direction, hence she is arbitrary in her views of government, bigoted in religion and exclusive in society." [4] They also understand that if woman were to be man's equal she would have to occupy the same positions and do the same work. Susan B. Anthony persistently reminded the social purity movement that "whoever controls work and wages, controls morals. Therefore we must have women employers, superintendents,

[2] Elizabeth Boynton Harbert, "Mothers to the Rescue," *New Era*, I (September 1885), 282.

[3] Generation is not a very exact term, but when speaking of the suffrage movement it seems fair to say that there were three distinct waves of women involved over time. The founders surfaced in the 1830s and 1840s and dominated the movement until the seventies and eighties. These included Mrs. Stanton, Miss Anthony, Lucy Stone, Amelia Bloomer, and many others, some of whom retained authority to the century's end. The second generation developed in the 1880s and 1890s. It included women like Carrie Chapman Catt, Anna Howard Shaw, and Harriot Stanton Blatch, who led the movement to final victory. A third generation consists of the younger women who emerged in the twentieth century, were active in the last years of the struggle, but for reasons discussed later never enjoyed the cohesion or prestige of earlier generations.

[4] Elizabeth Cady Stanton, "Stand By Your Guns Mr. Julian," *Revolution*, January 14, 1869, p. 25.

committees, legislators; wherever girls go to seek the means of sub-
sistence, there must be some woman." [5] Although never very precise
about the means by which woman's liberation would be effected, the
founders always insisted that it meant "emancipation from all political,
industrial, social, and religious subjection." [6] But while feminism was
born out of a revolt against stifling domesticity, and nurtured in the
understanding that for women to be really free the entire fabric of
their lives had to be rewoven, by the end of the century most feminists had succumbed to what Charlotte Perkins Gilman called the
"domestic mythology." Home and family were so revered in the Victorian age that the temptation to exploit rather than resist the current
of opinion was irresistible. The original feminists had demanded freedom in the name of humanity; the second generation asked for it in the
name of maternity. What bound women into a selfless sisterhood, it
was now maintained, was their reproductive capacity. Over and over
again feminists asserted that "women stand relatively for the same
thing everywhere and their first care is naturally and inevitably for
the child." [7]

Maternity was not only a unifying force but the enabling principle
which made the entrance of women into public life imperative. As
another suffragist put it in 1878, "The new truth, electrifying, glorifying American womanhood today, is the discovery that the State is but
the larger family, the nation the old homestead, and that in this national home there is a room and a corner and a duty for 'mother.' " [8]
Not only was the nation a larger home in need of mothering, but by
impinging upon the domestic circle it made motherhood a public role.
Jane Addams was a persistent advocate of this doctrine:

> Many women today are failing properly to discharge their duties
> to their own families and households simply because they fail
> to see that as society grows more complicated it is necessary that
> woman shall extend her sense of responsibility to many things
> outside of her own home, if only in order to preserve the home
> in its entirety. [9]

[5] "Social Purity," an address first given by Miss Anthony in 1875, in Ida H.
Harper, *Life and Work of Susan B. Anthony* (Indianapolis, 1898–1908), II, p.
1008.

[6] Ibid., p. 1011.

[7] Mrs. Ellis Meredith at the 1904 convention of the NAWSA, *History of Woman
Suffrage*, V, 101.

[8] Elizabeth Boynton Harbert in *History of Woman Suffrage*, III, 78–79.

[9] Jane Addams, "Woman's Conscience and Social Amelioration," in C. Stelzle, ed.,
Social Applications of Religion (Cincinnati, 1908), p. 41.

So the effort to escape domesticity was accompanied by an in-vocation of the domestic ideal—woman's freedom road circled back to the home from which feminism was supposed to liberate her. In this manner feminism was made respectable by accommodating it to the Victorian ethos which had originally forced it into being.

Given the plausibility and elasticity of this contention, women were, inevitably perhaps, lured into using it to secure their immediate aims. Yet in retrospect it does not seem to have been a completely successful ploy. One historian has recently hailed Frances Willard's "supreme cleverness" in using the WCTU "to advocate woman suffrage and child labor laws and other progressive legislation always in the name of purity and the home." [10] But the history of the WCTU illustrates the weakness of an argument that begins by accepting the opposition's premise. In conceding that better homes were of equal importance to antifeminists and feminists alike, these women reduced their case from one of principle to a mere quarrel over tactics. To redeem itself the opposition had only to prove that its tactics were superior. This is apparently what happened to the Temperance Union after the death of Frances Willard (which coincided with a significant change in its social composition), when new leaders came to believe that temper-ance was more crucial to the home than suffrage, child welfare, and other progressive causes.[11] Perhaps this new orientation would have come about in any event, but the suffragists in the WCTU made it all the easier by their willingness to use the cult of domesticity in pursuit of quite separate and distinctively feminist objectives.

The truth was that while feminists resented the demands made upon them in their roles as wives and mothers, they were not alert to the danger of even a partial accommodation to the maternal mystique. They gravely underestimated the tremendous force generated by the sentimental veneration of motherhood, and assumed they could manip-ulate the emotions responsible for the condition of women without challenging the principles on which they rested. Moreover, while denying that under present circumstances mothers could be held ac-countable for the failings of their children, they implied that once emancipated, women could properly be indicted for the shortcomings of their progeny. In 1901 Susan B. Anthony herself went so far as to say that:

[10] Andrew Sinclair, *The Better Half* (New York, 1965), p. 223.
[11] On the Union's changing character, see the unpublished doctoral dissertation by Janet Z. Giele, "Social Change in the Feminine Role: A Comparison of Woman's Suffrage and Woman's Temperance, 1870–1920" (Radcliffe College, 1961).

Responsibilities grow out of rights and powers. Therefore before mothers can rightfully be held responsible for the vices and crimes, for the general demoralization of society, they must possess all possible rights and powers to control the conditions and circumstances of their own and their children's lives.[12]

Her remark would seem to mean that once granted political equality, mothers would have to answer for all the ills of society—a great weight to lay on posterity. Such statements contributed to the unhealthy and unrealizable expectations which feminism encouraged.

A further hazard stemming from the feminist emphasis on motherhood was the support it gave to the notion that women were not only different from men, but superior to them. Julia Ward Howe, a moderate and greatly admired feminist, persistently reminded women that emancipation was intended to make them better mothers as well as freer persons.

Woman is the mother of the race, the guardian of its helpless infancy, its earliest teacher, its most zealous champion. Woman is also the homemaker; upon her devolve the details which bless and beautify family life. In all true civilization she wins man out of his natural savagery to share with her the love of offspring, the enjoyment of true and loyal companionship.[13]

Definitions like this left men with few virtues anyone was bound to admire, and inspired women to think of themselves as a kind of super race condemned by historical accident and otiose convention to serve their natural inferiors.

[12] *History of Woman Suffrage*, V, 5–6.
[13] Florence Howe Hall, ed., *Julia Ward Howe and the Woman Suffrage Movement* (Boston, 1913), p. 158.

WOMEN'S LIB: THE WAR ON "SEXISM"

by Helen Dudar

After a while, when friends asked what I was working on these days, I would say, "Oh, this and that," and then hurriedly ask about the children. One more curdled dinner, one more snarling exchange between a man and a woman whose life together had always seemed so friendly became an insupportable prospect. At the beginning, even before anyone asked, I often broached the subject myself. If the couple knew what the women's liberation movement was, there would be an immediate argument, he looking wounded and murmuring between clenched teeth, "But honey, whadya mean you're thinking of joining —don't you feel free?" and she responding with soothing persistence, "Yes, yes, but I just have this feeling I should make an existential commitment." If they had not yet heard of women's liberation, I would explain, and then an argument would follow. Sometimes it was *he* who might ask whether valid questions were not being raised, while *she*, facing attack on her roles as mother, wife, keeper of the hearth, rose in perplexed anger at alien ideas that suggested she had invested her entire life in triviality.

So I discovered almost at once how swiftly the subject assaults the emotions. No one is immune. Suffragettes were those funny ladies in rickety newsreels who tied themselves to lampposts to win the vote. America's New Feminist is the neighbor's college-educated daughter coolly announcing she does not intend to marry. She is Judy Stein, 16, founder of the women's lib at New York's High School of Music and Art, paying her way on dates. ("Otherwise, it's like the guy is renting you for the evening.") She is also Ti-Grace Atkinson, long past the stage of denouncing marriage and motherhood, now writing elegant analyses of the need to give up sex and love, both, in her view, fundamental male means of enslaving females. Finally, the New Feminists are thousands of women with lovers, husbands, and children—or expec-

From Helen Dudar, "Women's Lib: The War on 'Sexism'," Newsweek, March 23, 1970, pp. 43–49. Reprinted by permission of Newsweek.

tations of having a few of each—talking about changes in social attitudes and customs that will allow every female to function as a separate and equal person.

Toy: That, of course, is not how the American woman sees herself now. She is, in the labored rhetoric of the movement, a "sexual object," born to be a man's toy, limited and defined by her sexual role rather than open to the unbounded human possibilities held out to men—or at least, to some men. Usually she is not yet out of diapers when she learns that girls play with baby dolls, boys build things. If she is smart, grown-ups begin early to warn her against being too smart. "When you turn out to be a mathematical genius," reported a young woman at Columbia University, "your mother is the one who says 'put on some lipstick and get a boyfriend.'"

She becomes a secretary, a teacher, a nurse, and only occasionally a doctor, a lawyer, or a chief of anything. Whether she works in a factory or makes it in one of the elite professions, she earns less than men and has fewer prospects for promotion, no matter how superior she may be; women, by definition, are less superior than men. When she has children, she is chained to their needs for most of the years of her vigor and youth. She is Fred's wife and Jenny's mother and, beyond that, she may realize one late day, she has no other identity.

Image: The makers and sellers of consumer items pamper her with goods and attention concentrated on reinforcing a sexual image. "We're basically invisible," says Jo Freeman, a Chicago political scientist. "I look at the TV screen and the ads, and there is this person who's either sexy or shrill, and that's what's called a woman. I'm not that person, nor is any one of my friends. But you never see any of us." Nanette Rainone, who produces what may be the only female-liberation radio program in the country for WBAI in New York, says that, finally, to be a woman is to be nothing. "The guy on the assembly line doesn't want to be a woman. It's not that the work at home is worse than at the factory. It's that he realizes it's nothingness, total nothingness."

What has come racing along to fill the vacuum is the women's liberation movement, a very loose designation for a multiplicity of small groups led by a multiplicity of women who decline to call themselves leaders. The membership is mostly young (under 30), mostly middle class in origin, mostly radical and almost exclusively white, black women having chosen to remain within the confines of the civil-rights struggle. Because many of its founders came out of the New Left with its violent distrust for hierarchy, groups tend to be localized, unstructured and unconnected, although they all make common cause on such immediate issues as abortion-law repeal and establishment of day-care centers for children.

Women's lib has sprouted a growing periodical literature which includes No More Fun and Games, Tooth and Nail, and Aphra (named for Aphra Behn, the first English female novelist); it also boasts a feminist repertory-theater group; at least one dramatist—Myrna Lamb, whose play "The Mod Donna" [was] produced by the New York Shakespeare Theater—and it has inspired at least a dozen new books, finished or in the writing stage. But estimating the movement's menbership is a frail numbers game. One regular lecturer on the movement told me with surprised pride, that at least 10,000 women must be in women's lib. Another insisted that 500,000 was a conservative estimate. Most fair-size cities have one or more groups and so do most campuses. The movement is flourishing in Canada, England, and the Netherlands, where Provo-like "Crazy Mina" groups have augmented the U.S. program with demands for female public urinals and a twenty-hour workweek that would enable husbands and wives to share the burdens of child-rearing.

Growth: Of a certainty, the new feminist wave is building. Marlene Dixon, a radical sociologist whose failure to win reappointment at the University of Chicago set off take-over protest fourteen months ago, is now at McGill University, and almost every weekend she flies somewhere in the U.S. in the interests of the movement. "For five months after I left Chicago," she says, "I worked full time organizing groups. In the late spring of last year, I went down to Iowa City and met with a group of ten women consisting of two students and eight faculty wives—an unikely group to start a movement. Recently, I was back there for a conference they had organized, and they had 400 women. In the last few months, I've been to ten conferences, mostly in the Midwest, and none was under 300."

Plunging into the movement can mean a new life style. Some women give up make-up; a lot of them fret over whether to give up depilation in favor of furry legs. A few of them are a bouncy-looking lot, having given up diets and foundation garments. And virtually all those in the movement light their own cigarettes and open their own doors. "Chivalry is a cheap price to pay for power," one lib leader commented. In any event, the small masculine niceties now appear to liberationists as extensions of a stifling tradition that overprotects woman and keeps her in her "place."

For a newcomer to women's lib, the truly jolting experience is the first encounter with the anger that liberationists feel toward men. It bristles through the literature of the movement and it explodes into conversation in great hot blasts of doctrinaire invective. "There is no such thing as love between an adult male and a child," a feisty working-class liberationist with four grown daughters told me. "Between mother and infant, there is a bond. But in the father there is no such thing as affection, love, or any human emotion, other than the sense of power and property."

This kind of hostility, one young ideologue insisted, is healthy—"a gut reaction to a real situation" and without any of the guilts stirred by psychoanalysis. But it is also gravely infectious. I came to this story with a smug certainty of my ability to keep a respectable distance between me and any subject I reported on. The complacency shriveled and died the afternoon I found myself offering a string of fearful obscenities to a stunned male colleague who had "only" made a casual remark along the lines of "just-like-a-woman." "How do you control the hostility?" I kept asking, because in the beginning it came nervously close to interfering with normal routine. "I've been absolutely overwhelmed by feelings of hostility that scare the hell out of me," a twenty-four-year-old nursery-school teacher told me in San Francisco. But, she went on, much of the anger was "victim's rage" and it could be alleviated through constructive women's liberation activity. She also found it helped to stay away from men.

No Men: That is the solution recommended for all militants by Ti-Grace Atkinson, who is part of a hard-line New York group, The Feminists. Ti-Grace will no longer appear with a man except as a matter of "class confrontation"—a TV debate, a public platform—and she says that total separation works wonders since it dissolves ambivalence, and it is ambivalence that fosters rage.

Sardonically, she observes, "The basic issue is consistency between belief and acts. Of course, you know that every woman in the movement is married to the single male feminist existing. That's why we're funny. Contradiction is the heart of comedy. A woman saying men are the enemy with a boyfriend sitting next to her is both humiliating and tragic."

Ridicule has pursued the feminist down the corridors of time like some satanic practical joker; it is almost a relief when the hilarity turns to anger. "My male friends used to find us funny," said one activist. "I guess they've started taking us seriously; now they get mad." In the movement, there is a fidgety expectation of eventual backlash, supported even now by an occasional burst of male violence. Last December, when the Chicago chapter of the National Organization for Women (NOW) demonstrated against a traditional men-only lunch place, a

large and angry man pushed a small, bespectacled matron in the face.
NOW filed a complaint of assault. "In court," said Mary Jean Cillins-
Robson, the chapter president, "the prosecutor laughed, the public
defender laughed and the judge, who happened to be a black man,
laughed and threw the case out."

Among the many things that incite movement women to fury are the
liberties men take in addressing them on the street—whistles, "Hey,
honey" greetings, obscene entreaties. Casual annoyances to the un-
enlightened, this masculine custom becomes, in the heightened atmosphere of women's liberation, an enraging symbol of male supremacy
reflecting man's expectation of female passivity and, more important,
his knowledge of her vulnerability. "We will not be leered at, smirked
at, whistled at by men enjoying their private fantasies of rape and
dismemberment," announced a writer in a Boston lib publication.
"WATCH OUT. MAYBE YOU'LL FINALLY MEET A REAL CAS-
TRATING FEMALE."

Karate: Her point was part of a plea for the study of karate, a
fashion that inspires men to helpless ho-ho-ho's. The lib view is that
most girls, discouraged from developing their muscles, grow up soft,
weak, and without any defense reflexes to speak of. A little karate can
go a long way in a woman's life according to Robin Morgan, a poet, a
wife, a mother, and the designer of the movement's signet—a clenched
fist within the circle of the biological symbol for female. "Walking
alone at night on the street," she says, "there is always that feeling of
muted terror—and utter panic if you think someone is following you.
Knowing a small bit of karate is really remarkable—you may be afraid,
but you don't feel impotent."

In the new feminist doctrine, karate is not merely a physical or psychological weapon. It is also political, an idea that makes sense if you
agree that rape is a political act. And rape becomes political if you
accept the premise that women are a class, probably the original oppressed class of human history; that their oppression is a conscious
expression of the male need to dominate; and that a sexual attack is
a display of power allowed by a "sexist" society.

Sexist is the women's lib term for male supremacist and an offense
to the language we will have to learn to live with. Its kinship with
racist is obvious and probably inevitable in a movement that draws
much of its rhetoric and spirit from the civil-rights revolution and that,
like America's first feminist wave, evolved out of the effort to liberate
blacks.

Suffrage: Born out of the abolitionist struggle, nineteenth-century
feminism exhausted itself in seventy-two years of painful effort during

which a wide-ranging effort to change the status of women was finally narrowed down to a compromise drive for suffrage. The vote for women arrived in 1920, along with a few other reforms that went part way toward converting women from property to people. But the ballot "means nothing at all if you are not respresented in a representative democracy," writes Kate Millett, a Barnard College teacher and leading theoretician of today's movement.

The modern feminist movement has grown along two parallel lines. The first derived from Betty Friedan's *The Feminine Mystique*, published in 1963. Reflecting on the post-World War II stress on the "creativity" of homemaking, Mrs. Friedan told women that a male-dominated, consumer-oriented society had conned them into producing more children than their mothers had, into giving up career hopes, into lives deadened by trivia and, finally, into a mystified struggle with the emptiness and malaise that came upon them in middle age.

"The Feminine Mystique" spawned NOW, headed by Mrs. Friedan since its inception in 1966 [until her resignation] to return to writing. NOW, which is also open to men, currently has about thirty-five chapters. Early announcements described it as the NAACP of women's rights and, in fact, NOW is reformist in approach, attacking job inequalities and other injustices through court action and legislative lobbying. In New York, it is starting a drive to bring more women into public office.

The elective process has scant interest, however, for the members of women's liberation—the second and more radical wing of today's feminist movement. Around the time the Friedan book appeared, scores of young women in the civil-rights movement and in the infant New Left were learning what it was to have a college education and to be offered a porter's job. Their contributions seldom were allowed to go beyond sweeping floors, making coffee, typing stencils, and bedding down. "The New Left has been a hellhole for women," says a Berkeley veteran. "It's the most destructive environment sexually I've ever encountered, going as far as Norman Mailer's anti-birth control posture. You know: I don't want my chicks using pills—that demolishes my immortal sperm."

Hoots: As a result of all this, female caucuses congealed in civil-rights and student groups, struggling against "hoots, laughter, and obscenities" to persuade male revolutionaries that American society and its men oppressed women. The atmosphere was so oppressive, however, that the women took to meeting separately. And finally, in mid-1967, starting in Chicago, they began breaking away from the parent organizations entirely.

Since then, women's lib groups have multiplied like freaked-out amebas, sometimes under sardonic titles, often nameless. San Francisco has Sisters of Lilith, the Gallstones, and SALT (Sisters All Learning Together). Several cities have WITCH (Women's International Terrorist Conspiracy from Hell), which produces mocking guerrilla theater on such pillars of the system as Wall Street and claims ancestral feminist kinship with the witches of old. Boston has Bread and Roses, a name derived from an early women's mill strike in Massachusetts. New York is a splinter-group paradise—WITCH, Redstockings, Media Women, The Feminists, the newborn Radical Feminists, and a host of special-interest caucuses in such unexpected places as City Hall.

Trust: The differences among women's lib groups are often Jesuitical, but they do suggest the range of possibilities open to women in rebellion. Nomenclature notwithstanding, The Feminists, who take a hard line against marriage, are perhaps more radical than the Radical Feminists. But the Radical Feminists, too young to have been active in much of anything yet, may wind up more active politically than the Feminists; the Radicals see themselves eventually dealing with issues in "pragmatic terms." The Feminists, in fact, are less concerned with personal self-discovery than with analysis of the social institutions that oppress women. By contrast, self-discovery is a prime goal for the members of Redstockings which has been defined as neither revolutionary nor reformist but committed to "what is good for women." As for WITCH, whose members insist on anonymity, it seems to be open to all possibilities—"theater, revolution, magic, terror, joy, garlic, flowers, spells."

Often a women's lib organization is simply described as "my little rap group," and that is substantially what the movement has been about up to now—five to fifteen women meeting weekly in an exchange of ideas and experiences. In these "consciousness-raising" sessions, rage spills out, anxieties are dissected, and women learn how similar are their lives and problems. They also learn to like other women. "For the first time, I've begun to trust women," a book editor told me. "I look at them more closely. Even a woman I find obnoxious, I can see as a person, not as a stereotype."

Breakups: But women's lib members sometimes stereotype men. "Your husband is a writer, too?" a woman asked me. "Isn't he jealous?" I said no; she looked skeptical. Participation in the movement, in fact, can be hard on pairings. Marriages and settled affairs have come apart over the woman's newly developed anger or the man's newfound prejudices.

Yet a lot of women I met were married to men they felt were relatively free of the burdens of "machismo"; in these cases, maleness did not stand in the way of sharing the drudgery of tending house or babies. And a few couples manage exceptional partnerships. In New York, I met a husband and wife who both have part-time jobs so that each can spend half the day with their infant son. In Berkeley, I heard of a woman editor with a "house-husband." She went out each day to a job she liked; he cheerfully gave up one he hated to stay home with the baby. But these are essentially private solutions. For all its talk of abolishing marriage and motherhood, much of the movement is focused on the liberating possibilities of a network of child-care centers staffed by men and women who will take drudgery out of child-rearing.

Nor is this simply a utopian illusion. "I would like a revolution," New York reporter Lindsy Van Gelder told me. "But realistically, I suppose I would settle for what Sweden has." Which is a fair beginning. For as the result of an intense debate during the past decade, Sweden is now undergoing a wave of feminist reform. Fourteen percent of its parliamentary seats and two of its Cabinet ministries are held by women. Women run cranes, cabs, and buses; fathers must support children, but divorced wives are expected to pay their own way. There are compulsory coeducational classes in metalwork, sewing, and child care; a new tax structure virtually forces wives to go to work; a start has been made on day-care centers and, this year, a government-ordered revision of textbooks is expected to begin eliminating stereotyped images of both sexes.

Sex: But Swedish-style reforms, though admired in the movement, are hardly a subject of active debate. The recurrent preoccupation of rap sessions is sex: the disappointments of sex, the failures of orgasm, the ineptitudes of men. The discussions seem endless, and the obsessive literature the subject has produced fuels an obsessive male view— what I have to call the Big Bang theory of women's liberation. Men seem transfixed by the notion that all any of these women need is really swell copulation. Few men pause to ask whether causing the earth to shake for a woman each night will obliterate her boredom, frustration, and sense of injustice each day. And they are very puzzled by her complaint that the predominant male view of woman is sexual.

Lesbian-baiting is another favorite masculine exercise, and it has produced some interesting reactions among liberationists, including sober debates over whether lesbianism is a viable alternative to heterosexuality. "A woman who doesn't mind any other insult—'go home and take a bath,' 'what you need is a good screw,' 'dirty, Communist pinko'—will dissolve in tears because someone calls her a dyke," says Robin Morgan. So, women's lib has started asking why women react that way, to welcome lesbians into the movement as "our sisters," and to consider the idea of homosexuality as a means of population control and a path to equality.

Between the marriage abolitionists and the lesbian flirters falls a kind of moderate radicalism. Shulamith Firestone, a founder of the New York movement, and author of an uncoming theoretical work called "The Dialectic of Sex," says most women prefer sex with men and should have it, but without allowing themselves to become dependent or to be used as "doormats." Anne Koedt, another New York pioneer, is cautious about advising anybody to do anything. "You have to be honest with yourself," she says, "to take each step when it's real to you. We have just so much tolerance for change."

As I sat with many of the women I have discussed here, I was struck by how distorting the printed word can be. On paper, most of them have sounded cold, remote, surly, tough, and sometimes a bit daft. On encounter, they usually turned out to be friendly, helpful, and attractive. Meeting the more eccentric theoreticians, I found myself remembering that today's fanatics are sometimes tomorrow's prophets. Among the women I interviewed were careerists and intellectual hustlers; few of them, moreover, could resist sly put-downs of a competing group. Yet the total impact has been a quality of uncorrupted tenderness, a sense of unsentimentalized "sisterhood" threaded throughout the movement.

Free: It was refreshing to find women who weren't desperate to land a husband. But much of the talk of liberation from dependency seemed delusive. Who is truly independent, except the man or woman with no personal relationships at all? The newly free feminist, I would guess, draws support from her group—another form of dependency. Also, few of the women I met would allow that life itself is unfair. Most of them cherished an apocalyptic conviction that a society that assumed the drudgery of child-rearing would free women. Free them for what? For the jobs that millions of men now have and hate?

But millions of women do not even have the choice, and options are really what this revolt is about. I was startled to discover that the name of Dr. Benjamin Spock, which suggests sound baby-rearing and impassioned peace-seeking to me, evokes hisses at lib meetings because the movement associates him with keeping woman in her place. Always opposed to the working mother, Spock has taken to speaking unkindly these days about the aspirations of the educated girl. "Spock wasn't born to be a pediatrician," Nanette Rainone told a Columbia liberation teach-in last month. "He made a choice. Women are told it is their destiny to be mothers—the way to fulfillment. And if they want an abortion, fulfillment is forced on them."

Split: The way to fulfillment is spiky. After two years of talking, of self-discovery, no one has learned how to confront the issues. For the moment, the women's lib movement is split by competing ideologies—between pure feminists who want to go it alone and political feminists convinced they must work with other radical groups to bust the system. And there is a general fragmentation that suggests a more serious impediment. "I have a sense of an enormous kind of movement that isn't really organized," says Leslye Russell of Berkeley. She worries that it is "doomed to being a fad" unless it pulls itself together. "To be effective, there must be some kind of mass membership and some kind of structure. The point isn't structure, but structure that must be democratic."

Although not everyone agrees more organization is the solution, there are some signs of change in that direction. Most of Chicago's groups have just united under the Women's Liberation Union, with a citywide steering committee. New York's Radical Feminists, conceived by Shuli Firestone and Anne Koedt, is setting up small groups, each responsible for organizing another "brigade," each brigade to be represented by rotating delegates on a citywide coordinating body—the whole aimed at a mass-based movement with replicas in other cities.

No Power: There is, of course, territory hardly touched by the new spirit. Roxanne Dunbar, one of the movement's most important theoreticians, has just left her Boston group to try to organize Southern women, the women she knows best. She is looking to build something, but in common with most of the sisterhood has an aversion to defining it in terms of power. Power is what men have. "You can't overcome power with liberation power," she says, "because it would be a monster. What we want to do is build groups that isolate power." No sensible person, she suggests, wants to see women "liberated into the social role of men." She is out to destroy both roles.

The prospect fills me with joy, and—let me add at once—that is a world away from the position I held a few months ago. I have spent years rejecting feminists without bothering to look too closely at their charges. Stridency numbs me, and, in common with a lot of people, it has always been easy to dismiss substance out of dislike for style. When you think about it, though, my distaste for the presentation was silly: who listens to complaints in *pianissimo* anyway?

Pride: About the time I came to this project, I had heard just enough to peel away the hostility, leaving me in a state of ambivalence. We all thought—the men who run this magazine and I—ambivalence, Wow! What a dandy state of mind for writing a piece on the women's lib movement. Well, I suppose the ambivalence lasted through the first 57½ minutes of my first interview. Halfway through an initial talk with Lindsy Van Gelder, a friend and colleague, she said almost as a footnote that a lot of women who felt established in male-dominated fields resented the liberation movement because their solitude gave them a sense of superiority.

I came home that night with the first of many anxiety-produced pains in the stomach and the head. Superiority is precisely what I had felt and enjoyed, and it was going to be hard to give it up. That was an important discovery. One of the rare and real rewards of reporting is learning about yourself. Grateful though I am for the education, it hasn't done much for the mental stress. Women's lib questions everything; and while intellectually I approve of that, emotionally I am unstrung by a lot of it.

Never mind. The ambivalence is gone; the distance is gone. What is left is a sense of pride and kinship with all those women who have been asking all the hard questions. I thank them and so, I think, will a lot of other women.

6

AN EVEN NEWER LOOK FOR THE 1970s:
PROGRAMS AND PROPOSALS

In an ironically democratic way, women face exclusion and disparagement in every class, at all educational levels, and in all ethnic and religious groups. Thus the women's movement has attracted wide appeal and support and is rapidly growing in numbers. At the same time, many groups have been formed within the movement that present diverse definitions of the problems and different proposals for their solution.

The proposals range from policy recommendations drawn from scholarly analyses (including suggestions as to how the society might motivate young women toward higher aspiration and what kind of child care assistance ought to be provided) to political cries in favor of separate worlds for women and men.

All the views are radical in that they stress the need for basic changes in society, such as the ways we bring up our children, the social structure in which we live, how we choose the location of our homes or view the traditional organization of work.

Alice Rossi offers suggestions, adopted by most groups within the women's movement today, on how to raise boys and girls so that they will regard the sharing of work and home life as natural. Thus the belief in a traditional sexual division of labor that requires women to remain at home and men to work outside it would dissolve. She points out that the present social definitions of masculinity and femininity reinforce the sexual division of labor and narrow the expression of the full array of emotions and capacities of which both men and women are capable. Rossi's practical analysis shows that, if women are to be permitted options in combining home and work, then society must help, and not hinder, by creating a social organization that facilitates that choice.

Among her practical suggestions are these possibilities: reducing the geographical distance between home and work; abandoning the suburbanization of life, which places a large work burden on the woman; and encouraging the development of professional services and personnel to help the family, such as a corps of training experts in child care and home maintenance.

The "Statement of Purpose" of the National Organization for Women, a group that has become the largest and most heterogeneous group educated to the equality of women in the United States, states the underlying principles and conditions for the achievement of equality, and indicates the directions in which action must be taken. The proposals of NOW are considered the most moderate of any group, since it seeks to utilize such accepted channels for change as political action and education, and since it solicits the participation of men.

The manifesto of the Redstockings, a group of radical young women, located primarily in eastern university centers, places the blame for women's inequality upon men, and not upon women or the unintended consequences of the larger social structure. The manifesto aims at raising women's consciousness and alerting them to the source of their oppression and calls on men to abandon the privileges they have enjoyed because of the oppression of women. But consciousness-raising is not enough and may possibly be a wrong approach, asserts another radical women's group, The Feminists. In their probing document, they maintain that bringing women to an awareness of their plight is not sufficient; it is too passive. They argue further that the basic assumption of most women's groups—that women's lives will always be intertwined with men's—ignores an important option: instead, women might consider living separately from men and accept homosexual relations as an alternative to heterosexual relationships. A section of The Feminists' statement is included in this volume because it emphasizes the deep-seated resentment of many women, particularly young women, today; the extreme alterations they believe are necessary to effect basic changes in the society; and the intensity of their personal commitment to change. It offers another interpretation of the consequences of present social arrangements and calls for the destruction of existing institutions, such as marriage, in order to permit the redress of the power imbalance in the society.

Probably some combination of the elements offered by different groups must be put into effect if women are to achieve equality. Not all women may seek equality, as not all men prefer to; but at least the options offered will have to become real options if anything approaching democracy for women is to become real. Options to marry or not marry, to have children or not to have children, or to have a combination of all must eventually be backed up by new attitudes and by a facilitating set of services to men and women that will support those new attitudes.

EQUALITY BETWEEN THE SEXES:
AN IMMODEST PROPOSAL

by Alice S. Rossi

Institutional Levers for Achieving Sex Equality

In turning to the problem of how equality between the sexes may be implemented as a societal goal, I shall concentrate on the three major areas of child care, residence, and education. Institutional change in these areas in no sense exhausts the possible spheres in which institutional change could be effected to facilitate the goal of sex equality. Clearly government and industry, for example, could effect highly significant changes in the relations between the sexes. But one must begin somewhere, and I have chosen these three topics, for they all involve questions of critical significance to the goal of equality between men and women.

1. It is widely assumed that rearing children and maintaining a career is so difficult a combination that except for those few women with an extraordinary amount of physical strength, emotional endurance, and a dedicated sense of calling to their work, it is unwise for women to attempt the combination. Women who have successfully combined child-rearing and careers are considered out of the ordinary, although many men with far heavier work responsibilities who yet spend willing loving hours as fathers, and who also contribute to home maintenance, are cause for little comment. We should be wary of the assumption that home and work combinations are necessarily difficult. The simplified contemporary home and smaller sized family of a working mother today probably represent a lesser burden of responsibility than that shouldered by her grandmother.

This does not mean that we should overlook the real difficulties that are involved for women who attempt this combination. Working

From Alice S. Rossi, "Equality Between the Sexes: An Immodest Proposal," in Robert Jay Lifton, ed., The Woman in America (Boston: Beacon Press, 1967), pp. 119–40. Reprinted by permission of DAEDALUS, Journal of the American Academy of Arts and Sciences (Boston), 93 (Spring, 1964).

mothers do have primary responsibility for the hundreds of details involved in home maintenance, as planners and managers, even if they have household help to do the actual work. No one could suggest that child-rearing and a career are easy to combine, or even that this is some royal road to greater happiness, but only that the combination would give innumerable intelligent and creative women a degree of satisfaction and fulfillment that they cannot obtain in any other way. Certainly many things have to "give" if a woman works when she also has young children at home. Volunteer and social activities, gardening, and entertaining may all have to be curtailed. The important point to recognize is that as children get older, it is far easier to resume these social activities than it is to resume an interrupted career. The major difficulty, and the one most in need of social innovation, is the problem of providing adequate care for the children of working mothers.

If a significant number of American middle-class women wish to work while their children are still young and in need of care and supervision, who are these mother-substitutes to be? In the American experience to date, they have been either relatives or paid domestic helpers. A study conducted by the Children's Bureau in 1958 outlines the types of child-care arrangements made by women working full time who had children under twelve years of age.[1] The study showed that the majority of these children (57 percent) were cared for by relatives: fathers, older siblings, grandparents, and others. About 21 percent were cared for by nonrelatives, including neighbors as well as domestic helpers. Only 2 percent of the children were receiving group care—in day nurseries, day-care centers, settlement houses, nursery schools, and the like. Of the remainder, 8 percent were expected to take care of themselves, the majority being the "latchkey" youngsters of ten and twelve years of age about whom we have heard a good deal in the press in recent years.

These figures refer to a national sample of employed mothers and concern women in blue-collar jobs and predominantly low-skill white-collar jobs. Presumably the proportion of middle-class working mothers who can rely on either relatives or their husbands would be drastically lower than this national average, and will probably decline even further in future years. Many of today's, and more of tomorrow's, American grandmothers are going to be wage-earners themselves and not baby-sitters for their grandchildren. In addition, as middle-class

---

[1] Henry C. Lajewski, *Child Care Arrangements of Full-Time Working Mothers* (Washington, D.C.: U.S. Department of Health, Education and Welfare, Children's Bureau Publication No. 378, 1959); and Elizabeth Herzog, *Children of Working Mothers*.

women enter the occupational world, they will experience less of a tug to remain close to the kinswomen of their childhood, and hence may contribute further to the pattern of geographic and social separation between young couples and both sets of their parents. Nor can many middle-class husbands care for their children, for their work hours are typically the same as those of their working wives: there can be little dovetailing of the work schedules of wives and husbands in the middle class as there can be in the working class.

At present, the major child-care arrangement for the middle-class woman who plans a return to work has to be hired household help. In the 1920s the professional and business wife-mother had little difficulty securing such domestic help, for there were thousands of first generation immigrant girls and women in our large cities whose first jobs in America were as domestic servants. In the 1960s, the situation is quite different: the major source of domestic help in our large cities is Negro and Puerto Rican women. Assuming the continuation of economic affluence and further success in the American Negro's struggle for equal opportunity in education, jobs and housing, this reservoir will be further diminished in coming decades. The daughters of many present-day Negro domestic servants will be able to secure far better paying and more prestigeful jobs than their mothers can obtain in 1964. There will be increasing difficulty of finding adequate child-care help in future years as a result.

The problem is not merely that there may be decreasing numbers of domestic helpers available at the same time more women require their aid. There is an even more important question involved: are domestic helpers the best qualified persons to leave in charge of young children? Most middle-class families have exacting standards for the kind of teachers and the kind of schools they would like their children to have. But a working mother who searches for a competent woman to leave in charge of her home has to adjust to considerably lower standards than she would tolerate in any nursery school program in which she placed her young son or daughter, either because such competent help is scarce, or because the margin of salary left after paying for good child care and the other expenses associated with employment is very slight.

One solution to the problem of adequate child care would be an attempt to upgrade the status of child-care jobs. I think one productive way would be to develop a course of study which would yield a certificate for practical mothering, along the lines that such courses and certificates have been developed for practical nursing. . . .

A longer-range solution to the problem of child care will involve the establishment of a network of child-care centers. Most of the detailed plans for such centers must be left for future discussion, but there are several important advantages to professionally run child-care centers which should be noted. Most important, better care could be provided by such centers than any individual mother can provide by hiring a mother's helper, housekeeper or even the practical mother I have just proposed. In a child-care center, there can be greater specialization of skills, better facilities and equipment, and play groups for the children. Second, a child-care center would mean less expense for the individual working mother, and both higher wages and shorter hours for the staff of the center. Third, these centers could operate on a full-time, year-round schedule, something of particular importance for women trained in professional or technical fields, the majority of which can be handled only on a full-time basis. Except for the teaching fields, such women must provide for the afternoon care of their nursery school and kindergarten-age children, after-school hours for older children, and three summer months for all their children. Fourth, a child-care center could develop a roster of home-duty practical mothers or practical nurses to care for the ill or convalescent child at home, in much the way school systems now call upon substitute teachers to cover the classes of absent regular teachers. . . .

I have begun this discussion of the institutional changes needed to effect equality between the sexes with the question of child-care provision because it is of central importance in permitting women to enter and remain in the professional, technical, and administrative occupations in which they are presently so underrepresented. Unless provision for child care is made, women will continue to find it necessary to withdraw from active occupational involvement during the child-rearing years. However, the professional and scientific fields are all growing in knowledge and skill, and even a practitioner who remains in the field often has difficulty keeping abreast of new developments. A woman who withdraws for a number of years from a professional field has an exceedingly difficult time catching up. The more exacting the occupation, then, the shorter the period of withdrawal should probably be from active participation in the labor force. If a reserve of trained practical mothers were available, a professional woman could return to her field a few months after the birth of a child, leaving the infant under the care of a practical mother until he or she reached the age of two years, at about which age the child could enter a child-care center for daytime care. Assuming a two-child family, this could mean not more than one year of withdrawal from her professional field for the working mother.

2. The preferred residential pattern of the American middle class
in the postwar decades has been suburban. In many sections of the
country it is difficult to tell where one municipality ends and another
begins, for the farm, forest, and waste land between towns and cities
have been built up with one housing development after another. The
American family portrayed in the mass media typically occupies a
house in this sprawling suburbia, and here too, are the American
women, and sometimes men, whose problems are aired and analyzed
with such frequency.[2] . . .

The geographic distance between home and work has a number of
implications for the role of the father-husband in the family. It reduces
the hours of possible contact between children and their fathers. The
hour or more men spend in cars, buses, or trains may serve a useful
decompression function by providing time in which to sort out and
assess the experiences at home and the events of the work day, but it is
questionable whether this outweighs the disadvantage of severely
curtailing the early morning and late afternoon hours during which
men could be with their children.

The geographic distance also imposes a rigid exclusion of the father
from the events which highlight the children's lives. Commuting fathers
can rarely participate in any special daytime activities at home or at
school, whether a party, a play the child performs in, or a conference
with a teacher. It is far less rewarding to a child to report to his father
at night about such a party or part in a play than to have his father
present at these events. If the husband-father must work late or attend
an evening fuction in the city, he cannot sandwich in a few family
hours but must remain in the city. This is the pattern which prompted
Margaret Mead to characterize the American middle-class father as
the "children's mother's husband," and partly why mother looms so
oversized in the lives of suburban children.

Any social mixing of family-neighborhood and job associates is reduced or made quite formal: a work colleague cannot drop in for an
after-work drink or a Saturday brunch when an hour or more separates
the two men and their families. The father-husband's office and work
associates have a quality of unreality to both wife and children. All

---

[2] William Whyte, *Organization Man* (New York: Simon and Schuster, 1956);
Robert Wood, *Suburbia, Its People and Their Politics* (Boston: Houghton Mifflin,
1959); John Keats, *The Crack in the Picture Window* (Boston: Houghton Mifflin,
1956); A. C. Spectorsky, *The Exurbanites* (Philadelphia: J. B. Lippincott, 1955);
and Nanette E. Scofield, "Some Changing Roles of Women in Suburbia: A Social
Anthropological Case Study," *Transactions of the New York Academy of Sciences*,
XXII (April, 1960), 6.

these things sharpen the differences between the lives of men and women—fewer mutual acquaintances, less sharing of the day's events, and perhaps most importantly, less simultaneous filling of their complementary parent roles. The image of parenthood to the child is mostly motherhood, a bit of fatherhood, and practically no parenthood as a joint enterprise shared at the same time by father and mother. Many suburban parents, I suspect, spend more time together as verbal parents—discussing their children in the children's absence—than they do actively interacting with their children, the togetherness cult notwithstanding. For couples whose relationship in courtship and early marriage was equalitarian, the pressures are strong in the suburban setting for parenthood to be highly differentiated and skewed to an ascendant position of the mother. Women dominate the family, men the job world.

The geographic distance between home and the center of the city restricts the world of the wife-mother in a complementary fashion. Not only does she have to do and be more things to her children, but she is confined to the limitations of the suburban community for a great many of her extrafamilial experiences. That suburban children are restricted in their social exposure to other young children and relatively young adults, mostly women and all of the same social class, has often been noted. I think the social restriction of the young wife to women of her own age and class is of equal importance: with very few older persons in her immediate environment, she has little first-hand exposure to the problems attending the empty-nest stage of life which lies ahead for herself. It is easy for her to continue to be satisfied to live each day as it comes, with little thought of preparing for the thirty-odd years when her children are no longer dependent upon her. If the suburban wife-mother had more opportunity to become acquainted with older widows and grandmothers, this would be pressed home to her in a way that might encourage a change in her unrealistic expectations of the future, with some preparation for that stage of life while she is young.

If and when the suburban woman awakens from this short-range perspective and wants either to work or to prepare for a return to work when her children are older, how is she to do this, given the suburban pattern of residence? It is all very well to urge that school systems should extend adult education, that colleges and universities must make it possible for older women to complete education interrupted ten or more years previously or to be retained for new fields; but this is a difficult program for the suburban wife to participate in. She lives far from the center of most large cities, where the educational facilities tend to be concentrated, in a predominantly middle-class community, where domestic help is often difficult to arrange and transportation often erratic during the hours she would be using it.

It is for these reasons that I believe any attempt to draw a significant portion of married women into the mainstream of occupational life must involve a reconsideration of the suburban pattern of living. Decentralization of business and industry has only partly alleviated the problem: a growing proportion of the husbands living in the suburbs also work in the suburbs. There are numerous shops and service businesses providing job opportunities for the suburban wife. Most such jobs, however, are at skill levels far below the ability potential and social status of the suburban middle-class wife. Opportunities for the more exacting professional, welfare, and business jobs are still predominantly in the central sections of the city. In addition, since so many young wives and mothers in this generation married very young, before their formal education was completed, they will need more schooling before they can hope to enter the fields in which their talents can be most fruitfully exercised, in jobs which will not be either dull or a status embarrassment to themselves and their husbands. Numerous retail stores have opened suburban branches; colleges and universities have yet to do so. A woman can spend in the suburb, but she can neither learn nor earn.

That some outward expansion of American cities has been necessary is clear, given the population increase in our middle- to large-sized cities. But there are many tracts in American cities between the business center and the outlying suburbs which imaginative planning and architectural design could transform and which would attract the men and women who realize the drawbacks of a suburban residence. Unless there is a shift in this direction in American housing, I do not think there can be any marked increase in the proportion of married middle-class women who will enter the labor force. That Swedish women find work and home easier to combine than American women is closely related to the fact that Sweden avoided the sprawling suburban development in its postwar housing expansion. The emphasis in Swedish housing has been on inner-city housing improvement. With home close to diversified services for schooling, child care, household help, and places of work, it has been much easier in Sweden than in the United States to draw married women into the labor force and keep them there.

In contrast, the policy guiding the American federal agencies which affect the housing field, such as the FHA, have stressed the individual home, with the result that mortgage money was readily available to encourage builders to develop the sprawling peripheries of American cities. Luxury high-rise dwellings at the hub of the city and individual homes at the periphery have therefore been the pattern of middle-class housing development in the past twenty years. A shift in policy on the part of the federal government which would embrace buildings with three and four dwelling units and middle-income high-rise apartment buildings in the in-between zones of the city could go a long way to counteract this trend toward greater and greater distance between home and job. Not everyone can or will want to live close to the hub of the city. From spring through early fall, it is undoubtedly easier to rear very young children in a suburban setting with back yards for the exercise of healthy lungs and bodies. But this is at the expense of increased dependence of children on their mothers, of minimization of fathers' time with their youngsters, of restriction of the social environment of women, of drastic separation of family and job worlds, and of less opportunity for even part-time schooling or work for married women.

3. Men and women must not only be able to participate equally; they must want to do so. It is necessary, therefore, to look more closely into their motivations, and the early experiences which mold their self-images and life expectations. A prime example of this point can be seen in the question of occupational choice. The goal of sex equality calls for not only an increase in the extent of women's participation in the occupational system, but a more equitable distribution of men and women in all the occupations which comprise that system. This means more women doctors, lawyers, and scientists, more men social workers and school teachers. To change the sex ratio within occupations can only be achieved by altering the sex-typing of such occupations long before young people make a career decision. Many men and women change their career plans during college, but this is usually within a narrow range of relatively homogeneous fields: a student may shift from medicine to a basic science, from journalism to teaching English. Radical shifts such as from nursing to medicine, from kindergarten teaching to the law, are rare indeed. Thus while the problem could be attacked at the college level, any significant change in the career choices men and women make must be attempted when they are young boys and girls. It is during the early years of elementary school education that young people develop their basic views of appropriate characteristics, activities, and goals for their sex. It is for this reason that I shall give primary attention to the sources of sex-role stereotypes and what the elementary school system could do to eradicate these stereo-

types and to help instead in the development of a more androgynous conception of sex role.

The all-female social atmosphere of the American child has been frequently noted by social scientists, but it has been seen as a problem only in its effect upon boys. It has been claimed, for example, that the American boy must fight against a feminine identification this atmosphere encourages, with the result that he becomes overly aggressive, loudly asserting his maleness. In contrast, it is claimed that the American girl has an easy socialization, for she has an extensive number of feminine models in her environment to facilitate her identification as a female.

There are several important factors which this analysis overlooks. To begin with the boy: while it is certainly true that much of his primary group world is controlled by women, this does not mean that he has no image of the male social and job world as well. The content of the boy's image of man's work has a very special quality to it, however. Although an increasingly smaller proportion of occupations in a complex industrial society relies on sheer physical strength, the young boy's exposure to the work of men remains largely the occupations which do require physical strength. The jobs he can see are those which are socially visible, and these are jobs in which men are reshaping and repairing the physical environment. The young boy sees working-class men operating trucks, bulldozers, cranes; paving roads; building houses; planting trees; delivering groceries. This image is further reinforced by his television viewing: the gun-toting cowboy, the bat-swinging ball-player, the arrow-slinging Indian. Space operas suggest not scientific exploration but military combat, the collision and collusion of other worlds. In short, even if the boy sees little of his father and knows next to nothing of what his father does away from home, there is some content to his image of men's work in the larger society. At least some part of his aggressive active play may be as much acting out similar male roles in response to the cultural cues provided by his environment as it is an overreaction to his feminine environment or an identification with an aggressor-father.

And what of the girl? What image of the female role is she acquiring during her early years? In her primary group environment, she sees women largely in roles defined in terms that relate to her as a child—as mother, aunt, grandmother, babysitter—or in roles relating to the house—the cleaning, cooking, mending activities of mother and domestic helpers. Many mothers work outside the home, but the daughter often knows as little of that work as she does of her father's. Even if her own mother works, the reasons for such working that are given to the child are most often couched in terms of the mother or housewife role. Thus, a girl is seldom told that her mother works because she enjoys it or finds it very important to her own satisfaction in life, but because the money she earns will help pay for the house, a car, the daughter's clothes, dancing lessons, or school tuition. In other words, working is something mothers sometimes have to do as mothers, not something mothers do as adult women. This is as misleading and distorted an image of the meaning of work as the father who tells his child he works "to take care of mummy and you" and neglects to mention that he also works because he finds personal satisfaction in doing so, or that he is contributing to knowledge, peace, or the comfort of others in the society.

The young girl also learns that it is only in the family that women seem to have an important superordinate position. However high her father's occupational status outside the home, when he returns at night, he is likely to remove his white shirt and become a blue-collar Mr. Fixit or mother's helper. The traditional woman's self-esteem would be seriously threatened if her husband were to play a role equal to her own in the lives and affections of her children or in the creative or managerial aspect of home management, precisely because her major sphere in which to acquire the sense of personal worth is her home and children. The lesson is surely not lost on her daughter, who learns that at home father does not know best, though outside the home men are the bosses over women, as she can see only too well in the nurse-doctor, secretary-boss, salesclerk-store manager, space Jane-space John relationships that she has an opportunity to observe.

The view that the socialization of the girl is an easy one compared with the boy depends on the kind of woman one has in mind as an end-product of socialization. Only if the woman is to be the traditional wife-mother is present-day socialization of young girls adequate, for from this point of view the confinement to the kinds of feminine models noted above and the superordinate position of the mother in the family facilitate an easy identification. If a girl sees that women reign only at home or in a history book, whereas outside the home they are Girl Fridays to men, then clearly for many young girls the wife-mother role may appear the best possible goal to have. It should be noted, however, that identification has been viewed primarily as an either-or process— the child identifies either with the mother or the father—and not as a process in which there is a fusion of the two parent models such that identification involves a modeling of the self after mother in some respects, father in others. It is possible that those women who have led exciting, intellectually assertive, and creative lives did not identify exclusively with their traditional mothers, but crossed the sex line and looked to their fathers as model sources for ideas and life commitments of their own. This is to suggest that an exclusively same-sex identification between parent and child is no necessary condition for either mentally healthy or creative adults.

If I am correct about the significance of the father in the childhoods of those women who later led creative adult lives, then an increased accessibility of the middle-class father to his daughters and greater sharing of his ideas and interests could help to counteract the narrow confines of the feminine models daughters have. Beyond this, young girls need exposure to female models in professional and scientific occupations and to women with drive and dedication who are playing innovative volunteer roles in community organizations; they need an encouragement to emulate them and a preparation for an equalitarian rather than a dominant role in parenthood. Only if a woman's self-esteem is rooted in an independent life outside her family as well as her roles within the home can she freely welcome her husband to share on an equal basis the most rewarding tasks involved in child-rearing and home maintenance.

What happens when youngsters enter school? Instead of broadening the base on which they are forming their image of male and female roles, the school perpetuates the image children bring from home and their observations in the community. It has been mother who guided their preschool training; now in school it is almost exclusively women teachers who guide their first serious learning experiences. In the boy's first readers, men work at the same jobs with the same tools he has observed in his neighborhood—"T" for truck, "B" for bus, "W" for wagon. His teachers expect him to be rugged, physically strong, and aggressive. After a few years he moves into separate classes for gym, woodworking, and machine shop. For the girl, women are again the ones in charge of children. Her first readers portray women in aprons, brooms in their hands or babies in their arms. Teachers expect her to be quiet, dependent, with feminine interests in doll and house play and dressing up. In a few years she moves into separate classes for child care, cooking, and practical nursing. In excursions into the community, elementary school boys and girls visit airports, bus terminals, construction sites, factories, and farms.

What can the schools do to counteract these tendencies to either outmoded or traditional images of the roles of men and women? For one, class excursions into the community are no longer needed to introduce American children to building construction, airports, or zoos.

Except for those in the most underprivileged areas of our cities, American children have ample exposure to such things with their car- and plane-riding families. There are, after all, only a limited number of such excursions possible in the course of a school year. I think visits to a publishing house, research laboratory, computer firm, or art studio would be more enriching than airports and zoos.

Going out into the community in this way, youngsters would observe men and women in their present occupational distribution. By a program of bringing representatives of occupations into the classroom and auditorium, however, the school could broaden the spectrum of occupations young children may link to their own abilities and interests regardless of the present sex-typing of occupations, by making a point of having children see and hear a woman scientist or doctor; a man dancer or artist; both women and men who are business executives, writers, and architects.

Another way in which the elementary schools could help is making a concerted effort to attract male teachers to work in the lower grades. This would add a rare and important man to the primary group environment of both boys and girls. This might seem a forlorn hope to some, since elementary school teaching has been such a predominantly feminine field, and it may be harder to attract men to it than to attract women to fields presently considered masculine. It may well be that in the next decade or so the schools could not attract and keep such men as teachers. But it should be possible for graduate schools of education and also school systems to devise ways of incorporating more men teachers in the lower grades, either as part of their teacher training requirements or in the capacity of specialized teachers: the science, art, or music teacher who works with children at many grade levels rather than just one or two contiguous grade levels. His presence in the lives of very young children could help dispel their expectation that only women are in charge of children, that nurturance is a female attribute, or that strength and an aggressive assault on the physical environment is the predominant attribute of man's work.

The suggestions made thus far relate to a change in the sex-linking of occupations. There is one crucial way in which the schools could effect a change in the traditional division of labor by sex within the family sphere. The claim that boys and girls are reared in their early years without any differentiation by sex is only partially true. There are classes in all elementary schools which boys and girls take separately or which are offered only to one sex. These are precisely the courses most directly relevant to adult family roles: courses in sex and family living (where communities are brave enough to hold them) are typically offered in separate classes for boys and for girls, or for girls only. Courses in shop and craft work are scheduled for boys only; courses in child care, nursing, and cooking are for girls only. In departing from completely coeducational programs, the schools are reinforcing the traditional division of labor by sex which most children observe in their homes. Fifteen years later, these girls find that they cannot fix a broken plug, set a furnace pilot light, or repair a broken high chair or favorite toy. These things await the return of the child's father and family handyman in the evening. When a child is sick in the middle of the night, his mother takes over; father is only her assistant or helper.

These may seem like minor matters, but I do not think they are. They unwittingly communicate to and reinforce in the child a rigid differentiation of role between men and women in family life. If first aid, the rudiments of child care and of cooking have no place in their early years as sons, brothers, and schoolboys, then it is little wonder that as husbands and fathers American men learn these things under their wives' tutelage. Even assuming these wives were actively involved in occupations of their own and hence free of the psychological pressure to assert their ascendancy in the family, it would be far better for all concerned—the married pair and the children as well— if men brought such skills with them to marriage. . . .

I have suggested a number of ways in which the educational system could serve as an important catalyst for change toward sex equality. The schools could reduce sex-role stereotypes of appropiate male and female attributes and activities by broadening the spectrum of occupations youngsters may consider for themselves irrespective of present sex-linked notions of man's work and woman's work, and by providing boys as well as girls with training in the tasks they will have as parents and spouses. The specific suggestions for achieving these ends which I have made should be viewed more as illustrative than as definitive, for educators themselves may have far better suggestions for how to implement the goal in the nation's classrooms than I have offered in these pages. Equality between the sexes cannot be achieved by proclamation or decree but only through a multitude of concrete steps, each of which may seem insignificant by itself, but all of which add up to the social blueprint for attaining the general goal.

THE NATIONAL ORGANIZATION FOR WOMEN
(NOW)

Statement of Purpose

(Adopted at the organizing conference in Washington, D. C., October 29, 1966)

We, men and women who hereby constitute ourselves as the National Organization for Women, believe that the time has come for a new movement toward true equality for all women in America and toward a fully equal partnership of the sexes, as part of the worldwide revolution of human rights now taking place within and beyond our national borders.

The purpose of NOW is to take action to bring women into full participation in the mainstream of American society now, exercising all the privileges and responsibilities thereof in truly equal partnership with men.

We believe the time has come to move beyond the abstract argument, discussion, and symposia over the status and special nature of women which has raged in America in recent years; the time has come to confront, with concrete action, the conditions that now prevent women from enjoying the equality of opportunity and freedom of choice which is their right, as individual Americans, and as human beings.

NOW is dedicated to the proposition that women, first and foremost, are human beings, who, like all other people in our society, must have the chance to develop their fullest human potential. We believe that that women can achieve such equality only by accepting to the full the challenges and responsibilities they share with all other people in our society, as part of the decision-making mainstream of American political, economic, and social life.

We organize to initiate or support action, nationally, or in any part of this nation, by individuals or organizations, to break through the silken curtain of prejudice and discrimination against women in government, industry, the professions, the churches, the political parties, the judiciary, the labor unions, in education, science, medicine, law, religion, and every other field of importance in American society.

Enormous changes taking place in our society make it both possible and urgently necessary to advance the unfinished revolution of women toward true equality, now. With a life span lengthened to nearly seventy-five years it is no longer either necessary or possible for women to devote the greater part of their lives to child-rearing; yet child-bearing and rearing, which continues to be a most important part of most women's lives—still is used to justify barring women from equal professional and economic participation and advance.

Today's technology has reduced most of the productive chores which women once performed in the home and in mass-production industries based upon routine unskilled labor. This same technology has virtually eliminiated the quality of muscular strength as a criterion for filling most jobs, while intensifying American industry's need for creative intelligence. In view of this new industrial revolution created by automation in the mid-twentieth century, women can and must participate in old and new fields of society in full equality—or become permanent outsiders.

Despite all the talk about the status of American women in recent years, the actual position of women in the United States has declined, and is declining, to an alarming degree throughout the 1950s and '60s. Although 46.4 percent of all American women between the ages of 18 and 65 now work outside the home, the overwhelming majority— 75 percent—are in routine clerical, sales, or factory jobs, or they are household workers, cleaning women, hospital attendants. About two-thirds of Negro women workers are in the lowest-paid service occupations. Working women are becoming increasingly—not less—concentrated on the bottom of the job ladder. As a consequence full-time women workers today earn on the average only 60 percent of what men earn, and that wage gap has been increasing over the past twenty-five years in every major industry group. In 1964, of all women with a yearly income, 89 percent earned under $5,000 a year; half of all full-time year-round women workers earned less than $3,690; only 1.4 percent of full-time year-round women workers had an annual income of $10,000 or more.

Further, with higher education increasingly essential in today's society, too few women are entering and finishing college or going on to graduate or professional school. Today, women earn only one in three of the BA's and MA's granted, and one in ten of the PhD's.

In all the professions considered of importance to society, and in the executive ranks of industry and government, women are losing ground. Where they are present it is only a token handful. Women comprise less than 1 percent of federal judges; less than 4 percent of all lawyers; 7 percent of doctors. Yet women represent 51 percent of the U.S. population. And, increasingly, men are replacing women in the top positions in secondary and elementary schools, in social work, and in libraries—once thought to be women's fields.

Official pronouncements of the advance in the status of women hide not only the reality of this dangerous decline, but the fact that nothing is being done to stop it. The excellent reports of the President's Commission on the Status of Women and of the State Commissions have not been fully implemented. Such commissions have power only to advise. They have no power to enforce their recommendations; nor have they the freedom to organize American women and men to press for action on them. The reports of these commissions have, however, created a basis upon which it is now possible to build.

Discrimination in employment on the basis of sex is now prohibited by federal law, in Title VII of the Civil Rights Act of 1964. But although nearly one-third of the cases brought before the Equal Employment Opportunity Commission during the first year dealt with sex discrimination and the proportion is increasing dramatically, the commission has not made clear its intention to enforce the law with the same seriousness on behalf of women as of other victims of discrimination. Many of these cases were Negro women, who are the victims of the double discrimination of race and sex. Until now, too few women's organizations and official spokesmen have been willing to speak out against these dangers facing women. Too many women have been restrained by the fear of being called "feminist."

There is no civil rights movement to speak for women, as there has been for Negroes and other victims of discrimination. The National Organization for Women must therefore begin to speak.

We believe that the power of American law, and the protection guaranteed by the U.S. Constitution to the civil rights of all individuals, must be effectively applied and enforced to isolate and remove patterns of sex discrimination, to ensure equality of opporunity in employment and education, and equality of civil and political rights and responsibilities on behalf of women, as well as for Negroes and other deprived groups.

We realize that women's problems are linked to many broader questions of social justice; their solution will require concerted action by many groups. Therefore, convinced that human rights for all are indivisible, we expect to give active support to the common cause of equal rights for all those who suffer discrimination and deprivation, and we call upon other organizations committed to such goals to support our efforts toward equality for women.

We do not accept the token appointment of a few women to high-level positions in government and industry as a substitute for a serious continuing effort to recruit and advance women according to their individual abilities. To this end, we urge American government and industry to mobilize the same resources of ingenuity and command with which they have solved problems of far greater difficulty than those now impeding the progress of women.

We believe that this nation has a capacity at least as great as other nations, to innovate new social institutions which will enable women to enjoy true equality of opportunity and responsibility in society, without conflict with their responsibilities as mothers and homemakers. In such innovations, America does not lead the Western world, but lags by decades behind many European countries. We do not accept the traditional assumption that a woman has to choose between marriage and motherhood, on the one hand, and serious participation in industry or the professions on the other. We question the present expectation that all normal women will retire from job or profession for ten or fifteen years, to devote their full time to raising children, only to reenter the job market at a relatively minor level. This, in itself, is a deterrent to the aspirations of women, to their acceptance into management or professional training courses, and to the very possibility of equality of opportunity or real choice, for all but a few women. Above all, we reject the assumption that these problems are the unique responsibility of each individual woman, rather than a basic social dilemma which society must solve. True equality of opportunity and freedom of choice for women requires such practical and possible innovations as a nationwide network of child-care centers, which will make it unnecessary for women to retire completely from society until their children are grown, and national programs to provide retraining for women who have chosen to care for their own children full-time.

We believe that it is as essential for every girl to be educated to her full potential of human ability as it is for every boy—with the knowledge that such education is the key to effective participation in today's economy and that, for a girl as for boy, education can only be serious where there is expectation that it will be used in society. We believe that American educators are capable of devising means of imparting such expectations to girl students. Moreover, we consider the decline in the proportion of women receiving higher and professional education to be evidence of discrimination. This discrimination may take the form of quotas against the admission of women to colleges and professional schools; lack of encouragement by parents, counselors and educators; denial of loans or fellowships; or the traditional or arbitrary procedures in graduate and professional training geared in terms of men, which inadvertently discriminate against women. We believe that the same serious attention must be given to high school dropouts who are girls as to boys.

We reject the current assumptions that a man must carry the sole burden of supporting himself, his wife, and family, and that a woman is automatically entitled to lifelong support by a man upon her marriage, or that marriage, home, and family are primarily woman's world and responsibility—hers to dominate— his to support. We believe that a true partnership between the sexes demands a different concept of marriage, an equitable sharing of the responsibilities of home and children and of the economic burdens of their support. We believe that proper recognition should be given to the economic and social value of homemaking and child-care. To these ends, we will seek to open a reexamination of laws and mores governing marriage and divorce, for we believe that the current state of "half-equality" between the sexes discriminates against both men and women and is the cause of much unnecessary hostility between the sexes.

We believe that women must now exercise their political rights and responsibilities as American citizens. They must refuse to be segregated on the basis of sex into separate-and-not-equal ladies' auxiliaries in the political parties, and they must demand representation according to their numbers in the regularly constituted party committees—at local, state, and national levels—and in the informal power structure, participating fully in the selection of candidates and political decision-making, and running for office themselves.

In the interests of the human dignity of women, we will protest, and endeavor to change, the false image of women now prevalent in the mass media, and in the texts, ceremonies, laws, and practices of our major social institutions. Such images perpetuate contempt for women by society and by women for themselves. We are similarly opposed to all policies and practices—in church, state, college, factory, or office— which, in the guise of protectiveness, not only deny opportunities but also foster in women self-denigration, dependence, and evasion of responsibility, undermine their confidence in their own abilities, and foster contempt for women.

Now will hold itself independent of any political party in order to mobilize the political power of all women and men intent on our goals. We will strive to ensure that no party, candidate, president, senator, governor, congressman, or any public official who betrays or ignores the principle of full equality between the sexes is elected or appointed to office. If it is necessary to mobilize the votes of men and women who believe in our cause, in order to win for women the final right to be fully free and equal human beings, we so commit ourselves.

We believe that women will do most to create a new image of women by *acting* now, and by speaking out in behalf of their own equality, freedom, and human dignity—not in pleas for special privilege, nor in enmity toward men, who are also victims of the current, half-equality between the sexes—but in an active, self-respecting partnership with men. By so doing, women will develop confidence in their own ability to determine actively, in partnership with men, the conditions of their life, their choices, their future, and their society.

REDSTOCKINGS MANIFESTO

I

After centuries of individual and preliminary political struggle, women are uniting to achieve their final liberation from male supremacy. Redstockings is dedicated to building this unity and winning our freedom.

II

Women are an oppressed class. Our oppression is total, affecting every facet of our lives. We are exploited as sex objects, breeders, domestic servants, and cheap labor. We are considered inferior beings, whose only purpose is to enhance men's lives. Our humanity is denied. Our prescribed behavior is enforced by the threat of physical violence.

Because we have lived so intimately with our oppressors, in isolation from each other, we have been kept from seeing our personal suffering as a political condition. This creates the illusion that a woman's relationship with her man is a matter of interplay between two unique personalities and can be worked out individually. In reality, every such relationship is a *class* relationship, and the conflicts between individual men and women are *political* conflicts that can only be solved collectively.

III

We identify the agents of our oppression as men. Male supremacy is the oldest, most basic form of domination. All other forms of exploitation and oppression (racism, capitalism, imperialism, etc.) are extensions of male supremacy: men dominate women, a few men dominate the rest. All power structures throughout history have been male-dominated and male-oriented. Men have controlled all political, economic, and cultural institutions and backed up this control with physical force. They have used their power to keep women in an in-

From the "Redstockings Manifesto," in Notes from the Second Year (*Radical Feminists, 1969*), *pp. 112–13. Reprinted by permission of Karen Rappaport.*

ferior position. *All men* receive economic, sexual, and psychological benefits from male supremacy. *All men* have oppressed women.

IV

Attempts have been made to shift the burden of responsibility from men to institutions or to women themselves. We condemn these arguments as evasions. Institutions alone do not oppress; they are merely tools of the oppressor. To blame institutions implies that men and women are equally victimized, obscures the fact that men benefit from the subordination of women, and gives men the excuse that they are forced to be oppressors. On the contrary, any man is free to renounce his superior position provided that he is willing to be treated like a woman by other men.

We also reject the idea that women consent to or are to blame for their own oppression. Women's submission is not the result of brainwashing, stupidity, or mental illness but of continual, daily pressure from men. We do not need to change ourselves, but to change men.

The most slanderous evasion of all is that women can oppress men. The basis for this illusion is the isolation of individual relationships from their political context and the tendency of men to see any legitimate challenge to their privileges as persecution.

V

We regard our personal experience, and our feelings about that experience, as the basis for an analysis of our common situation. We cannot rely on existing ideologies as they are all products of male supremacist culture. We question every generalization and accept none that are not confirmed by our experience.

Our chief task at present is to develop female class-consciousness through sharing experience and publicly exposing the sexist foundation of all our institutions. Consciousness-raising is not "therapy," which implies the existence of individual solutions and falsely assumes that the male-female relationship is purely personal, but the only method by which we can ensure that our program for liberation is based on the concrete realities of our lives.

The first requirement for raising class-consciousness is honesty, in private and in public, with ourselves and other women.

VI

We identify with all women. We define our best interest as that of the poorest, most brutally exploited woman.

We repudiate all economic, racial, educational, or status privileges that divide us from other women. We are determined to recognize and eliminate any prejudices we may hold against other women.

We are committed to achieving internal democracy. We will do whatever is necessary to ensure that every woman in our movement has an equal chance to participate, assume responsibility, and develop her political potential.

VII

We call on all our sisters to unite with us in struggle.

We call on all men to give up their male privileges and support women's liberation in the interest of our humanity and their own.

In fighting for our liberation we will always take the side of women against their oppressors. We will not ask what is "revolutionary" or "reformist," only what is good for women.

The time for individual skirmishes has passed. This time we are going all the way.

July 7, 1969

DANGERS IN THE PRO-WOMAN LINE
AND CONSCIOUSNESS-RAISING

by The Feminists

A Revolutionary Organization: Theory and Action

What the feminist movement needs now, in the face of increasing disunity and vacillation, are women who are willing to put *radical* feminism before any other commitment and a group capable of gathering together all the useful ideas and methods diffused throughout the movement and utilizing them effectively in the service of revolution.

The type of group we need is one which tends toward leaderlessness. Not that distinctions among members are ignored or suppressed, so that leadership exists but is not recognized as in consciousness-raising groups. Rather the group must be structured in such a way that these distinctions are destroyed. It is only demagogic flattery to proclaim that all women are presently equal. Nor can consciousness-raising, in which all personal testimony is assumed to be equally relevant, efface existing inequalities among women. The retelling of personal experience involes not merely the experience itself but facility in expression and it is here that the verbal ability and poise of the upper-middle-class women establish their dominance.[1] But if the movement is to spread to *all* classes of women, recognizing differences and inequities is of *primary* importance and methods of dealing with them must be sought.[2]

Leaderlessness is necessary for a strong and enduring revolutionary group. What it actually involves is raising the competence of all members to the level required by leadership in other groups. This situation

From Jeanne Arrow, "Dangers in the Pro-woman Line and Consciousness-Raising," ideas of The Feminists, mimeographed (November, 1969). Reprinted by permission of The Feminists.

[1] Also very often the upper-middle-class style is so ingrained in our imagination that another style is experienced as annoying or stupid.

[2] I will return to these methods further on.

ensures two eventualities. First, that every member of the group will become proficient in all aspects of theory and action so that initiative will be equally distributed over the entire membership. Thus more minds are utilized in the service of the movement rather than just more bodies. Such increased mental activity gathers momentum and the work[3] of the group multiplies rapidly, creating the need for more and more members. Leaderlessness thus implies unlimited fertility in the development of the movement.

Secondly, a leaderless group of highly competent individuals strengthens the group by making it impossible to destroy it by the method of picking of important individuals. Neither can any individual or clique become so disproportionately valuable to the group that they can take over, divert the group for their personal ambition, or seriously threaten the group by breaking away. The group consists of those members present at any time and is able to function on that level.

For the members of a really leaderless group the pressure toward greater participation and development is powerful and constant. Since the high competence of every member is necessary to the survival of the group, each individual is urged and encouraged by the rest to develop their full capacity in all political activities.

Another quality of a revolutionary group is the transformation of its members into professional revolutionaries. Although at this point the movement can support few, if any, of its members for full-time work in the movement, this is something that we ought to be working for, if we want to progress as rapidly and efficiently as possible in the work to be done. As it is now most of our time is spent at earning a living. Group activity must be squeezed in at night and on weekends. Even so this time *must* be completely taken up by movement work. No revolution can be successfully completed by people meeting once a month (as in NOW) or even once a week. The Feminists meet twice a week on a regular basis. Besides this there are extra workshops and committee meetings. Actions require almost daily meetings. Besides each member is required to read two hours a week at hard data relating to feminism and to submit a three-page paper once a month.

Before new members are admitted into the group they must understand the nature of the group and what will be expected of them. They must have reached a certain point in the evolution of their thinking to be prepared for the time-consuming work involved, to be ready to forfeit what many people treasure but what we cannot afford—a "private" life. The movement is the first commitment of all members. Each

[3] Theorizing, organizing, writing, speaking, planning, and executing actions.

member must be able to identify her future with that of the movement. No escape hatches are left open through which to flee in times of emotional stress. In this way a mutual dependence and trust is developed among the members, not centered on any one person in the group but all the members generally.

Further, a professional revolutionary is one who has become extremely proficient at the work of the movement. But this can happen only in an organization that will enable each woman to develop and *apply* her abilities to the fullest. She must be constantly acquiring new experience and increasing knowledge both of theory and tactics. She must have the opportunity to observe those of more developed skills and strive to rise to that level herself. She must *combine* her profound knowledge of oppression as a woman with professional skill. This is the only way we will be able to struggle against our highly organized and skilled enemy.

Both professional ability and equality among members is achieved by means of a number of mechanisms utilized in the group—the essential one being the use of the lot system. The lot system is called essential because it is the only system that insures full participatory democracy in the group. All tasks, both the creative and tedious ones, are assigned by drawing lots. This means that no work is beneath any member of the group no matter what her background or claims to special genius. In this way exploitation is eliminated in the group. When the volunteer system is employed it usually results in the most oppressed volunteering or being suggested for the most oppressive tasks. Leaders can always cop out of these jobs simply by refusing to do them or threatening to leave the group when pressure is brought to bear on them. Others, wanting badly to participate in some way, will usually take up the worst jobs. When the lot is employed, jobs cannot be pawned off on any other than the person chosen for the task.

Creative tasks are also chosen by lot. This may involve an initial loss of efficiency but, as it is essential to the development of the individual and the group itself, this loss of time or convenience is sustained by the group. It has also been suggested that quality will suffer drastically by use of the lot. This, however, has not been found to be the case. All women can acquire the skills necessary for revolutionary theory and action with only minor differences in performance. As experience is gained in the group, these discrepancies become even less important. The crucial idea here is that the lot system functions in a way to equalize members by promoting similar experiences, whereas the volunteer system tends to perpetuate differences since very few people will be moved to volunteer for a job they've never handled before, especially when there are "experts" present. The lot system, further, encourages cooperation and inhibits competition among women. At the same time, since each task is the ultimate responsibility of the person chosen, initiative and independence are not lost. Through the lot every woman is given both the opportunity and the obligation to learn and develop as an individual.

Continuity

The first function of a revolutionary group is to preserve continuity. The experience of the past, both in the acts of individuals and of the group, as well as the theoretical work of the group, is not lost to the movement and to history. In the loose-structured group, where there is a constant turnover of members, and where writing things down rests on individual initiative alone, there is a danger that many ideas and experiences will go unrecorded. We must be more aware of the fact that it is the memory of ourselves and our actions that *we* manage to preserve that will be the foundations of future work and future movements. There must be a consistent drive to get it all down, to move regularly from fact to theory to history. Only a strong, ongoing group has the continuity required to preserve the memory of itself and the movement for all women.

In a revolutionary group every idea is developed and incorporated into the body of theory or modifies that theory in a rational manner. Because of this the theory of the group and its history can be communicated immediately to new members. The same ground will not have to be gone over again and again and they will begin on an equal footing with older members.

Consistent theory is also the foundation for consistent and meaningful action. An analysis maps out the primary sources of oppression, separating the superstructure from the real foundations. Flailing at the superstructure is hopeless because these details can very well be changed without disturbing the oppressor/oppressed relationship at all and he *knows* it. Many actions in the movement have been about the particular style of the oppression rather than hitting at the oppression itself. . . . Take care of the substance and the incidentals will take care of themselves. But many of us are still reluctant to deal with this substance, to see our oppression in terms of those institutions invented solely with the object of keeping women in their place. It is only by challenging simultaneously these institutions that we can force men to give way. We do have to *force* them; we will never convince them, nor will they give it up of their own accord. Even if men decided to abandon the institution of marriage, let's say, if they did this on their own they would also work out an alternate plan of oppressing us. *We* must destroy marriage, motherhood, and prostitution ourselves. *We* must make the blueprints of the future, with or without male agreement. . . .

The Group: Work and Power

Lastly, a revolutionary group creates work for its members and power for itself. As a highly organized group grows, it creates work and activity by making use of the full capacity of all its members. This type of organization must be the focal point of the movement. Other kinds of groups can exist but they must never presume to lead the movement or to pretend that anything other than a well-organized group governed by discipline and total commitment can be the model for the movement. Conservatism also must never be allowed to get the upper hand. Conservatism, not wishing to stir up revolutionary sentiment, does not make full use of members but rather discourages initiative and full development because these lead to the desire for radical change. It is both the conservatism and the anarchy of the movement which have caused us not to make use of the many people whose names fill our files, because we have no place for them, no work for them to do. Conservatism wants power in order to bargain with the establishment; revolution creates power to destroy the establishment. The more women we have whose capacities are fully developed and utilized the more work we will have to do and the sooner we'll be a threat to the male power-structure. Only a well-organized group can fully develop and utilize its members. Only these kinds of groups should be the concern of the movement at this point. It is the moderate groups that will destroy us if we do nothing to expose them now, if we do not begin to build a strong central movement now.

I believe that The Feminists realize these dangers and are beginning to deal with it. But the rest of the movement *must* begin with us. Together, committed and growing stronger, we can attract more and more women over to us. We must all begin to be revolutionaries. There is no other alternative. Life at suvival level is tedious and pathetic. The masters of destruction, war, and oppression must be shown that we will not tolerate anything short of freedom; that this is how we are.

Jeanne Arrow,

November 1969

from the ideas of THE FEMINISTS

OTHER BOOKS OF INTEREST

THE ADMINISTRATIVE REVOLUTION: NOTES ON THE PASSING OF OR-GANIZATION MAN, by George E. Berkley

THE ECOLOGICAL CONSCIENCE: VALUES FOR SURVIVAL, edited by Robert Disch

THE FELON, by John Irwin

INSTITUTIONAL RACISM IN AMERICA, edited by Louis Knowles and Kenneth Prewitt

THE NEW SOCIAL DRUG: CULTURAL, MEDICAL, AND LEGAL PER-SPECTIVES ON MARIJUANA, edited by David E. Smith

OUR CRIMINAL SOCIETY: THE SOCIAL AND LEGAL SOURCES OF CRIME IN AMERICA, by Edwin M. Schur

THE UNEMPLOYED: A SOCIAL-PSYCHOLOGICAL PORTRAIT, by Donald W. Tiffany, James R. Cowan, and Phyllis M. Tiffany

THE UNIVERSITY AND REVOLUTION, edited by Gary R. Weaver and James H. Weaver

WHO RULES AMERICA?, by G. William Domhoff